NFC

A Wiley Brand

by Robert P. Sabella and John Paul Mueller

A Wiley Brand

NFC For Dummies®

Published by: **John Wiley & Sons, Inc.**, 111 River Street, Hoboken, NJ 07030-5774, www.wiley.com

Copyright © 2016 by John Wiley & Sons, Inc., Hoboken, New Jersey

Media and software compilation copyright © 2015 by John Wiley & Sons, Inc. All rights reserved.

Published simultaneously in Canada

For general information on our other products and services, please contact our Customer Care Department within the U.S. at 877-762-2974, outside the U.S. at 317-572-3993, or fax 317-572-4002. For technical support, please visit www.wiley.com/techsupport.

Wiley publishes in a variety of print and electronic formats and by print-on-demand. Some material included with standard print versions of this book may not be included in e-books or in print-on-demand. If this book refers to media such as a CD or DVD that is not included in the version you purchased, you may download this material at http://booksupport.wiley.com. For more information about Wiley products, visit www.wiley.com.

Library of Congress Control Number: 2016933642

ISBN: 978-1-119-18292-4

ISBN 978-1-119-18296-2 (ebk); ISBN ePDF 978-1-119-18293-1 (ebk)

Manufactured in the United States of America

10 9 8 7 6 5 4 3 2 1

Contents at a Glance

Table of Contents

Introduction

Ask most people what *NFC* stands for and they will probably answer "the National Football Conference." But the NFC in this book is far more important than football. It stands for Near Field Communication, a technology that has the potential to significantly change how you interact with the people and things around you. The exciting news about NFC is that we haven't even scratched the surface yet of how this technology is going to change our lives. That's why you need *NFC For Dummies*. This book is your introduction to the larger world of NFC, and it helps you see why this technology is so amazing.

About This Book

NFC For Dummies begins by introducing you to NFC. You discover that NFC is already used all over the place, and you might not have even realized it.

Discovering how this technology has been hiding in plain sight is a good starting point. The second part of the book tells you how NFC actually works and why it needs to work in this specific way. You may initially find some of this material a little technical, but if you want to use NFC to the fullest extent possible, you need to know what makes it special.

After you know how NFC works, it's time to see it in action. The next part of the book discusses many of the ways in which you can use NFC to perform useful tasks. Each chapter introduces another area in which NFC is in use today. Amazing as these uses are, they're really just the tip of the iceberg, and the links in these chapters will lead you to still more resources.

Every technology comes with a few implementation issues. Some set of technical circumstances inevitably causes problems. Fortunately, this book tells you about those issues and tells you how to fix them. You end up looking really smart because while your buddies are sitting there not doing much, you've already fixed the problem and are doing something useful with NFC.

A single book can't even begin to tell you about everything NFC has to offer. In fact, you could probably read several books and still not begin to exhaust this topic. That's why the Parts of Ten is there. It gives you access to resources that will keep you reading for quite some time to come. When you finish it all, you'll become an NFC guru, and everyone around you will be looking to you as the NFC expert.

To make absorbing the concepts even easier, this book uses the following conventions:

>> When you see terms in the text in *italics*, the surrounding text provides a definition for that term.

>> Web addresses appear in monofont. If you're reading a digital version of this book on a device connected to the Internet, note that you can click the web address to visit that website, like this: http://www.dummies.com.

Foolish Assumptions

You might find it difficult to believe that I've assumed anything about you — after all, we haven't even met yet! Although most assumptions are indeed foolish, I made these assumptions to provide a starting point for the book.

Of course, you do need to have some desire to work with NFC to solve some sort of problem or address a need. In many cases, the problem or need is business or task specific, but you might be amazed at the ways in which you can use NFC to address personal needs as well. The point is that you need to have some anticipated purpose for using NFC to get the most out of this book.

You should also understand some basics of technology. For example, if you aren't on speaking terms with your smartphone, this book might not be a good fit for you. You do need some level of technical savvy to make good use of the material, even though the bar isn't set very high.

This book also assumes that you can access items on the Internet. Sprinkled throughout are numerous references to online material that will enhance your learning experience. However, these added sources are useful only if you actually find and use them.

Icons Used in This Book

As you read this book, you see icons in the margins that indicate material of interest (or not, as the case may be). This section briefly describes each icon in this book.

TIP

Tips are nice because they help you save time or perform some task without a lot of extra work. The tips in this book are time-saving techniques or pointers to resources that you should try in order to get the maximum benefit from NFC or in performing NFC-related tasks.

WARNING

I don't want to sound like an angry parent or some kind of maniac, but you should avoid doing anything that's marked with a Warning icon. Otherwise, you might find that your NFC application fails to work as expected, you get incorrect responses from seemingly bulletproof configurations, or (in the worst-case scenario) you lose data or damage equipment.

TECHNICAL STUFF

Whenever you see this icon, think advanced tip or technique. You might find these tidbits of useful information just too boring for words, or they could contain the solution you need to get an NFC solution running. Skip these bits of information whenever you like.

REMEMBER

If you don't get anything else out of a particular chapter or section, remember the material marked by this icon. This text usually contains an essential process or a bit of information that you must know to work with NFC successfully.

Beyond the Book

This book isn't the end of your NFC experience — it's really just the beginning. I provide online content to make this book more flexible and better able to meet your needs. That way, as you send me email about the book, I can address questions and tell you how updates to NFC affect book content. In fact, you gain access to all these cool additions:

>> **Cheat sheet:** You remember using crib notes in school to make a better mark on a test, don't you? You do? Well, a cheat sheet is sort of like that. It provides you with some special notes about tasks that you can do with NFC. You can find the cheat sheet for this book at http://www.dummies.com/cheatsheet/nfc. It contains really neat information such as the NFC operating modes and tag types.

>> **Updates:** Sometimes changes happen. For example, I might not have seen an upcoming change when I looked into our crystal ball during the writing of this book. In the past, this possibility simply meant that the book became out-dated and less useful, but you can now find updates to the book at `http://www.dummies.com/extras/nfc`.

In addition to these updates, check out the updated content at `https://www.nfcbootcamp.com/`.

>> **NFC Bootcamps:** After reading this book and checking out all the updates online, you may want to take your NFC knowledge to the next level. For that, I conduct NFC Bootcamps — one- and two-day, hands-on training seminars in locations around the world. If you want to attend one of these, just check out the NFC Bootcamp website at `http://www.nfcbootcamp.com`.

Where to Go from Here

It's time to start your NFC adventure! If you're completely new to NFC, you should start with Chapter 1 and progress through the book at a pace that allows you to absorb as much of the material as possible.

If you're a novice who's in an absolute rush to get going with NFC as quickly as possible, you can skip to Chapter 3 with the understanding that you may find some topics a bit confusing later. Skipping to Chapter 4 is possible if you already have some experience with NFC, but you may find that some terms are confusing if you do.

Readers who have some exposure to NFC and already have a good idea of how it works can save reading time by moving directly to Chapter 6. You can always go back to earlier chapters as necessary when you have questions. Starting at Chapter 6 will get you moving with NFC as a real-world solution to your particular need. Of course, skipping all the preliminary chapters may also mean that you skip some really amazing information about NFC that you didn't know existed.

1
Getting Started with NFC

IN THIS PART . . .

Discovering how NFC came into being

Understanding why NFC is such a cool technology

Obtaining a brief overview of how NFC works

Seeing NFC from the user perspective

Differentiating NFC from other wireless technologies

Chapter 1

Introducing Near Field Communication (NFC)

N ear Field Communication (NFC) is an amazing technology that helps you interact with both the people and things around you in ways that you can't really imagine until you start using the technology. When using NFC to tap things (physically place your NFC-enabled device against something like an NFC tag), you gain advantages in efficiency that save both time and money. In addition, you can rely on NFC to help reduce costly errors that can cause problems for both you and your organization. Unlike older technologies, NFC is also quite flexible and can be found in almost all new smartphones today, so you can use it in more ways and places than you might initially think. Everyone can use NFC — developers, hobbyists, and the average person on the street. This chapter helps you gain an understanding of how NFC came to be and how it can give your organization a competitive advantage. Throughout this book, you gain insights into how you can use NFC to perform useful tasks. This chapter begins with the concept of using NFC to enable digital wallets — a topic that is in all the headlines. Using NFC means that you can make purchases with greater confidence and with a smaller chance of having to deal with issues such as identity theft. In fact, you'll be amazed at all the ways in which you can use NFC wallets to make your life easier. So, although you might initially think about all the ways you can use NFC to make things easier for your organization, you also need to think of all the ways you can use it to help yourself. After all, you do have a life outside of work that NFC can and will affect!

This chapter ends by providing you with a quick overview of how NFC works. You don't have to endure a long lecture about all the bits and bytes of NFC technology, nor do you have to become an electrical engineer. Rather, this chapter provides an introduction to the technology so that you can talk about it with other people and make a few simple decisions about how you might use NFC as an individual or within your organization. In addition, you gain insights into how NFC can make your life simpler because you now have a better idea of where you've already seen NFC used in real-world applications.

Presenting a Quick History of NFC

As with most technologies, NFC didn't just appear on the horizon one day. Various companies spent a good deal of time putting the specifics for NFC together. In addition, these companies used existing technologies, in this case Radio Frequency Identification (RFID), as a starting point. (RFID was a 1983 invention of Charles Walton, but its origins can be traced back to WWII. You can find an excellent history of RFID at http://www.rfidjournal.com/articles/view?1338.) NFC is actually a technology that overlaps RFID — it uses a shorter operating distance for the sake of security. Figure 1-1 shows the key dates for NFC milestones that have affected how the technology has changed over time. Even though the NFC effort started in 2002, the International Standards Organization (ISO) didn't approve NFC as an acceptable standard until 2003.

As shown in Figure 1-1, *NFC tags* — small sticker-like devices used to store information or data in a manner that an NFC-enabled device can read or optionally write — didn't come in a standardized form until 2006. When an NFC-enabled device moves over the tag, it can retrieve the information the tag contains. However, don't worry about how the hardware works for now. All that is important to remember at this point is that NFC tags use a standardized form so that any NFC-enabled device can interact with any NFC tag — making NFC exceptionally easy to use.

One of the technologies that truly distinguishes NFC is the use of *SmartPoster* technology (a kind of visual display that incorporates both traditional poster content and digital content that an NFC-enabled device can read or optionally write). This standardized technology also appeared in 2006. You use it to provide digital information in a physical printed poster for people to access. Passing a smartphone or other NFC-enabled device over specifically marked areas of the poster provides viewers with details they can take with them. The first use for SmartPosters that comes to mind is for public venues such as trade shows — no more need to waste money printing take-away brochures that end up on the floor anyway (see companies such as Poken, http://www.poken.com/, and ITN, http://www.itnint.com/, for examples of this use). However, SmartPosters can appear in all sorts of places, such as bus shelters, malls, and airports (see BlueBite, at http://www.bluebite.com/, for an example of these uses).

February 2006 saw the introduction of the first NFC-enabled cellphone, the Nokia 6131 NFC. (Not all versions of the Nokia 6131 provide NFC support.) This phone started the whole idea of being able to pass the phone over a tag and obtain information from it. By the time the Samsung Nexus S appeared on the scene in 2010, NFC support became a standard feature and the capabilities of NFC had improved significantly.

One of the significant additions to NFC is its capability to provide peer-to-peer support. In addition to reading information from tags, you can exchange information with another person by bringing your NFC-enabled smartphones closely together. Instead of having to deal with bulky business cards, NFC-enabled smartphones let you keep your connections in a place where they're easily found, used, and managed. In addition to business connections, your peer-to-peer connection can also exchange data such as pictures, movies, and music.

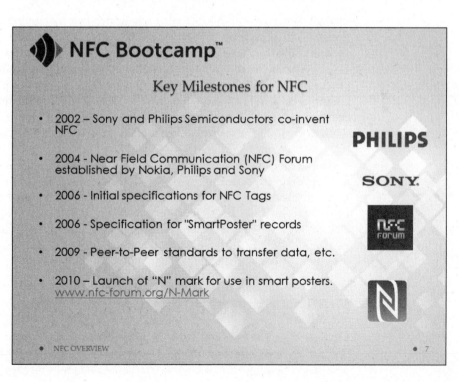

FIGURE 1-1:
Significant accomplishments in NFC technology.

TIP

NFC is growing significantly. It's predicted that within five years, half or more of all phones made will have NFC support. Within ten years, people will use NFC data exchange as a preferred method for obtaining publicly available information from physical objects; although, the use of NFC will remain completely optional.

Defining the Need for NFC

NFC solves all sorts of problems, and throughout this book you get introduced to a lot of these solutions. However, before you spend time reading about NFC, you might like to know how you can use it to meet your needs immediately. In fact, you might be surprised to learn that you already use NFC and simply don't know it. NFC appears all over the place. The following sections provide you with a quick summary of some of the most interesting uses. As you progress through the book, you find additional uses described in more detail.

Interacting with devices using simpler methods

Imagine being able to interact with any device just by tapping it with an NFC-enabled device such as your smartphone. For example, you tap your portable speakers, and the music currently playing on your smartphone starts playing out of the speakers instead. You get the full effect of those high-quality speakers you purchased, but with the music that you like from your smartphone. Bluetooth pairing of devices is normally a painful process when done manually. NFC makes the pairing possible with a single tap. Even though the music still relies on Bluetooth to get from the device to the speakers, the pairing is done with NFC.

The same concepts hold true with your television. A single tap is enough to make a connection with your smartphone so that you can see the pictures or video currently displayed on the smartphone, but at television size and resolution. Sony and other companies are currently engaged in making NFC connectivity happen in all sorts of ways. You can read about some of the latest Sony offerings at `http://venturebeat.com/2013/01/12/nfc-makes-it-easy-to-connect-sonys-devices-with-one-touch/`.

Buying products with ease

You walk up to the cash register with a cartful of goods you want to buy. Whether the cash register is actually manned by someone is unimportant (some stores are now experimenting with self-serve checkouts that really do save the store money and make the shopping experience much faster for most people). The goods are swiped across the scanner to get prices. When you have a coupon for an item, you simply tap your phone to add it to the register. You can be sure that the coupon actually reduces your cost because you can see the reduction immediately after you tap the phone. When it comes time to pay for the goods, another tap of your smartphone is all you need to pay for them using your credit or debit card. No more paper exchanging hands, and the level of convenience is amazing.

REMEMBER

Even though all these tasks can be performed with other technologies, the important issue is how NFC handles security. When using NFC, the cards, fobs, phones, stickers, watches, and other NFC-enabled devices all talk to the Point of Sale (POS) terminal used for payment in the exact same way using the exact same security.

WARNING

Remember that not every NFC transaction is completely secure. MIFARE transit fares and NFC payment are secure because the application supplies the required security. However, reading a tag isn't inherently secure, except for the natural level of security that NFC provides (such as a short reading distance). Security concerns are covered in later chapters, such as Chapter 6, where you can read about mobile wallet security requirements.

Products can also extend to services. For example, a common use for NFC is to pay for a train or a bus. London uses the Oyster card (`https://tfl.gov.uk/fares-and-payments/oyster`) to give people the capability to tap their card to gain access to the required transportation services. NFC makes using transportation of all sorts a lot easier.

Launching a marketing campaign

Getting people to buy your product is an essential part of any business venture. After all, if no one buys your product, you'll quickly be out of business. The problem is making your product stand out from all the other products out there. Of course, you could pay someone to ride in one of those cheesy trucks and blare out over a sound system, "Buy my product!" but that strategy is bound to fail. A better option is to provide people with information sources they can interact with, such as signs and kiosks. When people can enter a store, see the big poster with your product on it, and touch their smartphones to it to learn more, you gain a significant advantage over your competition that's relying on signs alone.

For a merchant, the NFC advantage is that full interactive communication with your customer, including tracking and accountability, can be initiated with a simple, digital gesture that's as natural as pointing at a product or display. This means that you can determine how many people have checked out your ad and know which locations are better suited to selling your product. Also, you can determine how people interacted with your ad so that you know which sales pitches work better. And you can learn which ads converted to sales. Therefore, it's no longer a matter of putting up a sign and hoping it sells something for you. Using NFC means that you can determine precisely how a marketing campaign is progressing and make changes as needed to ensure success.

Building your personal network quickly and easily

Networking is essential in today's world. Look at the emergence of online sites such as LinkedIn (https://www.linkedin.com/). Some people get most or even all their work based on contacts they make with these kinds of sites. Having a list of the right people at your fingertips makes you more efficient and better able to react to changing conditions. In short, you need connections today to be a success in business. With this in mind, NFC helps you create a personal network in two important ways, discussed next.

Exchanging business cards

One reason to use NFC is to make interacting with people easier. Of course, you have the option to exchange information simply by tapping smartphones. Information can include more than just name, address, and telephone number. You can exchange all sorts of information, including media of any sort that your smartphone can handle.

Exchanging other contact information

Thinking outside the box is important when exchanging information with someone else. For example, you might decide to create a presentation that fits on a smartphone. Tapping your phone with that of a potential client creates the connection that transfers the presentation and lets the client play it later at her leisure. No longer do you have to rely on a quick sales pitch to do all the work for you. Now you can concentrate on gaining the other person's interest and then make the sales pitch later using a full multimedia presentation through which you can convey all the facts.

Creating ad-hoc wireless connections

In times past, you often needed to jump through hoops to connect two devices in a secure manner. You can use the security that NFC provides for tasks such as banking because it carries only a low risk of eavesdropping and offers no practical way for an outsider to influence the content of your NFC transmissions (even if he's standing right there with you). NFC offers you the simplicity of a wireless connection, but its limited range offers added physical security not available to other forms of wireless communication. With this in mind, just about anything you can do with a wired connection, you can also do with NFC. However, unlike a wired connection, you don't have to do anything special to accomplish the task — simply bring the NFC device close to a tag or other device.

Having fun with games

Interestingly enough, you can even use NFC to enhance the gaming experience. For example, Skylanders (https://www.skylanders.com/), a toys-to-life game series published by Activision, integrates interactive figurines that you use to play a game. To use a figurine, you place it on the Portal of Power, which has an NFC reader in it, to register it. The Portal of Power reads the figurine's NFC tag to determine the characteristics that the corresponding character has. These are console games that use the gaming console for connectivity so that you can interact with other players. Theoretically, the gaming console you use doesn't matter, and you can even connect the Portal of Power to your PC.

REMEMBER

This game use of NFC is interesting because all the information about your character resides in the figurine. Using NFC means that your figurine contains the intelligence that you can rely on to hold information about your character between sessions.

Discovering Where NFC Wallets Are Used Most

One of the most exciting ways to use NFC is to pay for things — all sorts of things. It would be nice to say that NFC has completely penetrated absolutely every market out there, but the fact is that NFC is still a new technology. Consequently, you find NFC used quite a bit in some areas of the country and not nearly enough in other areas.

An *NFC wallet* lets you make payments using a variety of sources. In addition, with your NFC wallet, you can gain points on your loyalty card. The application used to make this functionality happen offers built-in security, so you can assign a PIN to every payment option your wallet includes. These features make NFC wallets different from other technologies, such as contactless cards, which don't provide the flexibility and security that the NFC wallet offers. The following sections describe where you can make NFC purchases quite easily and show the sorts of things that people buy using NFC today.

Of course, these figures are current as of the time of writing. Make sure you check out the NFC Bootcamp site at `https://www.nfcbootcamp.com/` for updates as they become available. You may be surprised at just how fast the use of NFC for making payments grows.

Viewing NFC wallet use by area

Where you live partially determines how much NFC you see. It definitely determines how much NFC you use (seeing it doesn't mean you get to do anything with it, though). Figure 1-2 shows a map of the places that currently use NFC the most. If you live in one of the larger cities in California, there is a good chance that you'll not only see but also use NFC regularly. The same holds true in Texas and New York (followed by Illinois and Florida). However, if you're a buyer in Wyoming, you might as well get used to not using the NFC features of your credit card for a while (until local businesses catch up).

Other states will see that NFC is making a huge difference to the bottom line of states like California, and businesses in other states will follow suit. The point is that NFC is catching on, and if you can start implementing it sooner than later, you'll gain a competitive advantage. Early adopters can see a huge increase in sales by using new technologies that have already proven their worth in other areas. NFC is such a technology.

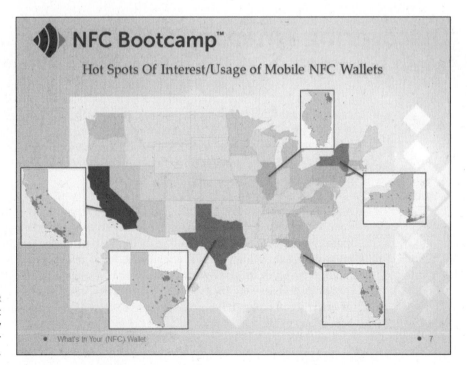

FIGURE 1-2:
Places that commonly use NFC for purchases today.

Viewing NFC wallet use by purchase type

It matters not only where but also how you use NFC. Many companies have already found that NFC is an indispensable part of their business environment, as shown in Figure 1-3. Of course, this figure doesn't show all the companies that use NFC, but it does show some of the larger organizations. Even in places like Wisconsin (one of the lighter areas in Figure 1-2, shown previously), you can go into a Subway, tap your card, and pay for your dinner. So, it's not impossible to find NFC usage wherever you go because these larger companies are already using it.

Figure 1-3 shows the relative strength of NFC by purchase area. Look for these numbers to change dramatically for the better as more national and global companies start to use NFC at the cash register. The article at `https://www.nfcbootcamp.com/near-field-communication-more-than-mobile-marketing/` provides you with more details on just how much of an impact NFC is starting to make in other industries.

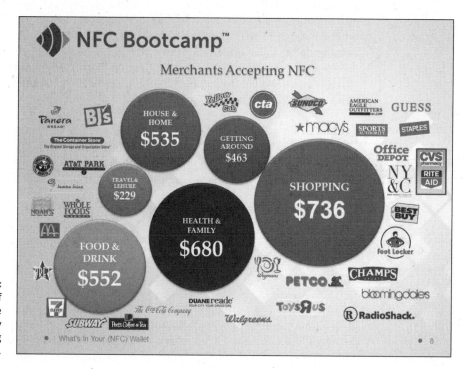

FIGURE 1-3: Types of items that are commonly purchased using NFC.

Presenting a Simplified View of NFC

It isn't essential to know every aspect of a technology in order to use it, but having some idea of how things work can be helpful. For example, you know that your cellphone requires a cell tower in order to gain access to the network so that you can make a call. You don't know all the details of how this happens, but you have some idea of what is involved at a high level. The following paragraphs provide you with this sort of high-level information. By the time you get done reading this material, you know enough about NFC to understand the essentials of what makes it such an amazing technology.

Considering what is needed for NFC

One of the reasons that NFC is so successful is that it's a relatively simple technology (well, at least if you're a propeller head). Figure 1-4 shows the basic elements of an NFC communication in most cases. As you can see, you have an NFC-enabled device that uses a wireless connection to power and then interact with some sort of NFC information source (a card). The technology relies on the same basic principle as those RFID readers and tags that you see all over the place in the stores right now. The main difference is that NFC operates at a shorter distance, provides secure communication, and allows for bidirectional communication (peer to peer), so it's like an RFID solution on steroids.

It's important to know that NFC-enabled devices can be either readers or cards. For example, when you use NFC to exchange information between two smartphones, the first smartphone begins by acting as a reader, and the second smartphone acts as a card. After the initial information exchange, they reverse roles. Now the first smartphone is a card and the second smartphone is a reader.

NFC tags can't act as readers. They are "passive," which means that they have no power source. So they always act as information sources, as shown in Figure 1-5. The NFC-enabled device sends power and commands to the tag, which then responds with data.

In addition, you can use any NFC-enabled device such as a smartphone to write data to a tag using a special command. This means that you can update the tags as needed to hold new information. As the book progresses, you see how this technology works and why NFC tags can do so many remarkable things.

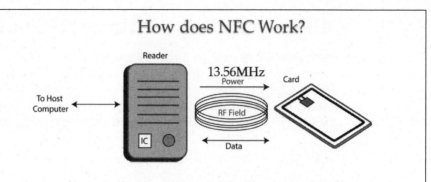

How does NFC Work?

- Operates on the same principle as contactless smart cards and RFID tags (e.g. access control badges)
- A reader initiates an RF communication and captures data from the card (or programs data into the card)
- With NFC, a phone can be either a reader or a card

FIGURE 1-4:
Types of items that are commonly purchased using NFC.

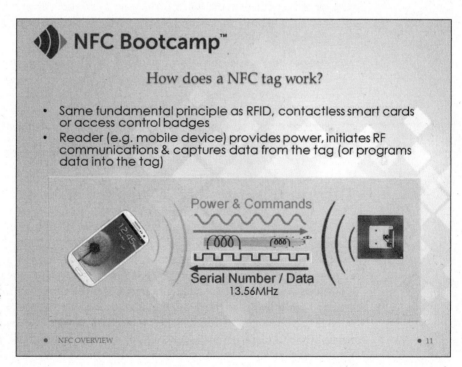

FIGURE 1-5:
Types of items that are commonly purchased using NFC.

Understanding the three NFC modes

NFC provides three basic modes of operation. These modes make NFC different from other wireless technologies such as RFID; they provide NFC with the flexibility needed to create an environment in which you can use NFC for a huge array of communication needs. The following list gives you an overview of the three NFC modes (which appear several times in the book in more detail):

>> **Card emulation:** Provides the means to replace a credit or debit card with an NFC-enabled device. Rather than use a credit or debit card, you rely on the NFC-enabled device to make the transaction. This mode also includes other sorts of card-type applications, such as identification cards, motel pass cards, loyalty cards, ticketing, access control, and any other sort of card-related task you can think of.

>> **Discovery (read and write):** Allows a user to interact with various information sources. This form of NFC application provides interaction with smart advertising, downloading coupons, getting information from kiosks, and using all sorts of other information sources that rely on both tags and smart posters. It is also possible to write information to these smart information sources using the right NFC-enabled device.

>> **Peer-to-peer communication:** Creates connectivity between two NFC-enabled devices. When you exchange information with any other smartphone user or create an ad-hoc network to collaborate on tasks, you're using the peer-to-peer mode of NFC. Using NFC in this mode is like having a secure network in your pocket that you can use in any location with complete peace of mind.

Discovering the NFC actors

NFC operates within a business ecosystem. An ecosystem is simply a set of rules that determines the behavior of the actors within that system. Originally, the term referred to natural environments where factors such as food availability, birth rate, and the number of predators determined the ability of a species to survive. In a business ecosystem, you must look at other factors, such as the productivity that a technology provides to those using it, and determine whether the technology can survive the onslaught of competition. In the case of NFC, you must consider the actors who interact with the technology:

>> **Consumer:** An entity (human or technological) who relies on NFC as an information source. Whether the consumer uses that information to make a purchase, obtain facts from a kiosk, or gain access to a resource, the entity

relies on NFC to provide the required information (outgoing or incoming). Think of a gazelle placidly browsing on the Serengeti.

>> **Producer:** An entity who creates NFC technologies for sale to a customer. Because NFC is still an emerging technology, you can count on finding more producers providing interesting products in the future. Think of Mother Nature using evolution to create interesting new food sources for the gazelle.

>> **Customer:** An entity who uses NFC to create information for a consumer or obtain information from a consumer. Someone who wants to sell something to someone will begin by offering information about the product and potentially provide coupons at a kiosk or other location. When the consumer decides to make the purchase, the customer will obtain the consumer's credit or debit card information. Of course, this scenario takes place in all sorts of other ways, too. Think of the customer as the food source for the gazelle.

>> **Competitor:** An entity who wants to keep NFC sales to a minimum and convince you that other technologies work far better. Competitors are the lions of the business ecosystem — it's best just to stay out of their way.

>> **Other stakeholders:** The NFC business ecosystem has all sorts of other actors that you'll meet as the book progresses. For now, think of them as the tourists and guides watching the gazelle and trying to determine whether the lion will eat it.

Chapter 2

Considering the NFC Difference

C hapter 1 helped you understand how Near Field Communication (NFC) originated from existing technologies, such as Radio Frequency Identification (RFID), but also added some interesting new functionality that you really need in order to make better use of the technologies available today. This chapter takes the next step. It begins by introducing you to the NFC Forum and the goals it had for NFC from the outset. By understanding these goals, you begin to understand why NFC is such an amazing technology.

It's also important to know that NFC isn't the appropriate technology for every need. NFC provides you with a new technology designed to meet specific needs that modern users have. Of course, you need to know a bit more about how NFC works before you can understand where it fits. Chapter 1 starts with an overview; this chapter gives you more specifics. After you know how the technology works at a lower level, you look at how NFC compares with other wireless communication technologies. You'll benefit from knowing where NFC fits into the picture and understanding that NFC has a specific niche that it fills.

NFC technology has evolved considerably since its introduction. This chapter also discusses some of this evolution and helps you understand why these changes are important.

The last part of the chapter is the most important of all. A major issue with most wireless technologies is that everyone can overhear your conversation. It's sort of like shouting from a rooftop when you meant only to contact the person across the hall. Wireless technologies tend to tell everyone everything, so they aren't private, and that's a problem. NFC is more like a whisper. You have to be up close, with your ear near the person's mouth to hear. No longer are you shouting from the rooftop and no longer is everyone able to hear you. NFC is a more secure solution precisely because it whispers your message to just the recipient that needs to hear it.

Understanding the NFC Forum Goals

The NFC Forum (`http://nfc-forum.org/`) is where you can go to discover all sorts of things associated with NFC. This is where you can go to learn about the latest NFC advances and why they're important to you. The home page highlights major NFC areas, so you can just click your way through informational sources. However, the NFC Forum does have specific goals in helping to promote NFC as a technology:

» **Developing specifications:** One of the most important functions of the NFC Forum is to define a modular architecture and interoperability parameters for NFC devices and protocols. Everyone has a set of rules to follow when creating products to ensure that every product works with every other product. Maybe you thought that making products that are interoperable was a common approach, but many technologies simply don't work that way, which is why you need that special high-priced widget from a vendor in order to get your new device to work.

» **Promoting the creation of new products:** Knowing that everyone is following the rules creates an open market in which even small vendors with just one great idea can compete. Creating this sort of atmosphere means that all the best minds can work together to help create great products that can enhance everyone's life.

» **Ensuring that everyone follows the specifications:** Of course, if you tell everyone that everyone else is following the rules, then you really do need to enforce those rules. Some vendors get the idea that the rules apply to everyone but them, so the Forum is there to help them remember that the rules are truly for everyone.

>> **Educating the public:** Keeping all the especially cool things that NFC can do a secret doesn't help anyone. The NFC Forum helps ensure that everyone knows about the latest NFC advances so that everyone can enjoy them. Most important, by knowing that a new advancement exists, other vendors can build on it to create even better products.

Considering NFC Wireless Communication Specifics

Before you can define the niche that NFC occupies in the pantheon of wireless technologies, you must know how NFC communication works to some degree. Chapter 1 gives you a great overview, but it isn't enough information to know how things work, just that they do. The following sections provide you with details about how NFC works as a wireless communication technology, so that you can better understand why NFC is such a great technology for private or personalized communications of all sorts.

Understanding selectivity

The term *selectivity*, when used in the context of NFC, means being able to ensure that a reader reads only the card you want to target. The reader and the card need to be close enough together to allow Radio Frequency (RF) communication between the two. If the reader read every card in the area, you would have a problem deciding what content to use or you might have to deal with a wealth of mixed content coming from all the cards simultaneously. Of course, the cacophony of information might be interesting for a little while, but you'd soon grow tired of it. Figure 2-1 shows how selectivity works with NFC. Notice that any card you want to read must be within the 4 cm to 10 cm reading distance — the NFC signal isn't strong enough to read all the other cards in the area.

Showing intent

NFC requires some sort of intent or gesture, an action on your part, to use it (after you set your device up to use NFC). The act of tapping your phone to the point of sale (POS) system at the cash register is a kind of gesture. Tapping the phone brings it in close proximity (within the 4 to 10 cm range) with the tag or other NFC-enabled device with which you want to interact. Unless you show specific intent to use NFC, by bringing an NFC-enabled device into close enough proximity with an NFC tag or other NFC-enabled device, NFC remains in sleep mode and you don't have any connectivity.

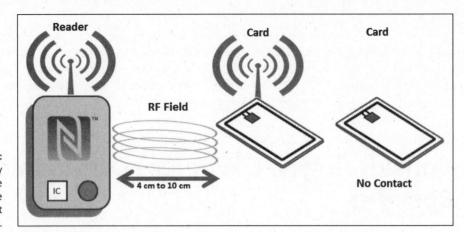

FIGURE 2-1:
NFC selectivity
is based on the
short distance
communication it
provides.

REMEMBER

You may see tapping referred to in other terms, such as *bumping, beaming, touching,* or *waving.* None of these terms adequately describes the gesture you must perform because of the real physical contact that is necessary to create an NFC connection. In order to work, the NFC-enabled objects must be close enough to establish an RF connection (which is 4 cm for NFC). It takes only milliseconds to make the connection, but finding the actual *interrogation zone* or *sweet spot* (the precise location between the two objects that allows for NFC connectivity) can sometimes be tricky for someone using NFC for the first time.

Creating secure access

The need for close proximity is what makes NFC secure — NFC requires a deliberate gesture to initiate a transaction, therefore nondeliberate transactions are difficult to initiate. You can't simply pass by someone's smartphone and read all the data from it. In order to read specific kinds of data from another person's smartphone, you have to be close enough to connect to it (which is too near for comfort). This means that you don't have to worry about some hacker coming along and simply stealing your data, as would be possible with other technologies that are more vulnerable.

TIP

It's important to realize that you do need to be proactive with every computer technology, and NFC is no exception. For example, you want to ensure that your smartphone or other NFC-enabled device has good password protection, just in case someone tries to gain access to it. A determined hacker will always find a way to gain access to data, but you can make things difficult, and perhaps the hacker will go bother someone else. You can read more about the potential vulnerabilities of NFC at http://electronics.howstuffworks.com/how-secure-is-nfc-tech.htm.

Understanding How NFC Compares to Other Technologies

NFC isn't the only game in town, nor was it ever intended to be. Other technologies provide functionality that makes them suitable for needs that NFC can't really address. Of course, choosing the right technology for a particular task can become confusing if you don't understand how it compares with NFC. Figure 2-2 provides a quick overview of the way in which NFC differs from other technologies when it comes to data rate and connection distance.

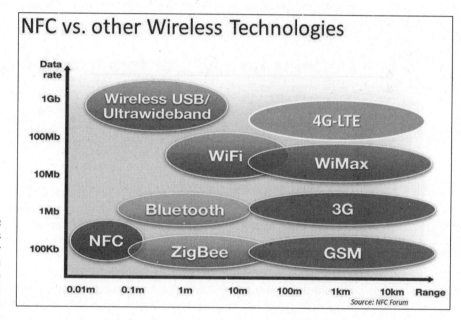

FIGURE 2-2: NFC differs from other technologies in both data rate and connection distance.

However, data rates and connection distances don't quite tell the whole story. The following sections compare NFC to these other technologies so that you can get a better idea of precisely when NFC is the best choice for your technology needs.

Defining how NFC differs from RFID

The first use of RFID occurred in the 1940s, during WWII, as a means of identifying friendly forces. Mario W. Cardullo received the first RFID patent on January 23, 1973. You can read a history of RFID development at http://www.rfidjournal.com/articles/view?1338.

NFC and RFID have completely different uses. Organizations generally use RFID only for tracking things — all sorts of things. Consequently, people generally use RFID for logistics, and it doesn't have a consumer or home use function because of the cost of the actual readers. RFID readers tend to be expensive, which keeps them out of the hands of the average person.

REMEMBER

When you think about RFID readers, imagine big trucks going through the inspection lanes on the highway. A reader picks up the truck's location from a large distance. RFID readers broadcast the signal widely (up to 25 meters). Contrast the wide area of RFID usage with the intimate, secure access provided by NFC, and you find that the two technologies serve different purposes. You can find an interesting infographic on the differences between NFC and RFID at http://www.nfcbootcamp. com/rfid-versus-nfc-whats-the-difference/.

Defining how NFC differs from QR codes

Quick Response (QR) codes or 2D bar codes are the little square black boxes that you see on some products or advertisements that look like someone spilled some ink onto the paper. They are similar to conventional UPC bar codes on products that get scanned when you buy something, but they can contain more information.

Most smartphones, even those that aren't NFC-enabled, can interact with QR codes. If the smartphone lacks the required app, you can download one. (QR readers aren't pre-installed in the United States, but they are in other countries.) To read the QR code, simply take a picture of it.

The advantages of QR codes are that they are extremely cheap to print and you can put them almost anywhere. The disadvantage of QR codes is that you need to have an app, open the app, and then take a picture of the QR code. Bad lighting or smudged ink can make QR codes difficult or impossible to read. NFC is different from QR codes in that it is native to the phone, meaning almost all phones have NFC pre-installed, and when you turn it on, all you need to do is to tap your phone on the tag (see the "Showing intent" section, earlier in this chapter, for details) to read it. No special app is needed.

NFC tags do cost more than just printing a QR code, but it is a cost versus convenience decision that you need to make for your specific use case. You can read more about the differences between QR codes and NFC at http://www.nearfield communication.org/qr-codes.html.

Defining how NFC differs from Bluetooth Low Energy (BLE)

One of the other proximity technologies getting a lot of attention these days is Bluetooth Low Energy (BLE), also known as Bluetooth Smart. BLE works by setting up *beacons* that are used to identify devices and then communicate with them. Think of an RFID reader that is always on and broadcasting its signal.

To use BLE, the user must turn on a device's Bluetooth. In addition, the user typically needs to download an app to receive and act upon specific actionable messages. The best example of BLE in action is when someone walks into a store, has that store's app loaded in the phone, and turns on Bluetooth support. When a beacon recognizes the active BLE support, it sends a message about what is on sale that day or information about a particular product. The phone can also receive a coupon for items that the merchant knows interests you. You can't (currently) use BLE to make a purchase.

The difference between NFC and BLE is one of infrastructure and task. BLE works at longer ranges (around 50 meters), transfers more data, and requires that you install the beacon infrastructure in order to work. The phone must have Bluetooth turned on, and for the best user experience, you need to install an app. NFC needs only a tag embedded in a smartposter, for example, and the user needs only to tap the phone in order for something to happen. In addition, most in the industry see NFC as the standard for making payments.

NFC AND BLE AREN'T MUTUALLY EXCLUSIVE

It's important to realize that the technologies in this chapter aren't mutually exclusive — you can use them together. For example, shoppers could walk into a store and see a poster welcoming them and asking whether they want to download the store's app. The app provides access to special deals and offers.

If a shopper decides that the offer is appealing, tapping the NFC tag on the poster automatically downloads the app for that shopper. Now that the BLE app is installed on the shopper's smartphone, she receives offers automatically, every time she comes into the store. The only requirement is that the shopper has Bluetooth turned on in her phone.

At a high level, you can compare these technologies as push versus pull, where BLE pushes you information and NFC pulls information. (See the infographic at `http://www.nfcbootcamp.com/location-becomes-part-mobile-technologies-like-beacons-nfc-can-provide-highly-accurate-location-data-intent/` for additional details.) Simply saying that you use one technology to push information and the other to pull information is a high-level comparison. For more details on the differences between the two view, this infographic at `https://ytd2525.wordpress.com/2014/02/17/ble-vs-nfc-vs-rfid-learn-the-differences/`. You can find a more detailed information on BLE, what it is, and how it works, at `http://www.smartcardalliance.org/resources/pdf/BLE101-FINAL-053014.pdf`.

Defining how NFC differs from powered chips (Wi-Fi)

Wireless Fidelity (Wi-Fi) is a communication technology that supports two-way conversations, just as NFC does. However, Wi-Fi provides significantly greater range than NFC, as shown previously in Figure 2-2. The advantage is that you can create an ad hoc network anywhere you need one and invite as many people as you like. The disadvantage is that everyone can hear you broadcast from a relatively great range. NFC is designed for private, personal communications, while Wi-Fi is designed to meet the requirements of group communications. You can learn more about the differences between Wi-Fi and NFC at `https://www.phonegurureviews.com/bluetooth-nfc-wifi-direct/`.

Following the Evolution from Smart Cards to Smartphones

We use smart cards for all sorts of purposes. Among the most common uses are riding the subway, buying something at the store, identifying ourselves, gaining access into a building, and securely sharing our health care records. The smart card technology saw its first use in 1970 and has gained acceptance since that time by many different institutions. You can find a history of smart cards at `http://www.cardwerk.com/smartcards/smartcard_history.aspx`.

The contactless technology that NFC provides emulates a smart card using card mode on a smartphone. That means that you don't need a separate card any longer when making smart card transactions. The smart card is *in* your phone. So all you really need is a single device — your smartphone with NFC-enabled technology.

When making a payment anywhere that accepts contactless payments, for example, you were previously limited to using just your NFC smart cards. These same locations now accept payments using your NFC phone.

This evolution from smart cards to smart phones is following the same generational and revolutionary trend toward everything going mobile, or more simply put, we can no longer live without our smartphones. The single best source of information on all things related to smart cards and NFC is the Smart Card Alliance (www.smartcardalliance.org). That organization continuously releases quality information on all these related topics, so I would check with it frequently.

Creating a Secure Environment

NFC is proactive in providing a secure environment for transactions. The "Creating secure access" section, earlier in this chapter, describes some of the ways in which the communication itself is secure. However, NFC needs more than simple security to get the job done. The following sections describe two methods for creating a secure environment.

Creating a secure environment on the device

One method of creating a secure environment comes in the form of special hardware. Figure 2-3 shows the construction of a generic NFC-enabled smartphone that includes a Secure Element (SE) to ensure that transactions remain safe.

REMEMBER

Credit card data is transmitted in the clear (unencrypted) for virtually all NFC card emulation specifications for companies such as Visa and MasterCard. The SE does not protect the data transmission; it protects the data only while it resides on the phone. The SE does protect the data, but only from On-Device attacks. Dynamic data appended to the credit card information protects the NFC data link, and the issuer needs to see this dynamic data to know that the transaction is real. Figure 2-4 shows how a typical credit card transaction would work.

As you can see, the bank or other financial institution sends the account information to a Trusted Service Manager (TSM) that encrypts the data. Nothing can easily decrypt the data without having a key, so now the data is inaccessible. The encrypted data goes from the TSM, through the user's data carrier, to the SE on the smartphone, where the account information is decrypted to make a purchase. The combination of wireless communication and physical security makes it unlikely that someone could steal the credit card data.

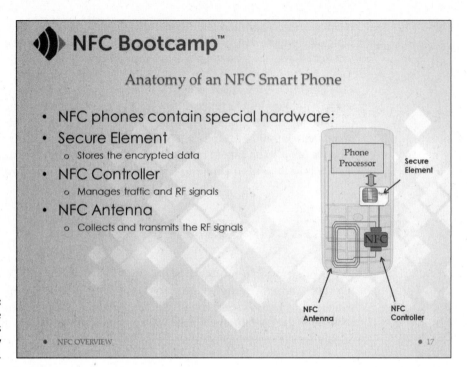

FIGURE 2-3:
The secure
element provides
physical security
for NFC.

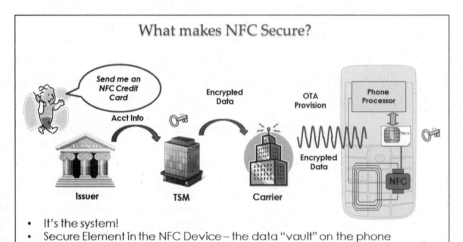

FIGURE 2-4:
Credit card
information
follows a secure
and encrypted
path to your
smartphone.

Creating a secure environment in the cloud

Another method is to rely on Host Card Emulation (HCE). When using HCE, you don't need an SE, although in some instances an SE can be used. When using HCE, an application running on the host processor of the mobile device performs the card emulation transaction with the external reader. The major benefits of using HCE are as follows:

>> Reduces application complexity for developers

>> Reduces hardware requirements, which opens NFC up to new applications

>> Makes provisioning card support for a mobile device easier and more flexible

>> Frees you from depending on the SE or Mobile Network Owner (MNO) owner

Of course, you don't get all these benefits free. You also have some downsides to consider with HCE:

>> Lack of hardware-secured data storage and credentials on the device

>> Dependence on the operating system used

>> Use of an alternative security setup, which increases backend complexity

As with most other technologies, HCE follows a process to secure your transactions. Here's a quick rundown on how the technology works:

1. Someone initiates an HCE payment.

2. The mobile device creates an NFC/in-app transaction.

3. The application creates an authorization message.

4. The authorization message travels to the cloud.

5. Various cloud applications route the message to provide the required response.

6. The mobile device receives the response message.

7. A host synchronization process occurs.

8. The payment issuer updates the user's credentials — making the payment.

Don't worry about knowing the details now. The "Defining Host Card Emulation (HCE)" section of Chapter 5 provides more details on how all this technology works. In addition, you can find more details about this approach at http://www.smartcardalliance.org/wp-content/uploads/HCE_Webinar_FINAL_061815.pdf. If you prefer a webinar, you can view it at http://www.smartcardalliance.org/activities-events-host-card-emulation-an-emerging-architecture-for-nfc-applications/.

2

Understanding NFC

IN THIS PART . . .

Considering the NFC standards

Understanding the NFC tag types

Defining how the NFC hardware works

Defining how the NFC software works

Chapter 3

Defining NFC

G aining an understanding of what NFC can do for you and why you need it as part of the solution for your organization is nice, but it's only a start-ing point. To understand what makes NFC special, you need more details.

REMEMBER

Some vendors produce nonstandard and proprietary NFC deployments that aren't technically compliant with NFC Forum standards. These products mostly work and look like NFC, but what they really use as an underlying technology is High Frequency Radio Frequency Identification (HF RFID) (see http://www.impinj. com/resources/about-rfid/the-different-types-of-rfid-systems/ for an explanation of different types of RFID systems). As an example, vendors kept tran-sit implementations, which are arguably the largest implementation of contactless payments, proprietary for competitive and security reasons. In addition, the NFC Forum standards weren't ready when they went to market. Another good example of this is the access control card made by HID Global (http://www.hidglobal. com/), which is the little white card that people use to enter buildings. This is a great example of proprietary use because it wants to control the security on its cards. The "Understanding the effects of proprietary technologies" sidebar, later in the chapter, discusses the effects of working with proprietary technologies in detail.

Newer NFC implementations rely on standards to ensure that everyone plays by the same rules and implements NFC in the same way. When you see NFC discussed in this book, what the book is referencing are the implementations that follow the NFC Forum specifications, which include the International Organization for Standardization (ISO) (http://www.iso.org/iso/home.html) and the International Electrotechnical Commission (IEC) (http://www.iec.ch/) standards. The beginning of this chapter discusses the most important NFC standards and helps you understand why standards are important for any viable technology.

NFC supports a number of operational modes. These modes help determine the kinds of tasks you can perform using NFC. One of these modes, card emulation, makes it possible to use NFC in the same way that you employ smart cards. For example, you can use NFC to make a payment. NFC can also read tags to obtain various kinds of information. In fact, there are four kinds of tags to ensure that you can get information in various ways. In addition to reading tags, NFC can also write information to tags under the right conditions. Exchanging data between two NFC devices requires a common language. For example, you can't hold a conversation with someone who speaks German very well if you speak only Greek. Likewise, two devices must speak the same language, which is NFC Data Exchange Format (NDEF) in this case. Understanding the different modes of operation gives you a much better idea of how NFC works and why it's an important technology.

The chapter ends with some sources of additional information. NFC is a huge topic, and you can't get every bit of information about it in a single chapter. The NFC Forum provides you with the resources you need to learn just about everything knowable about NFC. By the time you complete this chapter, you will know the basis for the claims that NFC makes and understand better just how NFC fits with your organizational needs.

Understanding the Need for Standards

It isn't possible to create a technology that everyone can use without also creating standards to govern that technology. *Standards* are simply rules that everyone agrees to abide by to ensure that everyone's products can interact. A standard contains a precise set of rules so that less doubt exists about how to implement them. For example, a standard might define precisely which frequency a device should use when communicating or determine how much power the device should generate to ensure that the signal is neither too weak nor too strong.

In addition, standards rely on committees to create them and groups to certify them. The use of committees ensures that everyone's ideas appear as part of the standard when those ideas make sense to the remaining committee members. A small company might have some great ideas that will turn the technology from a dud into something everyone wants to use. Having a committee set up increases the chance that the ideas from the small company will actually appear as part of the standard.

Groups ensure that standards follow similar formatting and go through a similar certification process. In the case of NFC, the main standards group is the NFC Forum. The NFC Forum built its specifications on top of the NFC standards produced by the ISO/IEC, which often work together to create, promote, certify, and manage standards.

For the purposes of this book, the NFC Forum is the overarching authority on specifications. It classifies NFC tags as types 1, 2, 3, 4, and 5, which incorporate the standards defined by the ISO and IEC. These tag types also follow NFC Forum compliance for tag types A, B, F, and V, as shown in Figure 3-2, later in this chapter.

REMEMBER

It's important to understand that standards control only issues that matter to the technology, not elements that a vendor could use to individualize a particular technology experience. For example, the standards for NFC don't dictate that NFC-enabled devices must be a certain size or use a specific case color. By focusing on just the important parts of the technology, standards allow vendors to innovate and create better products. Some of these innovations end up in updated versions of the standard, so everyone benefits.

Investigating the Two Main NFC Standards

When working with NFC, you need to know about two ISO/IEC standards (ISO/IEC 14443 and ISO/IEC 18000-3) that set the rules for most of the tasks you perform using NFC. Just by knowing something about these two standards, you can avoid potential problems with your NFC setup as well as know which vendors and services to use when working with NFC. Products and services that you obtain must also adhere to the standards or you can't be certain that they'll interact with each other correctly.

In addition, it's helpful to know about a Japanese standard, JIS 6319-4, that specifies the characteristic of the Type 3 tag (see the "Working with the Type 3 tag" section of this chapter for details). You see Type 3 tags used for Felicity Card (FeliCa) applications. *FeliCa* is a contactless smart card application from Sony that is used for electronic money cards. The following sections tell you more about these standards.

DEALING WITH THE THREE NFC MODES

NFC devices actually work in three different modes, as you discover in the "Considering NFC Operating Modes" section of Chapter 4. As a result, NFC also works with the ISO/IEC 18092 standard for peer-to-peer mode. This standard logically follows the ISO/IEC 14443 standard but works instead between two NFC devices. (The ISO/IEC 14443 standard specifies communication between one device and a tag or smart card.)

The ISO/IEC 18092 standard is necessary, but not sufficient to establish interoperability between popular consumer devices. The NFC Forum Digital Protocol Specification harmonizes the ISO/IEC 14443, JIS 6319-4, and ISO/IEC 18092 standards into a single interoperable digital protocol that uses the common air interface.

The digital protocol specification also explains how vendors can build devices that are sensitive to all these different standards at the same time. The specification defines a mode switch and polling loop that enables a device to switch rapidly between these different standard protocols many times a second, looking for a compatible combination in a well-ordered way. This approach increases the responsiveness and compatibility between two devices, a device and tag, or a device and card reader that follow the mode switch standard, and without requiring the user to choose between the combinations manually — an impractical alternative.

TECHNICAL STUFF

You can find lists of NFC-related specifications and standards on a number of sites online. For example, you can find a list of NFC Forum-related specifications at `http://members.nfc-forum.org/specs/spec_list/`. For the most part, these standards and specifications provide you with detailed information you might never even need to know. The standards discussed in this chapter actually provide enough detail for the vast majority of people using NFC for useful applications.

Considering ISO/IEC 14443

The ISO/IEC 14443 standard defines the requirements for proximity cards commonly used for identification purposes. The ISO/IEC differentiates these cards from close-coupled cards (ISO/IEC 10536), which provide extremely close distances with the coupling device, and vicinity cards (ISO/IEC 15693), which provide longer distances from the associated coupling device. The standard appears in four parts, as presented in the following list:

» **ISO/IEC 14443-1:2008 Part 1: Physical characteristics (**`http://www.iso.org/iso/iso_catalogue/catalogue_ics/catalogue_detail_ics.htm?csnumber=39693`**):** Specifies how the cards are put together physically.

The standard discusses two types of cards: identification cards conforming to ISO/IEC 7810, and thin, flexible cards conforming to ISO/IEC 15457-1. However, the standard also recognizes that the technology could appear in other forms.

» **ISO/IEC 14443-2:2010 Part 2: Radio frequency power and signal interface** (`http://www.iso.org/iso/home/store/catalogue_tc/catalogue_detail.htm?csnumber=50941`): Determines the characteristics of the fields used to provide power and bidirectional communication between proximity coupling devices (PCDs) and proximity cards or objects (PICCs). This specification doesn't determine the means used to generate the field. Type A, B, and FeliCa cards use different modulation methods and coding schemes. Chapter 4 discusses these differences.

» **ISO/IEC 14443-3:2011 Part 3: Initialization and anticollision** (`http://www.iso.org/iso/home/store/catalogue_tc/catalogue_detail.htm?csnumber=50942`): Defines how the communication process begins, proceeds, and ends. For example, this part of the standard describes how a device polls (looks for) potential connection and then initiates a command to start communications. Type A, B, and FeliCa cards use different protocol initialization procedures. Chapter 4 discusses these differences.

WARNING

Even though Parts 3 and 4 of the standard tells you how communications work, the techniques used have patent protection. To use the technology, you must negotiate a license with the patent holder. The previews at `https://www.iso.org/obp/ui/#iso:std:iso-iec:14443:-3:ed-2:v1:en` and `https://www.iso.org/obp/ui/#iso:std:iso-iec:14443:-4:ed-2:v1:en` provide you with details about the various patent holders. When you buy a product, the vendor who produced the product has already procured a license to use the technology, so this requirement isn't a concern unless you're creating a new product that relies on the technology. (When in doubt, ask a lawyer!)

» **ISO/IEC 14443-4:2008 Part 4: Transmission protocol** (`http://www.iso.org/iso/iso_catalogue/catalogue_tc/catalogue_detail.htm?csnumber=50648`): Defines a messaging protocol to be used for communicating with proximity cards. For example, this part describes the format of a message that would be used to read data from or write data to a card. The same messaging protocol applies to both Type A and B cards. FeliCa uses a different protocol defined in the JIS 6319-4 standard.

REMEMBER

The ISO/IEC requires that you purchase copies of the standards. However, if you look at the links provided in the previous list, you find that you can preview the standards by clicking the Preview button and then obtaining some standard details from the preview. You can get a better idea of how card emulation works by reading the "Considering Card Emulation" section of this chapter. The "Communicating Between Devices" section of Chapter 4 provides additional details on how the devices that implement this standard work.

Considering ISO/IEC 18000-3

The ISO/IEC 18000-3 standard (http://www.iso.org/iso/catalogue_detail.htm?csnumber=53424) defines the requirements for Radio Frequency Identification (RFID) for item management. It is actually Part 3 of the ISO/IEC 18000 standard. You need to consider only Part 3 when working with NFC. The standard has a number of goals:

>> Define rules for communication between devices using frequencies that are available in any country.

>> Specify the same set of rules for every acceptable frequency so that moving from one frequency to another doesn't pose technical problems.

>> Reduce both software and implementation costs.

>> Create a common method for performing system management and control, and information exchange tasks as much as possible.

This standard defines three modes of operation. The modes don't interoperate with each other, but they also don't interfere with each other. In short, the modes are completely separate. Each mode defines different speed characteristics for transferring data between devices using differing signal-encoding techniques. Because the mode transitions occur automatically, you don't really need to know much more than that they offer different speeds.

Considering FeliCa (JIS 6319-4)

The JIS 6319-4 standard was originally proposed as an ISO/IEC 14443 (Type C) addition, but the committee rejected it. Unlike the other standards in this chapter, the Japan IC Card System Application Council (JICSAP) (http://www.jicsap.com/) regulates this standard. Unlike the other standards mentioned in this chapter, you can download a copy of this standard from http://www.proxmark.org/files/Documents/13.56%20MHz%20-%20Felica/JIS.X.6319-4.Sony.Felica.pdf. Scanning the standard can be educational, but what you really need to know is that the tags work at the normal 13.56 MHz used by other NFC technologies and provides a 212 Kb/s data transfer rate.

Considering Card Emulation

It's possible to use NFC for card emulation (which can mimic a contactless smart card) for purposes such as those shown in Figure 3-1. Smart cards allow people to do all sorts of things, such as pay for goods, have access to various forms of transportation, and gain access control to buildings.

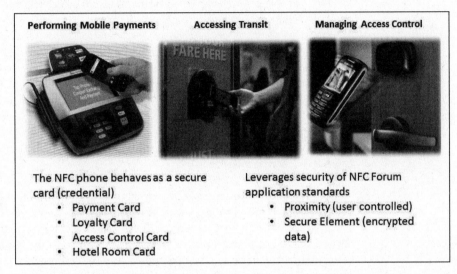

FIGURE 3-1: Examples of how NFC is typically used in card emulation mode.

Performing Mobile Payments

The NFC phone behaves as a secure card (credential)
- Payment Card
- Loyalty Card
- Access Control Card
- Hotel Room Card

Accessing Transit

Managing Access Control

Leverages security of NFC Forum application standards
- Proximity (user controlled)
- Secure Element (encrypted data)

You find smart cards all over the place, which really can become a problem. Filling your pockets with twenty or so smart cards makes working with them a nightmare. NFC-enabled devices solve this problem by storing the information needed in a single device that you can simply use in place of the smart card: The NFC-enabled device *emulates* (or mimics) the smart card you need. The following sections provide you with a more detailed look at how various card-emulation scenarios work so that you have a better idea of just how flexible NFC is in performing this particular task.

Performing mobile payments

When using your smartphone to make a mobile payment, you usually use an app to perform the task. (It is possible to use NFC to make payments without an app, such as when using a keychain fob, but most people find it easier to manage their payments using an app, and apps are common today.) You rely on the app to sign, encrypt, and decrypt the data packets that transfer financial information between the smartphone and the financial institution that makes the payment.

UNDERSTANDING THE EFFECTS OF PROPRIETARY TECHNOLOGIES

In most places in this book, you see NFC described from the perspective of technologies that follow the standards completely. The main reason to take this approach is that trying to describe all the exceptions to the rule would be confusing and not useful. Vendors are moving toward implementing the standards completely, so this book looks toward the future, rather than the past.

However, many tag technologies in existence today don't conform to the standard for various reasons. The most common reason is that manufacturers initially wanted to use their own proprietary system to implement tag technologies. Most people who encounter NFC in the real world today will actually see technologies that don't technically use NFC as defined by the NFC Forum specifications, but that are using the NFC frequency and a proprietary technology that predates any formal standard. As an example, the access control card from HID Global (http://www.hidglobal.com/), while technically not NFC, acts as though it is.

What all this means to you as you're reading this book is that some of the technologies you encounter will work like NFC, but won't actually use NFC specifications. In this case, things like NFC tag type have no meaning. These technologies don't implement an NFC tag type, but do interoperate with NFC devices in such a manner that the device can still read the tag by relying on a proprietary application. The same can be said of other NFC elements: These proprietary tags and associated applications don't use them, but do work with the NFC devices in such a manner that they appear to be NFC-specific. As with most technologies, NFC is enduring growth pains that will make understanding how the technology works now a bit confusing at times.

The apps come from many different vendors, including Apple Pay (http://www.apple.com/apple-pay/), Samsung Pay (http://www.samsung.com/us/samsung-pay/), Google Wallet (https://play.google.com/store/apps/details?id=com.google.android.apps.gmoney), PayPal (https://www.paypal.com/), and other merchant-branded apps. In addition, many banks are now getting into the picture. Chapter 9 discusses two kinds of payment systems: open loop and closed loop. For some people, the array of payment options is dizzying. However, having a range of payment options is much better than dealing with a one-size-fits-all approach. The best technologies will become standard at some point, but for now, innovation demands an assortment of choices in order to find out which technologies really are best to use. (The marketplace will decide.)

REMEMBER

The app is only part of the solution. When in card-emulation mode, the app provides the actual encryption of the data flowing between the smartphone and the financial institution. However, the encryption is based on tokens stored in the smartphone's Secure Element (SE) or by using Host Card Emulation (HCE). In addition, the app uses either SE or HCE to execute in a secure environment to ensure that outsiders can't access it. The "Creating a Secure Environment" section of Chapter 2 discusses these two strategies. HCE is definitely considered by many to be the wave of the future because it doesn't require any special hardware. Larger banks, such as Sberbank (http://www.sberbank.ru/en/individualclients), have adopted HCE using services from places such as Sequent (http://www.sequent.com/) because these companies support both SE and HCE seamlessly. You can read the details about why organizations would choose Sequent at http://www.sequent.com/europes-3rd-largest-bank-chose-sequent-hce-mobile-payments/.

A user must still initiate and participate in the transaction before a vendor receives payment. Of course, this means ensuring that the smartphone has NFC enabled (or turned on). The user must initiate the NFC conversation through an act such as tapping. The app will also ask the user for input — the user must select a payment option and approve the transaction. In many cases, the user must also provide some sort of credential — a fingerprint or Personal Identification Number (PIN). The actual process takes just a couple of seconds. The smartphone app typically displays some sort of progress indicator and then a message (such as Done) to indicate that the transaction was successful. Having standards as well as organizations that understand those standards makes the process simpler than using other technologies. The demo on the Apple Pay site (you simply click the Watch the Demo link at the bottom of the iPhone section) shows how fast and easy the process can be.

Accessing transit

You can find a number of transit schemes that rely on NFC. One of the simplest is the one offered by American Express (https://network.americanexpress.com/en/globalnetwork/transit/). (The Oyster Card (https://oyster.tfl.gov.uk/oyster/entry.do), for European travelers, is another popular example.) Any card that has the contactless indicator (or logo) makes travel easy. You can also use your NFC-enabled mobile device. The transit vendor must also support contactless payments. When this is the case, you simply tap your card or mobile device at the terminal in order to gain access to the mode of transportation. According to the American Express site, the entire transaction takes place in less than 500 ms. To use American Express, your mobile device must support the Android OS KitKat or later (https://network.americanexpress.com/en/globalnetwork/mobile-hce/ and https://www.android.com/versions/kit-kat-4-4/).

The American Express solution works well when you need to pay for your ticket. You need another solution when you rely on a transit pass for boarding transportation such as a bus. Most transit authorities currently use a physical transit pass that contains an NFC chip. However, companies like Apple want to replace those physical transit passes with smartphones that use special apps (http://www.cultofmac.com/301019/apple-wants-replace-transit-passes-iphone-6s-nfc/). In this case, your transit pass is actually stored on your smartphone so that all you need to do is tap at the ticket barrier to gain access. The Chicago Transit Authority (CTA) is currently experimenting with Ventra (https://www.ventrachicago.com/), a solution that lets people load transit tickets from anywhere (http://chi.streetsblog.org/2014/10/22/new-ventra-app-takes-very-small-step-towards-transit-fare-integration/).

When working with transit, understanding the role of the Trusted Service Manager is important. Companies such as Gemalto (http://www.gemalto.com/transport/mobile-nfc) provide access to the app required to make transit solutions work. In this case, the technology relies on a token that's transmitted to the NFC reader in the ticket barrier. A company such as Gemalto operates as the Trusted Service Manager (TSM) (http://www.gemalto.com/techno/inspired/nfc/tsm) to store the app, tokens, and other essentials required to make the transit solution work. Even though the TSM doesn't actually participate in the transaction, it does provide services such as enrolling new users, updating applications, and activating or deactivating services.

TIP

The role of TSMs is essential in making mobile payment and transit solutions work well. However, given the complexities of making these solutions work, only a few TSMs are available today. Here are the largest TSMs that you encounter:

>> **Gemalto (US):** http://www.gemalto.com/

>> **First Data (US):** https://www.firstdata.com/en_us/home.html

>> **Oberthur (Europe):** http://www.oberthur.com/

>> **Giesecke & Devrient (G&D) (Europe and Canada):** http://www.gi-de.com/usa/en/index.jsp

>> **SK C&C (Asia):** http://www.skcc.com/

Managing access control

Access control is all about identification. Knowing who is asking to interact with a particular resource is the essence of access control. For example, you don't want someone walking into a room to gain access to the items it contains until you know that the person is supposed to be there. Of course, the oldest form of access control is the key: When you hold the key, you also have the access. However, modern access control generally relies on something a bit better than a key. Smart cards provide access to all sorts of resources, such as hotel rooms or items like copiers.

NFCPorter (`http://www.nfcporter.com/`) and solutions like it make the process of managing access control a lot easier. In this case, a user taps her smartphone on an access panel to obtain access to some resource, such as a room. To use this setup, the user's smartphone must have the required app loaded and NFC enabled. The setup process is straightforward:

1. A configuration smartphone sends a pairing key to the reader mounted on the wall using a configuration app.

2. A user smartphone taps the reader.

3. The reader verifies the pairing key on the user smartphone and requests a unique user identifier.

4. After the user enters the unique user identifier, the reader sends the information to a superior system for rights validation and predefined action execution, such as opening a door. At this point, the system is configured for use.

To use the access control solution, the user must have the phone turned on and NFC enabled. Using the access control system follows these simple steps:

1. The user taps the phone on the reader.

2. The phone automatically starts the identification app.

3. The phone verifies the pairing key and sends the unique user identifier to the reader.

4. The reader sends the user identifier to the superior system for rights validation.

5. The system performs the predefined action, such as opening the door.

A process of this sort can provide access control for any resource. You can use NFC to perform tasks such as opening a car door, accessing a copier, or just about any other resource you can imagine. The steps are always the same — configuration, followed by access. These systems all have a pairing key setup of some sort and they all rely on unique user identifiers (which could be anything, such as a fingerprint). The point is that NFC makes access control easy, fast, and secure.

Defining the Five Tag Types

Tags let you perform various kinds of information-related tasks. For example, you can use a tag to store information on various topics at a kiosk. Each tag has specific functionality that lets you use the tag for particular tasks. NFC currently works with five tag types. The following sections discuss the five tag types you can use today and give you some ideas of how you might use tags in the future. The final section discusses the tag activation sequence so that you better understand that NFC always requires activation of some sort — the information isn't simply sent to your NFC-enabled device without your permission.

WARNING

It's important to remember that only the five tag types in use today are standardized and guaranteed to work with the NFC-enabled device you own today. Future tag types will require standardization and could potentially require some type of upgrade of your NFC-enabled device before you can read (or optionally write) them.

	NFC Forum Platform				
	Type 1 Tag NFC-A compliant	**Type 2 Tag** NFC-A compliant	**Type 3 Tag** NFC-F compliant	**Type 4 Tag** NFC-A, NFC-B compliant	**Type 5 Tag** NFC-V compliant
Compatible Products	Broadcom Topaz	NXP MIFARE Ultralight/ NXP MIFARE Ultralight C NXP NTAG 21s (F) NXP NTAG I2C	Sony FeliCa	NXP DESFire / NXP SmartMX-JCOP (MIFARE DESFire implementation) / ST Microelectronics	NXP ICODE SLI (x) / Texas Instruments Tag-It HF-I / EM423x / ST Microelectronics
Memory Size	454 Bytes	48 / 128 / 144 / 504 / 888 / 1904 Bytes	1, 4, 9 KBytes	2 / 4 / 8 KBytes / up to 144 Kbytes / 106 Kbytes	32 / 112 / 128 / 160 / 256 Bytes
Unit Price	Low	Low	High	Medium / High	Low / Medium
Data Access	Read/Write	Read/Write or Read-only	Read/Write or Read-only	Read/Write or Read-only	Read/Write
Active Content*	-	-	-	x / ▢	-
Operation Specification	ISO/IEC 14443-3 A	ISO/IEC 14443-3 A	JIS 6319-4	ISO/IEC 14443-4 A/B	ISO/IEC 15693

*Active Content refers to the ability for a developer to store and run small applications (called 'cardlets') on the tag. Only the Type 4, non-DESFire tags have this ability, all other tags are treated as static storage device .

MIFARE Ultralight, NXP MIFARE Ultralight C, MIFARE DESFire, SmartMX, NXP ICODE SLI(x) are registered trademarks of NXP B.V.
Tag-It HF-I is a registered trademark of Texas Instruments.
EM423(x) is a registered trademark of EM Microelectronic.

FIGURE 3-2: A quick overview of the tag types.

TECHNICAL STUFF

Notice the active content row of the table. This row tells you whether a tag can modify itself. For example, a tag based on Java Card technology (http://www.oracle.com/technetwork/java/embedded/javacard/overview/index.html) can include a self-incrementing counter that modifies the NFC Data Exchange Format (NDEF) content on the card. Every time someone reads the card, the counter increments itself. This means that you can determine how many times someone has read the card, even if you aren't the person using it. Only the 32 KB version of the Type 4 tag currently allows for active content. Don't worry precisely how NDEF works for now — the "Defining the NFC Data Exchange Format (NDEF)" section of this chapter fills in the details for you.

Working with the Type 1 tag

The NFC Type 1 tag is the simplest of the offerings. It's also the slowest chip, but because of the simplicity it offers, it's also possible to stuff more memory on this chip. Because these tags are simple, they also tend to be inexpensive, but can lack the functionality that you might need for some applications. You typically see these tags used for these types of applications:

>> One-time provisioning

>> Read-only applications

>> Business cards

>> Pairing devices with Bluetooth

>> Reading a specific tag when more than one tag is present

Working with the Type 2 tag

The Type 2 tag tends to be the most popular offering because it offers just enough functionality at the right price to meet a wide range of needs. The Type 2 tag is also faster than the Type 1 tag, so you can rely on it in applications in which a user expects nearly instant communication. You typically see these tags used for these types of applications:

>> Low-value transactions

>> Day transit passes

>> Event tickets

>> URL redirects

Working with the Type 3 tag

As mentioned in the "Investigating the Two Main NFC Standards" section of this chapter, the Type 3 tag relies on a different standard than the other tags in this group. The Sony FeliCa tag is a Japanese innovation and sees wide use in Asia. This is a sophisticated tag that provides a wide range of functionality, but also comes with a relatively high price tag. You typically see these tags used for these types of applications and used primarily in Japan:

>> Transit tickets

>> E-money

>> Electronic ID

>> Membership cards

>> E-tickets

>> Health care devices

>> Home electronics

Working with the Type 4 tag

The Type 4 tag offers the most flexibility and memory of all the tags. It comes with a moderate to high price tag, depending on the amount of memory you get. The most important reason to get this tag is security: It offers the functionality needed to perform true authentication. In addition, this is the only tag that provides support for ISO 7816 security (see http://www.iso.org/iso/catalogue_detail.htm?csnumber=54550) as well as allows for self-modification of NDEF content. Given the extra capability that this tag provides, you typically see it used for transit ticket applications.

Working with the Type 5 tag

The Type 5 tag offers support for the ISO/IEC 15693 specification (http://www.iso.org/iso/catalogue_detail.htm?csnumber=39694). In this case, the NFC Forum chose to support Active Communication Mode, which allows overall data transfer performance similar to the RF technologies already supported by NFC Forum. The reading distance is precisely the same as other NFC technologies. Because the standard mandates support for this mode, an NFC-enabled device that supports the Type 5 tag can read ISO/IEC 15693 tags. You typically see these tags used for these types of applications:

>> Library books, products, and packaging

>> Ticketing (such as ski passes)

>> Healthcare (medication packaging)

WARNING

Proprietary hardware can present compatibility issues and other dangers. For example, the proprietary tags you find in use generally require proprietary applications. In addition, these tags may look like NFC to the device that can access them, but the proprietary hardware often fails to implement NDEF or other NFC standards. Examples of this problem include MIFARE Classic for transit applications and DESFire for building access control. In short, even though these tags may look and even work like NFC tags, they really aren't NFC tags at all.

You'll eventually encounter some of these tags as you work with real-world applications. Fortunately, you don't have to try to figure out these tags and their intricacies on your own. The following list provides some resources you can use with dealing with these tag types:

» http://open-nfc.org/documents/STS_NFC_0707-001 NFC Tag Type 5 Specification.pdf

» http://open-nfc.org/documents/STS_NFC_0707-002 NFC Tag Type 6 Specification.pdf

» http://www.nxp.com/documents/application_note/AN1304.pdf

» http://www.nfcworld.com/2015/06/17/336050/nfc-forum-adds-support-for-type-v-tags/

Understanding the tag initiation sequence

When an NFC reader initiates a tag, the reader and the tag must follow a specific sequence to ensure proper operation. The reader and tag need to establish two things: that a specific tag is selected and what sort of tag is selected. Figure 3-3 shows how this sequence works for Type A cards. (Type B and F cards use a similar but somewhat different initiation sequence, but this sequence gives you an idea of how the initiation sequence will work.)

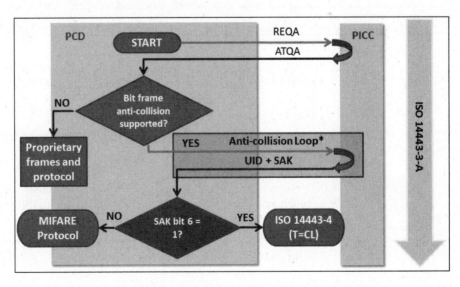

FIGURE 3-3: Performing a tag activation.

Whenever you work with NFC, there is a proximity coupling device (PCD) and a proximity inductive coupling card (PICC). The PCD emits a radio frequency (RF) signal that provides energy to the PICC. However, if more than one PICC is available within the required distance, all the PICCs respond, resulting in a collision. The initiation sequence ensures that the PCD selects only one PICC and communicates with it, preventing the collision from causing problems. When the PCD begins the initiation process by powering the PICC, it does so using the following steps:

1. The PCD sends a Request (REQA) command to the PICC. The REQA is specially constructed — it only has seven bits, it can't be confused with any other command. The PCD continues to send the REQA command until it receives at least one tag response. The intervals between these requests vary by vendor.

2. The PICC responds with an Answer to Request (ATQA) block. This block contains information such as a Unique Identifier (UID) prefix. It also tells the PCD whether the tag provides anticollision support. If not, the tag is proprietary — it doesn't provide standard NFC support. The UID prefix isn't the complete identifier; it contains only part of the UID.

3. When the tags provide anticollision support, the PCD sends a SELECT command that includes the UID prefix. Multiple tags can have the same prefix. If they do, the PCD detects this condition and sends another SELECT command with more prefix bits. As the PCD adds prefix bits, the number of responding tags becomes fewer until only one tag responds — the select tag.

4. The final step in the anticollision process occurs when the PCD sends out a SELECT command that includes the complete UID for the PICC.

5. The PICC responds by sending a Select Acknowledgement (SAK) command to the PCD. The PICC activates at this point.

6. The PCD must know how to interact with the PICC at this point. When bit 6 of the SAK contains a 1, the activated PICC supports the MIFARE protocol. Otherwise, the PCD can assume that the PICC provides standardized ISO 14443-4 support.

7. The PICC continues to process all commands until it receives a HALT command from the PCD. At this point, the PICC becomes disabled.

The REQA command works only on PICCs that aren't disabled — that is, that the PCD hasn't read before. In order to read disabled tags, the PCD instead issues a Wakeup (WUPA) command.

Defining the NFC Data Exchange Format (NDEF)

NFC really shines when it comes to peer-to-peer data exchange. However, just as with any other form of data exchange, the two devices have to agree on how to communicate. Think of it in human terms. If one person speaks German and the other French, neither party will understand the other and no communication can take place. It's the same for any communication, even between NFC-enabled devices. The two devices must agree upon a standardized method of communication as described in the following sections.

Understanding NDEF messages

NDEF messages provide a standardized method for a reader to communicate with an NFC device. The NDEF message contains multiple records, as shown in Figure 3-4. You get NDEF support only when working with standardized tags — proprietary tags typically don't provide this support. As previously mentioned, the NFC standard supports five tag types, all of which support the same NDEF message format.

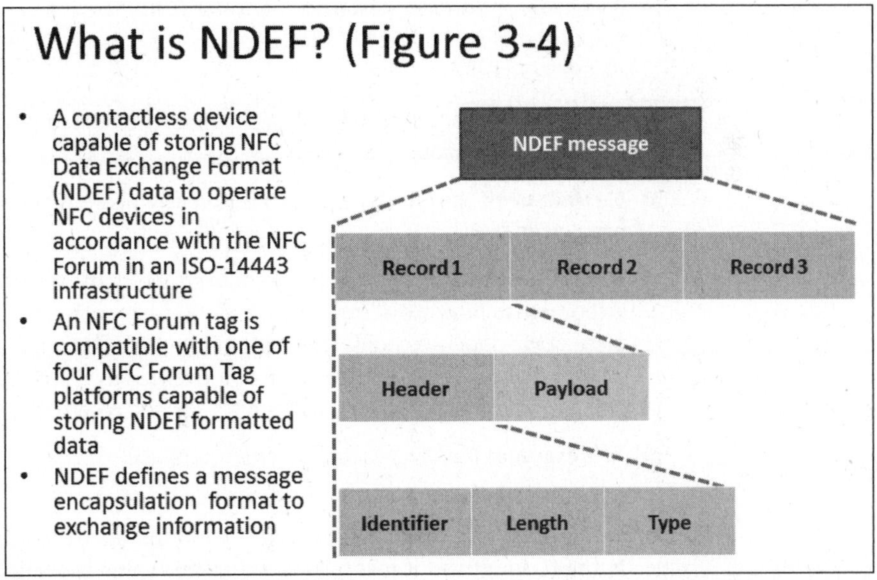

What is NDEF? (Figure 3-4)

- A contactless device capable of storing NFC Data Exchange Format (NDEF) data to operate NFC devices in accordance with the NFC Forum in an ISO-14443 infrastructure
- An NFC Forum tag is compatible with one of four NFC Forum Tag platforms capable of storing NDEF formatted data
- NDEF defines a message encapsulation format to exchange information

NDEF message

Record 1 — Record 2 — Record 3

Header — Payload

Identifier — Length — Type

FIGURE 3-4: Deciphering the NDEF messages.

Each record contains a header and a payload. The header contains useful information for the reader, such as the record ID, its length, and type. The type defines the sort of payload that the record contains. The payload is simply data.

Understanding NDEF records

The NDEF record contains quite a lot of information, as shown in Figure 3-5. The first eight bits actually contain flags that define how to interpret the rest of the record. Depending on how these flags are set, you can use various resources to discover what the record has to say to you. Of course, the easy way to get through this task is to have an application do it all for you, but the remainder of this section provides you with a useful overview.

The Type Name Format (TNF) field identifies the kind of content that the record contains. Here are the standard kinds of content that you could find in an NDEF record:

» **0 – Empty:** The record doesn't contain any information.

» **1 – Well-known:** The data is defined by the Record Type Definition (RTD) specification available from `http://members.nfc-forum.org/specs/spec_list/`.

» **2 – Multipurpose Internet Mail Extensions (MIME):** This is one of the data types normally found in Internet communications as defined by RFC 2046 (`http://www.faqs.org/rfcs/rfc2046.html`).

» **3 – Absolute Uniform Resource Identifier (URI):** This is a pointer to a resource that follows the RFC 3986 syntax (`http://www.faqs.org/rfcs/rfc3986.html`).

» **4 – External:** This is user-defined data that relies on the format specified by the RTD specification.

» **5 – Unknown:** The data type is unknown, which means that you must set the type length to 0.

» **6 – Unchanged:** Some payloads are chunked, which means that the data is too large to fit within a single record. In this case, each record contains a piece of the data — a chunk. This TNF indicates that this is not the first record in the chunk — it's one of the middle or the terminating records. The TNF is unchanged from the kind of data found in the first record of the chunked set.

» **7 – Reserved:** This value is reserved for future use.

The IL flag tells you whether the record contains an ID length field. It doesn't specify the ID length — it just tells you that this value is available.

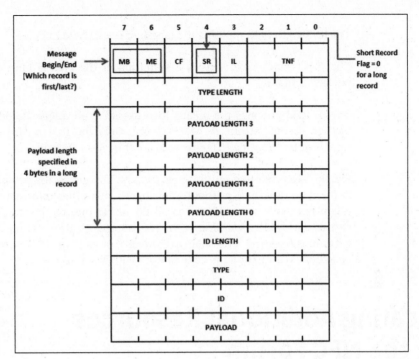

FIGURE 3-5:
Deciphering the
NDEF records.

The SR flag determines whether the record is a short record. A short record is one with a payload length <= 255 bytes. Normal records can have payload lengths exceeding 255 bytes up to a maximum 4 GB. Many use cases require the utmost economy of message size. The SR flag allows the use of a compressed record header by specifying the payload length in a single byte rather than requiring the normal four bytes. The CF flag tells you when a record is chunked. In other words, if you see this flag set, reading a single record won't provide you with all the data for that data item. You must read all the records associated with that data item to get the complete information about it.

An NDEF message can contain multiple records. The first record in a message has the MB (message begin) flag set to true so that you know that this is the first record. The last record in the message has the ME flag set so that you know this is the last record. All the intermediate records have both the MB and the ME flags set to false.

The Type Length field contains the length of the payload type in bytes. The payload type specifies the precise kind of data found in the payload. For example, just knowing that the TNF is a MIME data type isn't enough — you must know the precise MIME type (such as "text/plain") to process the data.

The Payload Length field contains the length of the payload in bytes. A record may contain up to 4,294,967,295 bytes (or 2^32 − 1 bytes) of data.

The ID Length field contains the length of the ID field in bytes.

The Type comes next. This is a definition of the precise kind of data that the payload contains.

The ID field provides the means for external applications to identify the whole payload carried within an NDEF record. Only the first record contains an ID; middle or terminating NDEF records don't have an ID field.

Finally, after defining all these particulars, you get to the payload. The payload is the data. However, without knowing all this other information, the payload might not make sense. You need all this other information to understand what sort of data you're working with. The tutorial at http://code.tutsplus.com/tutorials/reading-nfc-tags-with-android--mobile-17278 provides an example of how you might write code to work with NDEF records.

Locating Additional Resources on the NFC Forum

The NFC Forum (http://nfc-forum.org/) is one of the best places to obtain standardized information about NFC. The information applies to everyone. You find everything needed here to start your journey into using NFC in practical ways. The forum addresses all sorts of needs for users, marketers, implementers, managers, engineers, and developers. You can get a lot of information free, but to obtain the maximum benefit from the NFC Forum, you must become a member (see http://nfc-forum.org/about-us/join-the-forum/membership-overview/). The following list describes some areas of interest on the NFC Forum:

>> **What is NFC?** (http://nfc-forum.org/what-is-nfc/): This is an especially important area to visit when you first get started with NFC. Of special interest is finding out how to identify NFC (http://nfc-forum.org/what-is-nfc/identifying-nfc/). You may be surprised to find that it's all around you and you didn't even know it. It's also interesting to see NFC in action (http://nfc-forum.org/what-is-nfc/nfc-in-action/) because the material you see here gives you ideas of how you might employ NFC to meet your own needs.

>> **What is the N-Mark?** (http://nfc-forum.org/our-work/nfc-branding/n-mark/): NFC adherents use a number of symbols to indicate that their device or application relies on NFC. For example, you see variations of the NFC waves (http://www.clker.com/clipart-nfc-waves.html) used regularly. EMVCo payment acceptance devices — such as those that accept Apple

Pay — have their own distinct icon that incorporates the NFC waves symbol (see `http://tapatalk.imageshack.com/v2/14/10/22/66aa905911f00 8de14813122977b0f14.jpg`). In fact, all kinds of NFC symbols are out there, which makes things confusing. The N-Mark is a unifying logo that will eventually mark all uses of NFC. The "Getting the N-Mark logo" section of Chapter 9 discusses this issue in more detail.

>> **NFC Product Showcase** (`http://nfc-forum.org/nfc-product-showcase/`): Just in case you aren't convinced that NFC is everywhere yet, check out the NFC Product Showcase. The number and variety of products will astound you.

>> **NFC for Developers** (`http://tapintonfc.org/`): Interestingly enough, this particular feature isn't part of the actual NFC Forum — it resides on a supplementary site. This book doesn't show you how to write your own NFC application. However, if you want to write an application after seeing everything that NFC can do, you'll want to check out this site. It provides resources for Android, Blackberry, and Bluetooth developers.

TIP

It's important to realize that the NFC Forum isn't the only place a developer needs to visit. For example, if you want to build an Apple Pay application, you need to visit the Apple site at `https://developer.apple.com/apple-pay/`. Likewise, Android developers will want to visit the Android site at `https://developer.android.com/guide/topics/connectivity/nfc/ index.html` for detailed information.

>> **Specifications** (`http://nfc-forum.org/our-work/specifications-and-application-documents/`): One of the more important resources at your disposal is the list of specifications that the NFC forum supplies. You can get an overview of these specifications at `http://nfc-forum.org/our-work/specifications-and-application-documents/specifications/ nfc-forum-technical-specifications/`. However, to download the specifications, you must be a member (see `http://members.nfc-forum. org/specs/spec_list/`). These specifications help you to better understand how NFC works as well as provide a basis on which to make decisions about apps. They're also helpful in determining just how well vendors adhere to the standards and follow best practices. You don't need to memorize the specifications, but it's handy to know which specifications are available when you have questions.

>> **Certification** (`http://nfc-forum.org/our-work/compliance/ certification-program/`): Until now, The Open Group (`http://www. opengroup.org/certifications`) administered the certification process for NFC products. As of October 6, 2015, the NFC Forum took over this function. You want to be sure to get your product certified for a number of reasons — the most important of which is to ensure that it actually works with various NFC devices as it should. Of course, there is also the advantage of getting NFC Forum support and recognition.

REMEMBER

You may need to obtain additional certifications when performing certain tasks. For example, if you want to perform payment, you must get EMV certified. Additionally, some ticketing systems have their own certification processes. The NFC Forum certifies only that you are adhering to NFC standards, but it has nothing to do with the payments process.

Chapter 4

Considering NFC Hardware

S ome people view anything done by modern devices as a sort of magic. Poof! Suddenly you've made a purchase without much effort at all. All that's missing is a guy in a black cape and top hat. Actually, no magic is associated with NFC. Like the Wizard of Oz, there really is technology behind the magic that NFC seemingly performs. This chapter unveils the magic for you and helps you understand why things work as they do.

Don't get the idea that you need an engineering degree, however. The chapter makes things simple and understandable. You begin by looking at the physical hardware. After that, you discover how the hardware makes communication happen using Radio Frequency (RF) energy. Getting through this part means discussing NFC communication and operating modes.

The next few sections discuss some of the technical issues behind NFC. Knowing this information helps you get the big picture of why NFC is such a cool technology and why you need to perform certain tasks to make it work. Mostly these sections take the magic out of NFC by revealing that everything works in a logical manner.

The final two sections address tasks that you might eventually need to do based on your new knowledge. The first is to add NFC support to an existing device. The second is to develop your own NFC solution. You may never actually perform these tasks, but it's good to know that you can. The point is that this chapter is a gentle introduction to the insides of NFC so that you know that no magic is involved — just good technology that makes NFC cool to use.

Understanding NFC Hardware Basics

NFC hardware doesn't look very complicated, and it really isn't. You have a controller chip in the phone. Antennas appear in any device or tag that provides NFC support because you need an antenna to transmit the RF energy. Think of the antenna as a sort of speaker for your radio. You couldn't hear the music without a speaker; likewise, NFC cannot send a signal without an antenna. Of course, the antenna also receives signals, much the same as your ears receive sound from the radio. The last part of the picture is the tags and emitters that contain the information with which you want to interact. The following sections describe these hardware elements in more detail.

Considering the NFC controller chip

A *controller chip* (a kind of CPU) accepts instructions provided by software and then processes those instructions to allow for the completion of tasks. It also provides a certain level of order and management by ensuring that the right data ends up in the right place at the right time. Figure 4-1 shows the NFC implementation for a typical mobile device. Any mobile device you use will include other items, but Figure 4-1 shows a simplified view of how most mobile devices implement NFC so that you get a better idea of the controller chip's role in making NFC work.

REMEMBER

Everything starts with a user accessing an application or with an event (such as tapping the smartphone on a cash register) automatically starting an application. The software that makes up the application provides the user interface that the user interacts with to perform tasks. It also provides detailed instructions to the controller chip through the operating system.

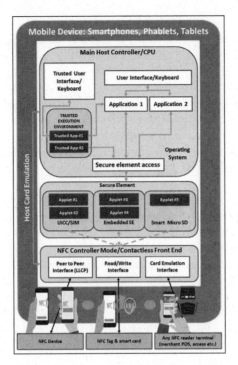

FIGURE 4-1:
An overview of the NFC hardware setup for a smartphone.

Even though the controller chip provides the means for performing tasks, it can't actually perform any tasks without software, and the software needs the user's direction (or some other type of input) on what sorts of tasks to perform next. The user might choose to transfer files. The act of telling an application to transfer a particular file starts a series of events in which the software provides detailed instructions to the controller chip on precisely how to perform the task. What the user sees is the act of making a connection and transferring the file — all the activity required to make these actions happen remain invisible to the user.

Some tasks require a secure connection. The "Creating a Secure Environment" section of Chapter 2 discusses two methods for creating a secure environment in which to perform sensitive tasks. The cloud-based security available when using HCE is one option. An alternative is to rely on the Secure Element (SE), with or without using HCE, to provide the required security. Figure 4-1 tells you more about the hardware used to make the secure access happen. The Main Host Controller can run both trusted (those that run with special protections) and untrusted (those that run without special protections) applications.

The trusted applications run in a special Trusted Execution Environment (TEE). A *TEE* is a secure area in the processor of a smartphone or other attached device that ensures that sensitive data is stored, processed, and protected in an isolated, trusted environment. The main idea is to enforce protected execution of authenticated code, confidentiality, authenticity, privacy, system integrity, and data access rights. You can read more about the TEE at `http://www.globalplatform.org/mediaguidetee.asp`.

REMEMBER

It is important to remember that the solutions for creating a secure environment are evolving as the technology evolves. The secure element solution was, for a time, seen as the best and only way to secure data. As the technology evolved, HCE was introduced as another potential solution. There are additional solutions that combine HCE and SE functions.

The SE is referred to as a storage location for data. Although this can be the case (and is true in some cases), the SE is actually a small processor that not only stores data securely but also runs special applications securely. When speaking of payments, for example, there is a requirement to have an application, and that application should be on the phone. For HCE, this is true: The application must marshall data between the phone and the cloud, and the application is what is actually talking to the payment reader, so the application is intimately involved in the transaction and must be much more complex. For an SE, the application on the phone is nothing but a switch to choose which card to use; the application that does the payment and the security runs completely on the SE. The application on the phone provides a second layer of security, in some cases, by asking for a pin or biometric before activating the switch.

REMEMBER

The SE is a physically separate element in the smartphone that can come in the following form factors:

>> **Universal Integrated Circuit Card (UICC)/Subscriber Identification Module (SIM):** Your mobile device (such as a smartphone) can have either a UICC (3G or 4G devices) or a SIM (2G devices) that is typically issued by the mobile carrier. Both chips store the International Mobile Subscriber Identity (IMSI) number and its related key used to identify your particular device. The chips can perform a number of tasks, such as storing contact information. Carriers can lock the SIM and prevent consumers from using it on other networks. A UICC has significant advantages over a SIM, and you can read about them at `http://www.justaskgemalto.com/en/communicating/tips/what-uicc-and-how-it-different-sim-card`. For the purposes of this book, all you need to know is that this chip provides identification information.

>> **Embedded SE:** An embedded SE provides all the elements of an SE as described in Chapter 2. However, the vendor permanently attaches it to the motherboard of whatever device uses it. Some people consider the permanent nature of embedded SE an additional security feature because the chip must stay with the original smartphone (making hacking harder).

>> **Smart Micro Secure Digital (SD) card:** The Smart Micro SD card is a removable flash memory card that stores identification information and communicates with NFC using the same Single Wire Protocol (SWP) used by UICCs and SIMs. Consumers typically obtain Smart Micro SD cards from service providers including banks, credit card companies, retailers, transportation providers, and governments. Unlike UICCs and SIMs, the consumer normally owns the Smart Micro SD card and can easily move it to another device. You can read more about the secure element options at http://www.secureidnews.com/news-item/nfcs-secure-element-war/.

DIFFERENTIATING BETWEEN NFC CONTROLLER AND NFC READER CHIPS

Depending on your level of involvement with NFC, the kinds of equipment you use, and the environment in which you work, you could find yourself using a device with an NFC reader chip inside, rather than an NFC controller chip. You need to know the difference because the chip chosen for a particular application affects the cost, size, power consumption, and, most important, the functionality of the product. The older the device, the more likely you are to encounter an NFC reader (which implements only ISO 14443-2), rather than an NFC controller chip (which implements the entire ISO 14443 standard).

When working with an NFC reader chip, the device designer must implement more of the NFC functionality through the Main Host Controller. An NFC controller chip handles the messy parts of features, such as

- Anticollision and selection process

- Additional framing required when using different tag technologies

- NFC operating modes such as card emulation and peer to peer

The bottom line is that when using an NFC reader chip, the designer must have a much greater knowledge of how NFC works. The additional requirements take time to implement, slowing the time to market for a device that uses an NFC reader chip in most cases. However, the trade-off is that an NFC reader chip costs less, consumes less power, and is generally smaller than an NFC controller chip.

No matter which form of security NFC uses, the signals end up at the NFC Controller (NFCC)/Contactless Front End, where NFC uses one of three modes to interact with external entities (devices, tags, cards, or anything else NFC can interact with). The NFCC acts as a gatekeeper — determining what mode to use to access the external entity and whether it requires HCE or SE for security needs (assuming the access requires security).

Communicating with the antenna

Every NFC device requires an antenna. You can't send and receive data without one. Figure 4-2 shows a typical antenna for a tag. The "Finding the Device Sweet Spot" section of Chapter 11 shows a similar antenna for a smartphone. In general, the antennas all look similar because they provide the same functionality no matter what sort of device you use.

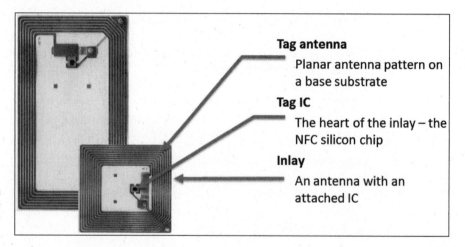

Tag antenna
Planar antenna pattern on a base substrate

Tag IC
The heart of the inlay – the NFC silicon chip

Inlay
An antenna with an attached IC

FIGURE 4-2: Viewing the antennas used for tags.

The antenna attaches to some sort of chip or Integrated Circuit (IC). For the tag shown, the chip is relatively simple — a smartphone would have more hardware associated with the antenna (as shown previously in Figure 4-1). The chip provides any memory, intelligence, and programming the tag requires.

Of course, you need something to hold everything together. The antenna wires won't tolerate much abuse, so the tag relies on an inlay to ensure that the tag remains functional. Don't get the idea that the inlay is always a simple piece of plastic (this is true for a dry inlay only). The inlay construction and materials vary according to the purpose of the tag. For example, an on-metal sticker has six layers of material that include a ferrite foil barrier to keep the metal used to hold

the tag from interacting with the antenna. You can see a number of inlay types at
`https://rapidnfc.com/nfc_tag_formats`.

Understanding tags and emitters

The hardware begins with two separate physical pieces, but NFC couples these pieces to form a unit using RF energy. Figure 4-3 shows the role of the emitter (a device such as a smartphone) and the tag (which could be anything the emitter wants to interact with, including another smartphone).

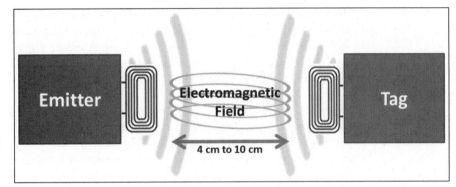

FIGURE 4-3:
Showing how emitters and tags work.

The combination of the two antennas and the air between them creates an air core transformer. The energy in the emitter creates an electromagnetic field that induces an electrical current in the tag. For NFC, the coupling takes place at a range between 4 cm and 10 cm. In order to work, the electromagnetic field produced by the emitter antenna must be strong enough to induce a current in the tag antenna. Otherwise, no communication can take place. Just knowing that the coupling takes place is enough information for working with NFC, but if you want to know more about the specifics of air core transformers, you can read about them at `http://www.ehow.com/how-does_4671982_air-core-transformers-work.html`.

TECHNICAL STUFF

Air core transformers are notoriously inefficient, which is one reason that the coupling distance between the two devices is so limited. The tuning of the antennas to provide matching between emitter and tag helps determine the connection range of the devices. When the emitter antenna is properly matched to the tag antenna, you obtain the maximum coupling possible. This concept is important to keep in mind as you read later chapters. Many of the problems associated with NFC tag interactions are the result of poor coupling, influenced by the presence of external factors, such as a metal mounting surface, the presence of an elemental factor (for example, water), or the distortion of the antenna in some manner, which affects tuning.

Considering NFC Communication Modes

The NFC communication modes determine how two NFC-enabled devices talk to each other. A communication consists of an *initiator*, which is the device that starts the communication, and a *target*, which is the device that receives the initial signal from the initiator. The following sections help you understand the two modes of communication.

Understanding active mode

When working in active mode, the initiator and target both have power supplies, so it isn't necessary for the initiator to send power to the target to allow the target to perform useful tasks. The two devices use alternate signal transmissions to send data to each other. In other words, both devices generate an RF field and send data by modulating that RF field.

When in active mode, the two devices use an Amplitude Shift Keying (ASK) modulation scheme (see `https://www.tmatlantic.com/encyclopedia/index.php?ELEMENT_ID=10420` for details on how ASK works). To avoid collisions, the receiving device turns off its field, so only one device is transmitting at any given time. Advantages of using active mode are that the data rate is usually higher and it's theoretically possible to work at longer distances.

Understanding passive mode

When working in passive mode, the initiator sends RF energy to the target to power it. The target modulates this energy in order to send data back to the initiator. Unlike active mode, the target relies on *load modulation* (making changes to the amplitude of the original signal) to transmit data (see `http://www.gorferay.com/energy-transmission/` for details on how load modulation works). It doesn't generate a field of its own, but rather changes the field of the initiator to transfer data.

Considering NFC Operating Modes

The operating mode determines the specific kind of task that NFC is performing at any given time. The devices interacting at the time allow for certain operating modes. The following sections describe each of the operating modes.

Working in card emulation mode

Card emulation mode places the NFC device in passive communication mode. The device acts precisely the same as a smart card. Figure 4-4 shows some of the ways in which you can use an NFC device in card emulation mode. It's important to remember that NFC security (through an SE or HCE) only protects the tokens used to identify the individual. You must still have an application that provides security for the data.

- The NFC phone behaves as a secure card (credential)
  - Payment Card
  - Loyalty Card
  - Access Control Card
  - Hotel Room Card

- Leverages security of NFC Forum application standards
  - Proximity (user controlled)
  - Secure Element (encrypted data)

FIGURE 4-4:
Using card emulation mode.

As described in Chapter 1, your NFC-enabled device can emulate more than one smart card, and the smart card support can include more than one form of identification. For example, the same digital wallet can hold loyalty cards and credit cards.

Working in reader/writer mode

When working in reader/writer mode, most NFC devices act as readers, as shown in Figure 4-5. The NFC device works in active mode to read the content of a tag. When it detects two or more tags, it relies on an anticollision algorithm to select just one tag. The NFC device must also detect the tag type (ISO/IEC 14443 A/B or FeliCa) and interact with it appropriately. The method used to perform anticollision depends on the tag type.

The application that interacts with the NFC data interprets the tag data and reacts accordingly. For example, when reading a tag containing a Uniform Resource Identifier (URI), the device opens a browser and the browser opens the content pointed at by the URI. All the user sees is a browser with web content displayed in it — the process for opening the URI remains hidden from view.

- The NFC Phone behaves as a card Reader
- Smart Posters/Displays contain NFC tags
- NFC Tag contains URL coded per NFC Forum standard
- Phone automatically jumps to URL
- User is presented with guidance and information
- Implementations include public transit, advertising ...

FIGURE 4-5:
Using reader/
writer mode.

REMEMBER

The originator of a tag can protect the tag content. Some tags provide for global locking, while other tags allow locking of selected data within a protected area of memory. When the tag remains unlocked, an NFC device can also write data to the tag. In order to write data to a tag, you must have a tag writer application, such as TagWriter (`https://play.google.com/store/apps/details?id=com.nxp.nfc.tagwriter`) installed on your device. After the application starts, you typically use steps like these to write data to a tag:

1. **Select an encoding type.**

The *encoding type* determines the kind of data that the tag contains. Here are some typical encoding types:

- Contact
- URI
- Plain text
- Short Message Service (SMS)
- E-mail
- Telephone
- Bluetooth

2. **Define a bookmark to hold the data.**

3. **Create the data.**

4. **Choose the encoding options, which can include:**

   - Locking the tag from further changes

   - Writing multiple tags using the same data

   - Confirming the overwriting of existing tag data

5. **Tap the tag to encode it.**

   The process will typically take a few seconds, so you must leave the device in place until the application tells you that encoding is complete.

Working in peer-to-peer mode

Two powered devices can engage in peer-to-peer mode, which is NFC specific. However, the initiator starts with its RF field turned on, and the target starts with its RF field turned off. (The target can also go into passive mode in order to reduce power usage.) The RF field state changes as the direction of communication changes. Figure 4-6 shows typical uses for peer-to-peer mode.

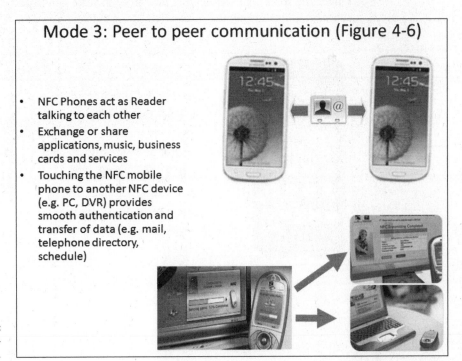

Mode 3: Peer to peer communication (Figure 4-6)

- NFC Phones act as Reader talking to each other
- Exchange or share applications, music, business cards and services
- Touching the NFC mobile phone to another NFC device (e.g. PC, DVR) provides smooth authentication and transfer of data (e.g. mail, telephone directory, schedule)

FIGURE 4-6: Using peer-to-peer mode.

REMEMBER

Be sure to note that NFC devices use a listen-before-talk protocol. The devices listen to ensure that no other device is transmitting before the device tries to transmit any information itself. Using listen before talk helps ensure that communication between devices doesn't suffer from interference from other devices. Given the short distances that NFC uses, the amount of interference is usually negligible, so listen before talk is the only protocol needed for this particular requirement.

During the initial communication, the two devices determine the communication parameters, such as data block size. The maximum data block size is 256 bytes. In many cases, peer-to-peer mode is used for pairing of the devices to use some other means of transferring the actual data, such as Wi-Fi or Bluetooth. This process is referred to as *Connection Handover*.

Differentiating Between Interrogators and Tags

When considering how two devices establish a connection, you can split NFC into interrogators and tags. It doesn't matter what the devices actually are; the terms reflect the roles that the devices play in the initial communication. Figure 4-7 shows graphically how the connection works between the two.

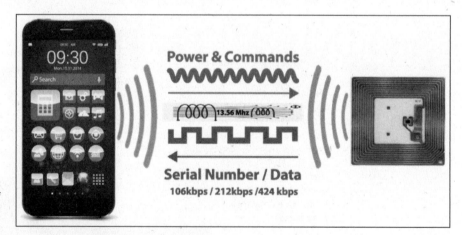

FIGURE 4-7:
The roles of interrogator and tag differ.

As you can see from the figure, one device is treated as powered, while the other isn't. The sequence of steps that interrogator and tag rely on is as follows:

1. The interrogator sends a signal to the tag. When the two devices are close enough, the signal powers the tag.

REMEMBER

The loosely coupled coils in the two devices actually create a high-frequency magnetic field between the two devices. After the field becomes established, the two devices can communicate.

2. The interrogator sends the first message to the tag to determine what sort of communication the tag uses (such as Type A or Type B).

3. The tag responds with the required information.

4. (Optional) The interrogator establishes a secure communication channel with the tag when required.

5. The interrogator sends out a command using the appropriate specification.

6. The tag receives the command and determines its validity.

   a. If the command is invalid, the tag doesn't do anything.

   b. If the command is valid, the tag responds with the appropriate data.

7. Steps 5 and 6 repeat as needed to complete the communication.

The interrogator modulates the RF signal at 13.56 MHz. Be aware that the data transfers at a different rate. Depending on the tag type, transmission can occur at

>> 106 Kbps

>> 212 Kbps

>> 424 Kbps

This is also the software view of the process. The initiator sends commands to the tag that interrogate the tag in various ways. The commands sent depend on the phase of the process and the application used to perform the communication. Depending on the command, a tag could respond with information such as a serial number or data contained within its memory.

Understanding the Transfer of Power

NFC antennas really do act as air core transformers and not truly as radiating sources. The low frequency of 13.56 MHz used by NFC means that the wavelength is about 22 meters (72 feet) long. To radiate the energy effectively as an antenna, the antenna length would have to be 11 meters (36 feet). You aren't going to fit a 36-foot antenna onto a smartphone, much less a tag. The radiation efficiency of an NFC antenna is essentially 0 (see http://www.antenna-theory.com/basics/gain.php for details on radiation efficiency), which means that you won't transmit anything in the traditional sense of the word.

What NFC is really using are loop-inductor antennas, as shown in Figure 4-8. Yes, they're called antennas, but you're talking about a specific kind of antenna, one that appears as a looped coil. The use of alternating current produces a continuous magnetic field from the smartphone. When that field gets close enough to the loop-inductor antenna in the tag, it induces a current in the tag loop-inductor. Inducing a current in the tag loop-inductor creates a *coupling* between the two antennas.

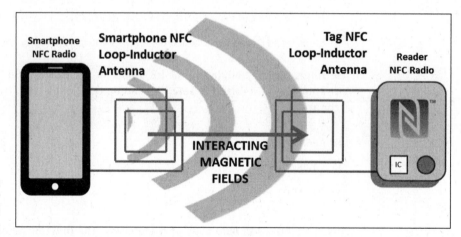

FIGURE 4-8: Inducing power from one device to another.

Now that the tag loop-inductor also has a current running through it, it also produces a magnetic field. What happens next is that you achieve mutual coupling of the two antennas, creating an air core transformer.

When the smartphone disrupts the current to the smartphone loop-inductor, the magnetic field collapses. The reader loop-inductor antenna still has a current running through it, however. As the reader loop-inductor antenna magnetic field collapses, it induces a current back into the smartphone loop-inductor antenna that the smartphone reads. The reader chip has modified the induced current from the reader loop-inductor antenna, so the smartphone sees a modulation change that reflects the data that the reader wants to transmit to the smartphone.

In general, the more turns of wire you can use to create the loop-inductor antenna, the better it performs. More turns means a larger magnetic field, which in turn means more induced energy. However, there are myriad reasons for creating loop-inductor antennas in a certain way that are well beyond the scope of this book. The number of turns is designed to make the antenna work best for this particular application.

The presence of metal (such as a ground plane on a PC board or a metal shield) near the wire also influences the magnetic field. Depending on the device, you may find that there is metal closer than you'd like. For example, the back of many smartphones contain metal. You must make the distance between the loop-inductor antenna and the metal as great as possible in order to improve the size of the magnetic field. This is why you often see a sheet of ferrite between the loop-inductor antenna and the back of a smartphone. You can read more about the math and electrical properties of NFC antennas at `http://www.antenna-theory.com/definitions/nfc-antenna.php`.

Communicating Between Devices

You need to understand the type of communication that occurs between devices. The kind of communication helps determine NFC functionality and the commands that the interrogator can send to a tag. Fortunately, standards define the communications in detail, so it's possible for one NFC device to interact with another.

To create a complete solution, an NFC device maker must support all the tag types: ISO/IEC 14443 Type A, ISO/IEC 14443 Type B, and FeliCa. Otherwise, each device implementation would need to come with instructions on which tag types it supports, and NFC couldn't make the inroads it does now. Even though there are three tag types, you can be sure that your NFC device supports all of them automatically (and invisibly). The following sections begin by defining some special communication principles and then continue with the various tag types.

Understanding what half duplex means

Imagine that you and your friend are trying to communicate using two tin cans and a string. Your friend talks into the tin can while you listen. You can hear your friend's voice just fine. The roles reverse and your friend can now hear your voice. The string between the two tin cans represents a channel — and there is only one of them. If you and your friend both decide to talk at the same time, neither of you can hear anything — because you both are talking and no one is listening. However, you can overcome this problem by adding two more tin cans and another string. Now there are two channels. You talk over one channel and listen over the other channel.

Devices that have just one channel can communicate only in *half-duplex* mode. One device must transmit while the other device listens. To get *full-duplex* capability, you must add a second channel. NFC provides half-duplex mode for communication. There is just one channel and it operates at 13.56 MHz. To add a second channel, NFC would require another frequency or some other means of providing that second string.

Working with ISO/IEC 14443 Type A tags

The ISO/IEC 14443 standard defines Type A tags, which are used in three different NFC tag types (as described in the "Defining the Five Tag Types" section of Chapter 3). An example of the Type A tag is the Oyster card (see https://oyster.tfl. gov.uk/oyster/entry.do for details). From an ISO/IEC 14443 standards perspective, the Type A tag has the following characteristics:

>> **Communication speed:** 106 Kbps, 212 Kbps, and 424 Kpbs

>> **Encoding:** 100% ASK, Manchester Encoding (see http://www.interfacebus. com/manchester-encoding.html for a description of how Manchester Encoding works)

>> **Bit order:** Least Significant Bit First (LSBF)

Working with ISO/IEC 14443 Type B tags

The ISO/IEC 14443 Type B tags work similarly to the Type A tags. They also are used in three different NFC Forum tag types. An example of the Type B tag is the Calypso ticket (http://www.calypsopark.com/en/waterpark/buy-online/).

The difference between a Type A and a Type B tag comes down to modulation. With all other factors the same, a Type B tag uses 10% ASK, Non-Return to Zero (NRZ) encoding. You can read precisely how NRZ encoding works at http:// whatis.techtarget.com/definition/NRZ-non-return-to-zero.

Working with FeliCa (JIS 6319-4) tags

The FeliCa tag type is a Japanese standard that you see used extensively in Japan and other Asian countries. This tag appears as the NFC Type 3 tag described in the "Defining the Five Tag Types" section of Chapter 3. An example of the FeliCa card is the Suica ticket (http://www.jreast.co.jp/e/pass/suica.html). The JIS 6319-4 standard defines these characteristics for the FeliCa tag:

» **Communication speed:** 212 Kbps and 424 Kpbs

» **Encoding:** 8-30% ASK, Manchester Encoding

» **Bit order:** Most Significant Bit First (MSBF)

Adding NFC to an Existing Device

The use of cloud strategies lets you add NFC to an existing device, assuming that certain conditions exist. In some cases, a device will never support NFC, and you can't do anything to change the situation. With this in mind, the following sections help you understand the requirements for adding NFC to an existing device so that you can obtain the benefits that NFC provides.

Ensuring the device supports NFC

You can't add full NFC support to every smartphone out there. However, a few companies produce kits to add NFC support to specific smartphones, such as the iPhone and Android. One such company is DeviceFidelity (http://www.credense.com/solutions/). It produced a microSD card and app that you can use to add NFC support to Symbian, Windows mobile 6.x, Blackberry, iPhone, or certain Androidmodels (http://www.tomsguide.com/us/Android-iPhone-NFC-MasterCard-PayPass,news-13857.html). Kili later purchased DeviceFidelity (http://www.nfcworld.com/2014/11/12/332607/kili-acquires-nfc-microsd-pioneer-devicefidelity/), which is now owned by Square (https://squareup.com/contactless-chip-reader). The reason you need to know this entire purchasing sequence is that the Internet hasn't quite caught up yet, and you may find resources you need under any of the three company names.

However, you can add limited NFC support to any smartphone that can run the required apps. Remember that NFC is a combination of the apps you use and hardware. By adding an NFC sticker to your smartphone and downloading the right app, you can create a workable solution for specific needs. These ad hoc solutions usually hinge on coupling the NFC sticker with another technology, such as Bluetooth. If your smartphone lacks an alternative connectivity solution, you really are out of luck.

Getting the right NFC add-on type

You aren't limited to just one way of adding NFC to your smartphone. In fact, you have several ways to do it:

>> External NFC Adapter

>> NFC Micro SD memory card

>> NFC sticker

The solution you use depends on how much you want to spend and the level of NFC support that you want. For example, the NFC sticker solution provides extremely limited support, but it also costs almost nothing to implement. The following sections describe the add-on types in more detail.

Using an External NFC adapter

The most popular way to add NFC support is to use a *dongle* (an externally attached device that extends the host device functionality). The advantage of this approach is that you don't have to modify or even open the device to add the required support. Using products such as the MobileMate card reader lets you add NFC functionality using the audio jack of your device (see `http://www.acs.com.hk/en/products/341/acr35-nfc-mobilemate-card-reader/` for additional details).

Using the Micro SD solution

The best solution in this category is Gemalto's Optelio (`http://www.gemalto.com/brochures/download/fs-microSD.pdf` and `http://www.gemalto.com/financial/cards/contactless-minitag`). However, DeviceFidelity CredenSE (`http://www.credense.com/solutions/`), Tyfone (`https://tyfone.com/technology/`), and Netcom provide a number of different solutions (`http://www.made-in-china.com/showroom/jblenetcom/product-detailebPmgkqyZNRY/China-Smart-Micro-SD-Card-with-Nfc.html`) for adding NFC support to your phone. The point is that you have numerous options to select from in this category, so ensuring that you get the add-on that works best for your smartphone, meets all your needs, and still keeps the cost low is important.

If you own an older iPhone, you may also want to look at the Gemalto Optelio iPay Cover(`http://blog.gemalto.com/blog/2014/12/18/how-to-nfc-enable-your-older-iphones-and-keep-up-with-the-iphone-6s-apple-pay-capabilities/`.

This solution won't work with Apple Pay, but you can use it with other NFC apps. It relies on a special cover to get the job done. However, with Apple integrating NFC into its newer iPhone versions, these cases are becoming hard to find.

Even if you choose not to use the DeviceFidelity solution, you owe it to yourself to view the video at https://www.youtube.com/watch?v=fWOKr5iC1WQ. The video demonstrates (quite quickly, in fact) that not all NFC add-on solutions are equal. Using some solutions forces you to rely on just one or possibly two sweet spots for creating an NFC connection. According to the demonstration on the video, CredenSE makes NFC a lot easier because you can hold the phone in nearly any position to make an NFC connection.

Using the NFC sticker solution

You can find instructions to provide extremely limited NFC support for just about any smartphone online. For example, the video at https://www.youtube.com/watch?v=cyPKdi5O9qc shows how to add NFC support using a special tag. The video maker emphasizes the need to use a tag that will work against a metal surface. This sort of addition may work on your smartphone, but you need to be aware that you still need an NFC application to make it work, and the level of support you receive is extremely limited.

Chapter 5

Considering NFC Software

ardware provides the means for performing tasks, but it doesn't actually perform the task. Think about a road. A road provides the means for getting from Point A to Point B, but standing on the road doesn't accomplish much. To get somewhere, you need transportation, such as a car. Likewise, software performs the tasks necessary to get somewhere using the means provided by the hardware. Chapter 4 discusses NFC hardware and helps you understand the means for performing tasks. In this chapter, you discover the software used to perform various tasks.

The chapter begins by telling you who is involved in NFC development. After all, you can't really get too far without knowing who's involved in the development process.

The next section describes how to turn NFC support on so you can begin using NFC in your device. Most devices come with NFC support turned off. To use NFC, you must turn on that support. You can turn it back off when you're finished, but most people just keep the NFC turned on for convenience because it doesn't use a significant amount of power and has a negligible impact on battery life. For Apple users, turning NFC on or off is not an option.

The next several sections describe various sorts of tasks. The first task is to use card emulation to do tasks like make a payment using Host Card Emulation (HCE). Part of working with HCE for payments is to ensure that the application encrypts data moving between two devices so that even if someone should manage to listen in, the data doesn't appear in clear text. Working with tags comes next. One section tells you how to write your own tags, while the next tells you how to perform various management tasks.

NFC actually relates to the Internet of Things (IoT). You find it used in many places that are identified with IoT usage. This section discusses what the IoT is all about in relation to NFC.

Finally, you discover the difference between web apps and mobile apps. Yes, there really are differences, even though clever coding can hide the differences from view. From a user's perspective, an app is an app, but from a development perspective, differences exist that you really do need to know about.

CONSIDERING THE NFC VIEW OF IOT

You might wonder why a book about NFC would contain anything about IoT. When people talk about IoT, they can mean a lot of things. At a high level, it is the connection of devices to the cloud. Many technologies can do this, and in the mobile setting, a connection can be made efficiently through something you could call *Proximity ID* technologies, which are comprised of RFID, NFC, and BLE. These technologies are cheap and extremely effective — they allow devices and people to connect to the cloud. These technologies will forever change the way people and things interact with each other. In fact, Proximity ID technologies represent the edge of IoT because they extend cloud computing out to the last 4 cm. That is, these technologies are used to connect people and things close by, from as far away as 50 m down to the last 4 cm, depending on the application.

Discovering the Key Players in NFC Development

Understanding the essentials of the NFC development environment is important because you want to know what sorts of options are available for making NFC work with your application. The following sections lead you through a process that helps you consider the various tools that NFC enables and how these tools end up on users' devices so that they can use them to perform useful tasks.

Creating the NFC ecosystem

The NFC Forum is the standards organization that supports the NFC ecosystem (see Figure 5-1). NFC Forum members inform and contribute to the development of NFC standards and technical specifications. However, even if you aren't a member, you can gain valuable information about NFC just by perusing the publicly available content. You can find more about the NFC Forum and its members on the Forum website (`http://nfc-forum.org/`).

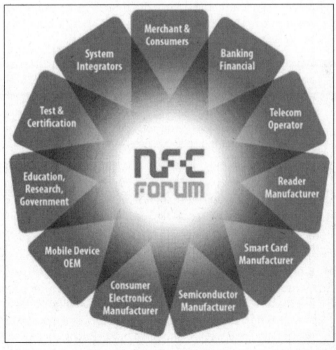

FIGURE 5-1:
Areas in which the NFC Forum provides a contribution to NFC development

Courtesy of NFC Forum.

REMEMBER

It's important to realize that the NFC ecosystem doesn't consist of just one particular group or meet one group's needs. It's a large number of different groups that work together to create NFC solutions. Yes, these solutions eventually end up in specific locations, but as you learn throughout the book, NFC is starting to crop up just about everywhere you can imagine.

The number of groups that make up the NFC ecosystem can be a bit overwhelming at first. If you simplify things a bit, though, you find that the groups make sense because they're the same groups that are part of many other computing environments today. The following list presents a simplified view of the NFC ecosystem that makes understanding where other groups might fit in easier:

>> **Low-level hardware:** Someone has to make the chips that go into the tags and other hardware used to create an NFC solution. The semiconductor manufacturer listens to the market (notably, input from business users and consumers) to determine the features that a chip set should provide. As these manufacturers obtain more input, the quality of the chips it provides improves.

>> **High-level hardware:** Manufacturers receive descriptions of various chips from low-level hardware manufacturers, choose the chips that work best for the solutions they provide, and then produce a product such as a tag or a reader. High-level hardware manufacturers include reader manufacturers, smart card manufacturers, consumer electronics manufacturers, and mobile device Original Equipment Manufacturers (OEMs).

>> **Developers:** Before the hardware can become useful, a developer must write an app to work with it. Developers create apps that perform all sorts of tasks with NFC. However, before you can be sure that the app will work in a reliable and secure manner, the app must go through a test and certification process. The NFC Forum provides guidelines on both the testing and certification process to ensure that the apps you receive are of the highest quality.

>> **Resellers:** You can buy NFC hardware alone and NFC software alone. In fact, you find many such situations here in the book. However, many buyers want a one-stop-shop solution. That's where the system integrator comes into play. A system integrator takes an NFC device, pairs it with appropriate software, creates any required documentation, and sells the entire package to either a business user or a consumer.

>> **Business users:** A business user is an individual or organization that purchases both hardware and software from a reseller. Most people think about merchants as business users, but you must also consider banking institutions and other financial groups, telecom operators, and that person giving the presentation next week. Many of the most exciting uses for NFC today appear as part of education, research, or government applications. All these people and groups fall within the business-user category.

>> **Consumers:** Consumers are people who purchase NFC products to improve their personal lives in some way. Increasingly, consumers are using NFC in their homes, cars, and even in a business setting. Consumers end the cycle of purchases within the NFC ecosystem.

Working with mobile payments

You can find many forms of NFC software today, all of which have their proponents and supporters. The software appears in many subcategories within a particular product category. For example, mobile payments appear in the five subcategories shown in Figure 5-2.

Notice that each of these subcategories provides a different kind of function when it comes to mobile payments. In addition, vendors tend to specialize in one particular field rather than embrace them all (which could be too much for any one vendor to handle).

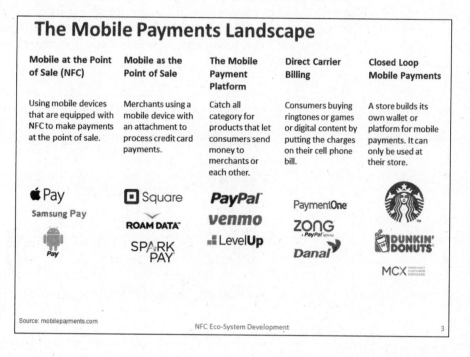

FIGURE 5-2:
Types of mobile payments and their supporters.

Members of the NFC ecosystem also tend to line up around a particular app type. Consumers likely want an app that addresses mobile at the point-of-sale needs. Merchants want a mobile app as the point-of-sale solution when working out of a kiosk or other mobile site. On the other hand, brick-and-mortar merchants, such as Starbucks, prefer to work with their own closed-loop mobile payment systems.

When researching your particular involvement with software development, you need to consider the area in which you want to participate and the kind of customer you want to attract. The organizations listed in Figure 5-2 can give ideas on how various companies implement these solutions. You can also research the organizations to discover best practices for your own development efforts.

Understanding how NFC is deployed in unique ways

The previous section discusses NFC as it applies to mobile payments. Mobile payment strategies are big now, but plan to see NFC in all sorts of other applications as well. Figure 5-3 shows how NFC might appear as part of a door-lock solution. You tap the door lock with your NFC-enabled device and it unlocks. No more worries about lost keys, passwords, or weird rituals. NFC makes things extremely simple and yet safe.

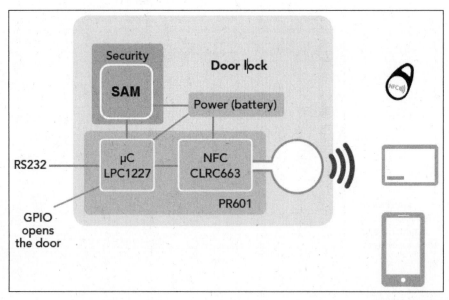

FIGURE 5-3: Considering the flow of a typical NFC deployment.

Courtesy of NXP B.V.

The door lock uses battery power. Trying to run an electrical circuit to the door lock would be difficult. In addition, a power failure would mean that you couldn't open the door using NFC.

The security for this setup is a combination of a Secure Access Module (SAM) and a TDA. (The TDA is the prefix for the TDA8026 chip or others in the TDA series that provides an ISO-7816 interface to the SAM, used primarily for smartcards.)

The NFC chip, CLRC663, acts as an NFC reader/writer front end. When a user provides a tag, smart card, or smartphone in card emulation mode that has the correct credentials, the NFC chip activates the LPC1227 microcontroller, which acts as a General Purpose Input/Output (GPIO) that opens the door. In addition, the LPC1227 provides all the logic for driving the CLRC663.

REMEMBER

A setup like this might seem overly complex, but modern technology makes it absurdly easy to copy standard keys and even some high-end metal keys. Smartcards have a proven record of accomplishment of protecting high-security assets. In addition, they're inexpensive. The lock itself is programmable. You can make it possible for cleaning staff to enter your home during specific hours, rather than allow them access 24 hours a day, as can be possible with a regular key. Programmable entry also means that you don't have to collect keys anymore — you just disable access for a particular key. You can also send someone a key using a nontraditional method, such as a Short Message Service (SMS) message to their smartphone. If you plan to have guests for the weekend, you can provide your guests with a temporary key to your home. Of course, this technology also works great in apartments, where the turnover rate is high, hotels, motels, or anywhere else that you need some means of controlling access using a door lock. Just think how this type of access control can be used by services like Airbnb.

This use of NFC demonstrates some basic principles used for just about every application. After you determine the call to action (what you are going to do/implement), you need the following items:

>> **Hardware:** As a starting point, you need an NFC-enabled reader, such as a smartphone. Then you need objects such as tags, cards, and smartposters that contain the information that you want read, and finally you need the hardware to encode the information into the tag's encoders for large jobs and its writers for small jobs.

>> **Coding software:** To write information to the tags/cards via the encoder/writer.

>> **Device software:** Software on a device that gives the device the intelligence it needs for a specific purpose. In this case, you need device software to make the lock work as a lock.

>> **Analytics software:** To provide data about the tag/card use, location access, opt-in, and so on.

Turning On Smartphone NFC Support

As mentioned in earlier chapters, you can't use NFC on your smartphone until you turn the support on (except in the case of Apple smartphones, for which support is always on, but in this case, you use NFC only for payments in the Apple operating environment). Having to turn the support on means that you can't accidentally start an NFC conversation (even though that's already difficult given the proximity required to start one).

However, it also means that you must take specific action to turn the support on before you can use NFC to perform tasks. In general, you need to perform these generic steps to turn the support on:

1. **Access the settings for your smartphone.**

2. **Locate the communication settings.**

3. **Change the NFC setting so that it reads on instead of off.**

TIP

Some smartphones, such as the Windows Phone, include separate settings for each NFC activity, such as sharing information and paying for products. You must turn each activity on separately.

4. **Exit the settings.**

Of course, your smartphone may require a little more interaction than these generic steps provide. Here are a few of the more common smartphone sites where you can find specific instructions for your phone:

>> **Android:** http://www.androidauthority.com/how-to-use-nfc-android-2-164644/

>> **HTC ONE:** http://www.htc.com/us/support/htc-one-m8/howto/465113.html

>> **Moto:** http://www.motorola.com/hc/3083/41/verizon/en-us/jcb1208131100.html

>> **Note 4:** https://support.t-mobile.com/docs/DOC-14676

>> **Samsung Galaxy:** http://www.att.com/esupport/article.jsp?sid=KB415822&cv=820

» **Windows Phone:** http://www.windowsphone.com/en-us/how-to/wp8/connectivity/nfc-on-windows-phone

TIP

You can find a listing of smartphones that provide NFC support at http://www.nfcworld.com/nfc-phones-list/. This listing provides links in most cases to the vendor sites where you can find additional information on how to turn on NFC support for a particular smartphone. The individual write-ups also tell you about the level of NFC support each smartphone provides so that you know what to expect from your smartphone in the way of tasks.

Performing Card Emulation Tasks

Rather than carry an endless assortment of credit cards with you, you can use your smartphone to make all payment transactions. Selecting the card you want to use on your smartphone is a lot easier than digging through the assortment of cards you own, looking for the one card you want.

Many people in the industry think that moving forward, the best way to provide NFC card emulation is to rely on Host Card Emulation (HCE). The "Creating a secure environment in the cloud" section of Chapter 2 provides you with a quick overview of HCE and defines the pros and cons of this approach.

REMEMBER

Although the examples in this section (and those that follow) use payments as an example, you can use HCE for many other purposes as well. Any NFC app that requires security potentially benefits from the use of HCE. The following sections give you additional details so that you can better understand why HCE is such a great idea.

Defining Host Card Emulation (HCE)

Host Card Emulation (HCE) has its genesis in the Interfaces Task Force of the NFC Forum, circa 2007. By 2010, all NFC controller vendors had incorporated support for HCE into their silicon. Blackberry 7 phones incorporated the first commercial version of HCE called Virtual Target Emulation, in the summer of 2011. But despite the hardware support for HCE in NFC chipsets, no developer access to HCE features existed in the other major smartphone or PC platforms that supported NFC.

Doug Yeager and Ted Fifelski, the founders of SimplyTapp, Inc. (https://simplytapp.com/), began experimenting with HCE in 2012. They modified a customized version of Android, called CyanogenMod (http://www.cyanogenmod.org), to enable the HCE features in the NFC controllers used in Android smartphones. Deploying and using their HCE features required *rooting* (also known as jailbreaking or simply becoming a superuser) an Android phone and replacing its operating system. But despite this commercial friction, they generated a lot of buzz in the NFC developer community by pioneering the OS changes required to make HCE work in Android.

Yeager and Fifelski's early work caught the attention of the Wallet team at Google and, subsequently, Google's Android team incorporated its own HCE functionality into the base Android Open Source Platform, making HCE available to all Android OEMs and developers. This Android HCE functionality was initially released with Android Kit Kat in the fall of 2013.

Prior to HCE, a smartphone required a Secure Element (SE) to complete a transaction, which increased complexity, added hardware requirements, and made smartcard emulation unavailable to less expensive devices. Most important, the previous way of doing things tended to limit the penetration of NFC in the marketplace. Figure 5-4 summarizes the changes that have occurred with the advent of HCE.

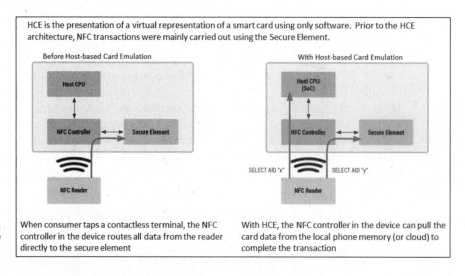

HCE is the presentation of a virtual representation of a smart card using only software. Prior to the HCE architecture, NFC transactions were mainly carried out using the Secure Element.

Before Host-based Card Emulation

Host CPU

NFC Controller ↔ Secure Element

NFC Reader

With Host-based Card Emulation

Host CPU (SoC)

NFC Controller ↔ Secure Element

SELECT AID "x"   SELECT AID "y"

NFC Reader

FIGURE 5-4: An overview of how HCE works.

When consumer taps a contactless terminal, the NFC controller in the device routes all data from the reader directly to the secure element

With HCE, the NFC controller in the device can pull the card data from the local phone memory (or cloud) to complete the transaction

REMEMBER

Even though HCE was available commercially in Android in 2013, it wasn't successfully implemented in OEM smartphones until 2014 when MasterCard and VISA both expressed their support for the technology. In December of that year, the Royal Bank of Canada (RBC) became the first bank to begin using HCE. HCE is still a new technology.

However, the newness of HCE hasn't stopped companies such as CardsApp (http://cardsapp.com/) from introducing a security-hardened version of HCE called HCE+, which mainly sees use in Eastern Asia. In this case, the update requires the addition of security policies such as online credit card tokenization and PIN code entry upon contactless payments. These updated forms of HCE are proprietary, of course, which locks you into using a particular vendor in many cases. The fact that these updates exist at all points to potential changes in HCE in the future: The updates could become part of the specification at some point if they prove useful and reliable. (You can read more about the CardsApp view of HCE and HCE+ at `http://blog.cardsapp.com/post/host-card-emulation-hce-explained`.)

Understanding interactions with devices

Unfortunately, HCE isn't available in every smartphone out there, even if the device is running Android (the platform initially targeted for HCE support). To detect HCE support, developers resort to a simple bit of code in their apps:

```
boolean isHceSupported =
  getPackageManager().hasSystemFeature(
  "android.hardware.nfc.hce");
```

Of course, this code works only for Android apps, but developers can detect the support and ensure that any device running their app has the required HCE support. The actual number of devices that currently support HCE is uncertain, but you can count on support from a number of devices, including the following:

>> Coolpad

- Coolpad 8971

- Coolpad 9970L

- VodafoneSmart4

>> Google: Nexus 4, 5, 7, and 10 series

>> HTC

- Butterfly S

- HTC6525LVW

- HTC6435LVW

- HTC 802t

- HTC 9060

- HTC Desire 601 series

- HTC One series

» LG

- Optimus G, GK, L9II, and LTE3 series

- LG G, G2, and Gx series

- VU3

» Motorola

- Droid series

- Moto X series

» Pantech: VEGA Secret series

» Samsung: Galaxy Mega 6.3, Note2, Note3, S3, S4, and S5 series

» Sony: Xperia Z, Z1, and Z2 series

Using Encryption to Secure Communications

Normally, if you want secure data transactions with NFC, you need to use the Secure Element (SE) to perform the task. HCE implementations support only a single logical channel by default, and they don't encrypt this channel. However, two concepts help secure HCE communications. The use of tokenization means that a transaction can rely on tokens that represent data, instead of using actual data, to perform tasks. In addition, some smartphones emulate ISO/IEC 7816-4 encryption, which makes it possible to establish encrypted and secured communication over the basic logical channel. The following sections discuss both approaches.

Understanding the concept of tokenization

The essential element of NFC tokenization is replacing a Primary Account Number (PAN) with a token. The token is a randomly generated 16-digit number that replaces the PAN, but it represents that PAN to everyone involved in the transaction. Because the token is simply a random number, and not a genuine PAN, someone listening in on the conversation will get the token, but it's useless outside the conversation currently taking place.

In addition to the tokenized PAN, the smartphone card-emulation software (either in a secure element or running in phone memory or in the cloud) generates a dynamic card verification value (dCVV, to use Visa's term for it). This dCVV is a cryptographic value that is unique to the single transaction and can be used only once.

A hacker stealing the token and the dCVV might attempt to use the token for some nefarious deed, but the dCVV's lifespan is so short that the amount of damage is significantly smaller than if the hacker had gained access to the PAN instead. And because the token is tied to a specific phone, it can't be used to prepare a counterfeit plastic card and can't be used to buy things on the web. Any transaction that includes the token but does not originate from the registered phone wallet is declined as fraud.

Payment applications that use NFC to communicate must also use the EMVCo Payment Tokenization standard (http://www.emvco.com/specifications.aspx?id=263) if they use HCE to store and route payment data according to Payment Network Operator (PNO) requirements. So to summarize, a *token* is a low-value item that represents a high-value item, akin to a poker chip representing money when playing cards.

Apple Pay uses a proprietary tokenization system; most other NFC wallets rely on the EMVCo Payment Tokenization standard. All current schemes tokenize the 16-digit PAN using a static token value issued by the token authority when the payment card is first registered in the NFC wallet. The token value never changes (unless it is compromised and reissued). This approach allows merchants and banks to identify particular customers for returns and loyalty programs in the same way they do now by hashing the card PAN. All tokenization schemes prevent anyone but the trusted authority from reversing the tokenization and revealing the true PAN of the card user.

You can use a token with any Cardholder Verification Method (a CVM might include a PIN, signature, or fingerprint). To keep the token from becoming a security problem, it has a specific expiration period, after which no one can use the token to represent the PAN — any new transactions require a different token. And tokens can be further restricted for use at specific merchants (for retail private-label cards or gift cards) or may contain other restrictions verified by the token authority.

REMEMBER

Some vendors also use tokens for their private-label card data. For example, you might see tokenization used for gift cards to ensure that the money on the card remains secure.

Using the ISO/IEC 7816-4 commands

Tokens provide a means to protect the user's PAN. However, tokens don't provide a method for protecting any transmitted data. In addition to using tokens, a secure transaction requires the use of encryption. The current gold standard for payments is Point-to-Point Encryption (PTPE). Data received by the NFC payment reader is immediately encrypted upon receipt, using one-time keys, prior to being transmitted to the merchant's bank for authorization.

However, at present no standardized encryption exists between the NFC reader and the NFC handset. All security over the NFC link is the responsibility of the application writer (such as Visa, MasterCard, American Express, Discover, JCB, or Union Pay). ISO/IEC 7816-4 specifies the syntax for smartcard commands, and it has been referenced by ISO/IEC14443 for use in contactless smartcards.

And although ISO/IEC 7816-4 specifies the commands and response messages, and even includes a form of channel security, most (if not all) application developers rely on their own application-level security methods for confidentiality, integrity, and authentication in NFC applications.

REMEMBER

This section refers only to encryption in the context of payment. You can and should use encryption in many other application areas.

The standard for NFC smartcard commands is ISO/IEC 7816-4 (http://www.iso. org/iso/catalogue_detail.htm?csnumber=54550). This standard originally defined the qualities of smartcards that allowed applications to interoperate in a variety of applications, so for NFC to use the same standard is not surprising. This standard defines the following elements:

>> Command/response pairs used to exchange data

>> Means used to retrieve data elements and data objects from the smartcard

>> Data used to describe the operating characteristics of the target smartcard

>> Information that describes the applications and data stored on the smartcard when viewed as a response to a command

>> Methods used to access data and files stored on the smartcard

>> Methods used to obtain the access rights for data and files stored on the smartcard

>> Techniques used to identify and access applications stored on the smartcard

>> Preferred methods to perform secure messaging (though actual details are often developed in specific applications)

>> Methods that access the algorithms used to secure data on the smartcard (subject to choices made by application developers)

WARNING

Even though the list of features that the standard defines seems comprehensive, vendors still have a lot of room to make modifications and to personalize implementations. For example, even though the standard defines how to access the algorithms used to secure the data, it doesn't define the actual algorithms. The standard also doesn't define smartcard physical characteristics or the method used to access the smartcard. It's important to read the standard carefully and not read anything that it doesn't contain into it.

Writing Tags

One of the especially appealing aspects of NFC is that you can write tags with relative ease. In fact, a number of low-cost methods are available for writing tags. Each of the options in the following sections has advantages and disadvantages. Simply select the option that works best for your needs.

TIP

You can use an Apple smartphone to write a tag; however, you must use an accessory reader/writer to perform the task. Apple enables NFC for card emulation only when working with an iOS device. If you want to write to an NFC tag using your iPhone, for example, you need to use an accessory, the most common being an audio jack dongle (see the "Using an External NFC adapter" section of Chapter 4 and the "Considering an audio jack" section of this chapter for more information on these accessories).

Using a smartphone

You can use your smartphone to write any sort of tag you need. Of course, you want to be sure that the tag is suitable for your particular need. A starter kit, such as the one found at http://rapidnfc.com/cat/15/nfc_starter_packs, may help you determine precisely what sort of tag to use. You also need a suitable app such as

TagWriter (`https://play.google.com/store/apps/details?id=com.nxp.nfc.tagwriter`). The actual process of writing the tag is quick and easy. The "Working in reader/writer mode" section of Chapter 4 gives you a procedure for performing this task using the TagWriter app.

Using an accessory reader/writer

You can perform reading and writing tasks from your PC. Doing so might actually make some tasks easier, depending on the devices you use to interact with the tags. Of course, the software that you get to go with the reader/writer devices makes a big difference in using the capabilities of a PC fully. PCs can provide you with flexibility you might not get with other devices.

REMEMBER

A main advantage of using a PC to read and write tags is speed. The device interfaces that a PC provides, coupled with a PC's processing power, tend to make reading and writing operations faster. The following sections consider two of the more popular PC options available to you.

Considering USB

A USB device attaches to your PCs USB port and is automatically recognized by the PC. Devices such as the ACR122U USB NFC Reader (`http://www.acs.com.hk/en/products/3/acr122u-usb-nfc-reader/`) make full use of the superior interface speed that a PC can provide. In this case, the device doesn't come with an ISO/IEC 7816-3 SAM, but you can add one as an option to ensure that any data you work with remains secure. You look for features of this sort to guarantee that you can interact with NFC tags and cards safely.

TIP

Besides the requirements for your NFC interactions, you also need to verify that the device will actually work with your PC. For example, you need to know that it provides you with support for the operating system of your choice and that you can obtain drivers for it. The vendor will usually tell you what sorts of tasks that the device normally performs. Make sure to look at all the details before purchasing the unit.

Considering an audio jack

You can find a number of unique solutions for reading and writing tags on the market. One such solution is the Flomio's FloJack NFC Mobile Reader (`http://flomio.com/shop/nfc-readers/flojack-nfc-reader/`). You literally plug this device into an audio jack on the mobile device. The device also requires a MicroUSB jack (used to charge the device's battery). You normally use this particular piece of hardware for e-payment purposes with smartcards that are compliant with ISO 14443 type A and type B, MIFARE, and FeliCa standards. If the Flomio solution doesn't meet your needs, you can find a whole host of audio jack devices at `http://www.alibaba.com/showroom/audio-jack-nfc-reader.html`.

TIP

Some of the audio jack devices you find online have just NFC reader support. You can find reader/writer solutions such as the Professional NFC Audio Jack p2 reader/writer from Advanced Card Systems `http://www.acr35.com/`. Just remember to read the specifications for whatever device you purchase carefully to ensure that it provides the capabilities you want.

Using a high-speed encoding system

Most of the material you read in the book discusses individual tags. The reason is simple: It's important to know how to write one tag correctly before you start to write a whole bunch of them. Of course, you eventually reach the point of needing to create a lot of tags quickly. To create a lot of tags, you need a high-speed encoding system. Many of these systems use a reel-to-reel setup. To make these systems work well for you, consider these issues:

>> **Tag size:** You can usually increase the recording speed when working with larger tags because the sweet spot is larger.

>> **Inlay type:** A smaller inlay usually requires more recording time. Special-purpose inlays may also require additional recording time.

>> **NFC chip type:** The kind of chip the tag contains affects reading and writing speed. The NXP NTAG series currently provides the fastest reading and writing times.

>> **Data size:** Because the transfer rate of NFC is fixed, the more data you write, the longer the transfer will take. Using larger data sets also affects reading speeds. Making data as small as possible improves tag performance.

>> **Locking:** If you choose to lock the tag, you must include a little additional time to write it. Locking doesn't affect the chip's reading speed.

>> **RF stability:** A human hand naturally shakes, causing instability in the RF field. Using high-speed equipment designed to stabilize the RF field improves both reading and writing time.

Smaller businesses may not be able to offset the costs of high-speed encoding systems. In this case, you want to use an encoding service, such as RapidNFC in Europe (`https://rapidnfc.com/rapidnfc_nfc_encoding`) or Cellotape in the US (`http://www.cellotape.com/`). To use this option, you just tell the company what to record and it sends you the tag — simple and efficient. The "Understanding the Need for Mass Production" sidebar in Chapter 12 gives you some additional options for mass producing tags.

Managing NFC Tags

Creating an NFC tag is the start of a process, not the end of a process. After you have a tag created, you can perform a number of management tasks with it, such as tracking how the tag performs. The following sections help you understand the sorts of management tasks you can perform using NFC tags.

Defining the management tasks

To get the most from your NFC investment, you need to manage the tags that you use to provide information to various groups. Many ways to manage tags exist, but the following sections detail three of the most common management tasks you must perform.

Tracking tag URLs

Tracking tags is essential if you want to know how users are interacting with the tags and whether the tags are successful in performing whatever task you have assigned to them. The most common use for tag tracking is to ensure that a campaign is successful so that you can make adjustments as needed, rather than wait until the campaign is over to assess its success. Companies such as Delivr (http://delivr.com/plans) and Qfuse (http://qfuse.com/learn-more/nfc) provide services that make tracking tags easier without resorting to specialized programming techniques.

If you determine that a campaign needs redirection, you can manage the tags in various ways. For example, most services let you change the tag Uniform Resource Identifiers (URIs) so that users get an updated experience. These services also make it possible to generate mobile landing pages quickly (or you can usually use your own). Without a compelling experience, the user will never follow through after tapping your tag.

Tracking and reporting tag performance

Real-time tracking of your tags is an important part of managing the tasks they perform. Without real-time management, you can't adjust how the tags interact with users quickly enough to make a difference. Here's some of the information you can usually track as part of a tag-management service (or by using custom programming):

>> How often users tap your tags

>> Where they are

>> What devices they're using

>> What users do after tapping the tag

Considering multichannel scenarios

Not everyone has NFC support yet. With this in mind, you need to manage tasks using multiple channels. For example, most services provide the means to combine QR codes with NFC. In some cases, you can also add iBeacons into the equation so that any user can participate. Companies like Smartwhere (`https://smartwhere.com/`) have such a system and would be worth looking into.

Determining whether you need an API solution

Using a service is quick and easy. In fact, it's the approach you should use for most campaigns because the effort of creating custom software may not provide a good return on investment (ROI), not to mention that it can delay your campaign and give a competitor a chance to steal potential customers. However, sometimes custom programming can provide you with some advantages. The following sections provide a quick overview of custom application program interface (API) solutions.

Considering the advantages of custom software

Using custom software does come with costs, such as development time, that you really do need to consider. However, it can also have some significant advantages when used appropriately. The following list offers some good reasons to use custom software to meet specific needs:

>> **Tailor made solution:** When you use software created by someone else, you're buying into that party's vision of what you need. In most cases, third parties do a great job anticipating the needs for a short-term campaign but are less proficient at building solutions for long-term needs. If you plan to monitor tag usage over a long period, a custom solution can provide flexibility and functionality that third-party solutions lack.

>> **Cost:** Depending on the terms you can get from a third party, a custom solution could end up costing you less over the long term if you can use the software to meet multiple needs. Software that you create yourself tends to pay for itself over the long term, assuming that you get enough benefit from it to offset development costs.

>> **Maintenance:** You need to weigh the cost of maintaining the software on your own against the cost of dealing with third-party updates. Any time a third party updates your software, you need time to incorporate the changes into your organizational structure. When working with custom software, you can time updates for convenient times to you and maintain your software indefinitely so that you don't have to worry about the potential for vendor lock in.

>> **Integration:** A custom solution will integrate well with multiple business processes and with your organization's policies. Third-party solutions can turn out to be the square peg fitting into a round hole at times.

>> **Support:** Third parties tend to keep costs down by reducing support costs as much as possible. When working with a custom solution, you decide how much support to provide. In addition, the support is specific to your organization, so you don't need to worry about things like travel time or conflicting policies.

Working with vendor-specific APIs

Most of the vendors you deal with for managing tags provide vendor-specific APIs. These APIs allow you to obtain many of the benefits of working with a third-party vendor without subscribing to the vendor's support software. You create a custom solution instead. The vendor still helps you manage your tag data, but you control the software used to perform the tasks.

REMEMBER

When it comes to marketing campaigns, so many low-cost solutions are available that building your own software or tying into someone's API doesn't make sense to even consider. Using vendor specific APIs is something that your business might consider for custom or other uses for NFC at the enterprise level.

Making NFC Part of the Internet of Things (IoT)

The Internet of Things (IoT) defines a set of technologies that relies on the Internet to perform interesting tasks. For example, your security system probably connects to the Internet, as does your car. IoT is at the convergence of mobility, cloud connectivity, cloud computing, and big data. People rely on the cloud to perform all sorts of important tasks, and big data is a component of all the features that people like about shopping online (such as getting recommendations of other products to buy). Using NFC with the IoT lets you perform an incredible array of interesting tasks. For example, you can create:

>> Smart railways

>> Agricultural tracking systems

>> NFC medical records

>> Interactive museums

>> NFC-enabled voting systems

What all these diverse technologies have in common is proximity ID technologies. When merged with cloud-based applications, proximity ID technologies enable complete interaction between the physical and digital worlds. You can read more about IoT and how it relates to NFC at http://proximityhack.com/at-the-intersection-of-proximity-id-technologies-and-the-internet-of-things/.

Differentiating Between Web Apps and Mobile Apps

NFC relies on apps to perform certain tasks. When working with a mobile device, you have a choice between web apps (which are really web pages that are launched by tapping an NFC tag or scanning a QR code) and mobile apps (which are applications that are downloaded onto the phone). What are the differences between the two? A *web app* relies on the same browser-based interface that any other web application does, which means using HTML pages. The formatting of a mobile web app favors the small screens that mobile devices possess and makes it easier to move around using the functionality that a mobile device provides. However, for the most part, it's still just a browser-based application. Web apps can support many phone features, including

>> Text content

>> Data

>> Images

>> Video

>> Click-to-call (to dial a phone number)

>> Location-based mapping

A *mobile app* is one that uses the native functionality of the mobile device. You download the app to your smartphone, just as you do any other mobile app on your device. Rather than use a browser, the mobile app has a custom interface that plays to the special features of the device that you're using. As a result, a mobile app tends to execute faster and provide better functionality than a web app (making it a favored choice for games). To gain these advantages, mobile apps tend to have reduced platform flexibility (you must create a version for each platform you want to support). Mobile apps favor tasks for which you have specific needs in mind, and a web app isn't capable of delivering the required functionality. For example, you must use a mobile app when you want the app to work even without an Internet connection.

When choosing between a web app and a mobile app, you need to consider issues such as the audience you wish to serve. If you can't adequately determine the devices your audience will use in advance, a web app has a definite appeal because it runs on any device that has a browser. A web app has these common advantages:

>> **Compatibility:** You can use web apps on any device that has a browser.

>> **Ease of updates:** You can update a web app instantly because you have the code stored on your server.

>> **Ease of sharing:** Two people can share a web app, even if they have different devices.

>> **Sustainability:** The costs associated with maintaining a web app are normally lower.

Using NFC

IN THIS PART . . .

Using NFC to make monetary transactions

Enhancing identification strategies using NFC

Employing NFC for health care tasks

Using NFC for all sorts of personal tasks

Making public appeals using NFC technology

Chapter 6

Using NFC for Payments

common — and popular — use of NFC today is to act as a mobile wallet. All the things that you normally stuff into your wallet are now stored in your smartphone. This functionality goes well beyond simply making payments — now you can store all your commonly used information in an NFC-friendly way. For example, when it comes time to use your loyalty card, you simply tap the cash register to send the required information and receive the proper credit.

Some of the items you store in your wallet aren't all that sensitive, but you don't want them to be public knowledge, either. Your receipts can tell quite a lot about you. For example, just four receipts can let someone figure out your identity and then use that information to make your life interesting in a bad way. (See the article at http://news.mit.edu/2015/identify-from-credit-card-metadata-0129.) Needless to say, you want to keep your credit card, debit card, and other sensitive information secure because gaining access to them would cause even bigger problems. The first topic for this chapter helps you understand the security requirements for a mobile wallet so that you can keep your personal business safe.

After you have some idea that your mobile wallet is safe, you can consider the solutions available for creating one. The next section of the chapter describes all sorts of technologies that are available when working with a mobile wallet. In fact, the flexibility of your mobile wallet is quite amazing.

Understanding Mobile Wallet Security Requirements

An essential aspect of making a mobile wallet work is ensuring that the data it holds remains secure. Just think about the sorts of information you keep in a real wallet. Figure 6-1 shows typical information sources. Many of these physical sources are quite sensitive, and the digital versions would be as well. For example, imagine what would happen if someone managed to obtain the information for one or more of your credit cards or the digital versions of any keys you own.

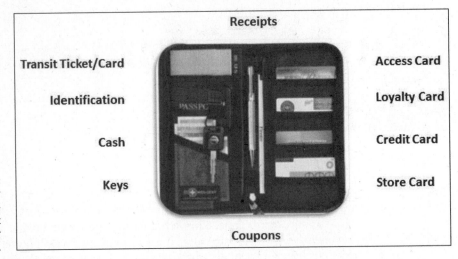

FIGURE 6-1: Potential uses for your mobile wallet require that you have proper security in place.

The following sections discuss the use of mobile wallets in more detail and describe the security requirements for these various uses. As you read through the material, consider how these security requirements affect your particular uses for mobile wallets. You do need to have a security plan in place before you implement or start to rely on any mobile wallet strategy.

Relying on Secure Element (SE)

It's important to understand the paths that information follows when it comes to data security. Figure 6-2 shows an example (one use case) of how banks and telecoms had initially envisioned using a secure element. This is just one way that NFC is used. (The "Performing mobile payments" section of Chapter 3 describes how you can also rely on Host Card Emulation for security, and the "Relying on Host Card Emulation (HCE)" section, later in this chapter, provides additional details.)

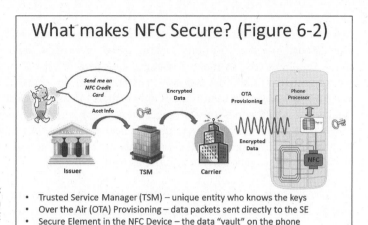

What makes NFC Secure? (Figure 6-2)

- Trusted Service Manager (TSM) – unique entity who knows the keys
- Over the Air (OTA) Provisioning – data packets sent directly to the SE
- Secure Element in the NFC Device – the data "vault" on the phone

FIGURE 6-2:
The data path
that makes the SE
secure.

In this case, a vendor combines NFC with a secure element. (The NFC Forum doesn't have any specifications related to secure elements.) The secure element is the add-on device that provides the high level of security. The focus of this process is to ensure that none of your data ends up transferred in the clear; it's all sent to your phone as encrypted data. The following sections describe the security components shown in Figure 6-2 in more detail, specifically the role of the Trusted Service Manager (TSM), Over the Air (OTA) provisioning, and the Secure Element (SE).

Considering the Trusted Service Manager (TSM)

The TSM plays a vital role in securing data by acting as the middleman. It coordinates the technical and business relationships of multiple stakeholders, such as Mobile Network Operators (MNOs), banks and other service providers, ticketing agencies, and other issuing authorities. The TSM makes communication between these various businesses possible. It also provides the means to deliver apps and services to the user's mobile device. The key function of a TSM is to provide all these services in a secure manner using encryption and authentication. It also provides a secure and authenticated way to actually install data into the secure element remotely, without having to actually have the mobile device in hand.

Understanding Over The Air (OTA) provisioning

OTA provisioning makes it possible to interact with a Subscriber Identity Module (SIM) card in a number of ways. An MNO can use it to

>> Communicate directly with the mobile device

>> Download applications to the mobile device

>> Manage the SIM card without physically accessing it

OTA relies on the client/server architecture in which one end is a back end system, such as customer care, a billing system, or an application server, and the other end is the SIM card. To make a change, the operator's back-end system sends service requests to an OTA Gateway. The OTA Gateway transforms the requests into Short Messages and sends them onto a Short Message Service Center (SMSC). Finally, the SMSC sends the messages to the SIM card. SMS wake up and SMS payload delivery are just one example of a mechanism for delivering data to an SE. Push wake-up messages and IP connectivity are another, and IP without any kind of wake-up message is currently in use as well.

REMEMBER

OTA provisioning, while it may refer to a specific implementation (just as NFC is specific to NFC Forum), is also generally used to refer to any technology for provisioning secure elements remotely. OTA provisioning can be used with any secure element, not just a SIM. Not all OTA provisioning uses the SMS architecture. The environment in which SMS is used is limited to SIM cards, but in a more general environment where other communication channels are used, any secure element can be the target.

Considering the security information locations

A secure element is a dedicated processor with its own memory and specific software dedicated to security functions. The SE stores data — like a credit card Primary Account Number (PAN) or token — and can act on that data isolated from any other processing that may be going on by its host, such as a smartphone. The SE data needs to reside somewhere. In many cases, it resides directly in your smartphone, but there are other options, as shown in Figure 6-3.

REMEMBER

Data may be encrypted going into an SE to prevent tampering or theft during the load process to the SE. Whether it is actually stored inside the SE in an encrypted way or transmitted out of the SE in an encrypted way depends on a specific use case. In the case of payments using Visa, MC, Amex, or Discover, a PAN or token is transmitted in the clear (without encryption) to the point-of-sale (POS) terminal. This lack of encryption is because of legacy issues of the payment networks. It is possible to capture payment data by spying on an NFC POS with a remote antenna; however, there are other parts of the transmitted message that are encrypted and are required to complete a transaction, thus mitigating the risk. The following sections discuss form factors that a secure element takes and help you understand their advantages and disadvantages.

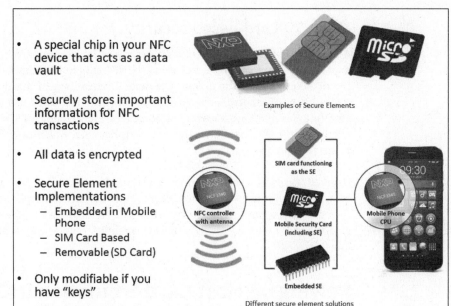

- A special chip in your NFC device that acts as a data vault

- Securely stores important information for NFC transactions

- All data is encrypted

- Secure Element Implementations
  - Embedded in Mobile Phone
  - SIM Card Based
  - Removable (SD Card)

- Only modifiable if you have "keys"

Examples of Secure Elements

SIM card functioning as the SE

Mobile Security Card (including SE)

Embedded SE

NFC controller with antenna

Mobile Phone CPU

Different secure element solutions

FIGURE 6-3: Storing the SE data.

Using embedded security

Embedded security is part of the smartphone when you buy it. The main advantage of using embedded security is that you don't need to buy anything special to obtain the security benefits because the SE silicon is directly soldered to the motherboard of the smartphone or is included as part of the NFC modem. In addition, because it's part of the smartphone, no one can take it out easily and put it in another smartphone.

Using SIM Card-based security

To use the SIM card — which is more currently referred to as the Universal Integrated Circuit Card (UICC) for 3G networks and above — option, you buy a UICC that includes Single Wire Protocol (SWP) support to communicate with the NFC modem in a smartphone. This option works with any smartphone, making it the easiest method to obtain the required support. However, the fact that it works with so many smartphones means that someone can potentially steal the card and use it in another smartphone. UICC/SIM with NFC has two configurations:

>> The UICC must support SWP, and the UICC connects to the NFC controller (which is external to the UICC and an internal part of the phone).

>> The UICC has a built-in NFC front end and either a built-in antenna or a connection for a flexible antenna, which is placed somewhere on the back of the phone.

Using SD Card-based security

A Storage Device (SD) card serves as memory for your smartphone. To use this approach, you buy an SD card that has an NFC chip in it or that can interface with the NFC controller in the phone. The main disadvantage of this option is the limited number of smartphones that it works with. You can't use this option with smartphones that have a metallic slot, unless you're using an SD card with a connection to the NFC controller in the smartphone (in which case, whether the slot is metal or not is irrelevant).

Using SD cards as a secure element, NFC modem and/or an NFC antenna is going away. The major use for SD cards was to retrofit older smartphones to allow them to make payments and perform other NFC-related tasks. However, almost all smartphones now have an SE with NFC capabilities built into the phones when you buy them.

Relying on Host Card Emulation (HCE)

There is a lot of interest recently in deploying Host Card Emulation (HCE) as part of the security solution for payments. Figure 6-4 describes the most common reasons that vendors are looking at using HCE. The sections that follow provide you with some additional input on why HCE is a good solution for secure transactions.

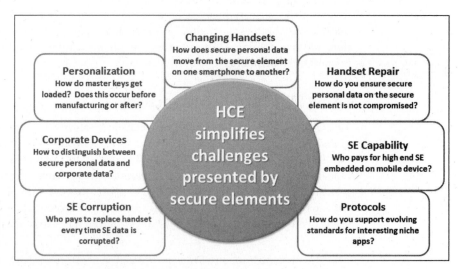

FIGURE 6-4: Considering some of the challenges with using SE.

Considering HCE security

HCE stores security credentials in the cloud, and the smartphone emulates a smart card. In contrast, SE stores the actual card credentials on the smartphone in the

SE. In short, the security that HCE provides relies on the idea that the credit card credentials are not stored directly on a person's phone. HCE happens in the cloud, and the smartphone receives only a one-time token that allows the user to pay merchants for things.

Considering the TSM

HCE doesn't require a TSM function, per se, but HCE introduces a tokenization authority into the issuing and authorization flows. Therefore, in some respects, it's different, but not necessarily simpler, technically. What is simplified is the business framework. With SE, someone has to act as the security owner, independent of applications and credential issuers. This entity becomes a gatekeeper role that in the early days became more of a troll taxing access to an essential transport asset.

Using Internet protocols

Using standardized protocols tends to make transaction processing and customization easier. HCE uses mostly Internet protocols in the value chain, without the need for specialized security assets at the edge.

REMEMBER

Access to the NFC radio can still be locked down (as Apple has done in iPhone) so that the hardware manufacturer insinuates itself into the application value chain. Apple has yet to provide the ability to use HCE — all card emulation must be through Apple's approved tokenization platform providers and only in support of approved applications (such as MasterCard, Visa, Amex, and Discover). Consequently, HCE doesn't simplify use of NFC on the Apple platform because it's unavailable for business reasons. However, Apple could offer HCE on existing NFC-enabled iPhones with a simple iOS update in a manner that doesn't disrupt Apple's primary business mission. It's important to remember that Apple must approve every app and app update on iOS. Many NFC apps don't need the security of an embedded smart card, and Apple could simply not approve payment apps or other apps that tried to use HCE outside Apple's golden path.

Considering connectivity

One thing that SE and HCE have in common is that the smartphone or other NFC-enabled device doesn't have to remain connected at all times. TSM-generated updates can wait in a queue until a device is back on Wi-Fi, which is the same technique used for app updates. In addition, an EMV point-of-sale (POS) terminal can apply scripts (digitally signed by the issuer) directly to an SE at the POS without relying on the smartphone apps or smartphone connectivity.

The same queuing technique applies to HCE. A magazine of ten or so keys can replace the dynamic limited-use keys that are at the heart of HCE security. This use of queuing enables offline spending without connectivity at the time of purchase, which was seen as one primary benefit of SE-based mobile payments and EMV payment cards. Therefore, in the modern smart-device world, limited but periodic connectivity is about as disconnected as a device ever gets.

Combining HCE and tokenization

The key to understanding HCE is tokenization — it reduces the value of the stored credentials by replacing genuine account data in the handset with worthless random values. The random token values are associated to the genuine data in the cloud. Matching occurs during an authorization transaction, when the token is supplied as part of a service request, but the matched genuine credential values are never exposed outside the token issuer's system. OAUTH (http://oauth.net/) and JSON Web Token (JWT) (https://tools.ietf.org/html/rfc7519) do this for web apps (enabling you to log into a web app using something like Google, Facebook, or Twitter credentials, but without disclosing those credentials to the web app) and there are analogs in payment and nonpayment NFC apps. (This information also applies to embedded SE.)

The thing to remember about tokenization is that the tokenizer is the only entity that knows both values (the token and the genuine data). So this is an inherently trusted and gate-keeping role.

WARNING

Developers need to exercise caution when depending on a third party tokenization service. It's important to remember that the third party could revoke your access at any time. In addition, an outsider could troll your credentials. In some cases, this issue is similar to the one faced by developers who work with app stores.

Understanding the role of Trust Zone

Trust Zone (http://www.arm.com/products/processors/technologies/trustzone/), which ships in all ARM processor-equipped smart devices, can be used as a halfway step between a dedicated SE and open HCE. The benefits of secure, integral, and confidential execution of selected algorithms used in an authorization process, together with Internet connectivity and direct OS support, might bring the best of both worlds to a future HCE implementation.

Trust Zone is the brand name for the generically-specified Trusted Execution Environment (TEE), a parallel execution environment and OS that runs inside every ARM CPU. No matter what the brand name might be, the TEE is a secure area of the main processor in a smart phone (or any connected device). It ensures that an app can store, process, and protect sensitive data in an isolated and trusted environment. The TEE's ability to offer isolated, safe execution of authorized security software (called a *trusted application*), enables it to provide end-to-end security by enforcing protected execution of authenticated code, confidentiality, authenticity, privacy, system integrity, and data access rights. The TEE also offers high processing speeds and a large amount of accessible memory when compared to other secure areas on the device. You can discover more about TEE at http://www.globalplatform.org/mediaguidetee.asp.

In some ways, the gatekeeper function discussed for the TSM (in the "Considering the TSM" section, earlier in this chapter) exists also for the TEE. Someone must provide access to the facility, and it's possible to deny access from the OS level. But because TEE is essentially a zero-cost asset, available in every handset CPU, and because ways exist to generate TEE security keys confidentially and anonymously in the OS without a TSM and for any app, a for-profit model of TEE administration is not sustainable. Trustonic (https://www.trustonic.com/), founded by leaders in both the mobility and security industries, provides processes for TEE and TrustZone access. Samsung Pay (http://www.samsung.com/us/samsung-pay/) is one of the companies that are making good use of the TEE and Knox environment.

Some classes of authentication, authorization, audit, and use accounting can all be built on HCE using traditional Internet architecture and protocols without a dedicated SE. Some of these apps might benefit from use of a TEE resource in the handset, when provably secure calculations are part of the application. But even with that additional requirement, HCE is still technically simpler and may be more business viable than relying on SE hardware.

Considering the Potential Mobile Wallet Solutions

The mobile wallet market is really just getting started, and many different solutions are already available. Figure 6-5 shows a few of the benefits from deploying a mobile wallet solution, but you can count on more of them coming soon. A challenge with the current benefits is that they work differently and have various features that don't transfer between product types or vendors.

REMEMBER

It's important to know how various mobile wallet strategies work. The following sections discuss the various mobile wallet strategies that are currently in use. Keep in mind that not every vendor provides the features required to access all these strategies. Choosing the right mobile wallet solution is important because you want to ensure that you have access to the features you need.

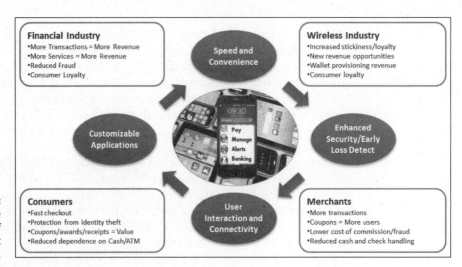

Using Magnetic Secure Transmission (MST)

Traditional plastic cards have a stripe of material on which it's possible to record data using magnetic methods. This information is static, which means that anyone who swipes the card can store the information for later use (such as identity theft), making the magnetic stripe open to attack. In addition, the data from a magnetic stripe is always available for reading. The *Magnetic Stripe Emulator (MSE)* is a flexible electronic planar array encased between the layers of the card. When you swipe the card for some reason (payment, identity, or some other use), the MSE lights up to present the signal of a regular magnetic stripe and then turns off when the swipe is complete. This process is called *Magnetic Secure Transmission (MST)*.

The content provided through MST is dynamic. It permits transmission of dynamic Card Security Codes (CSC) or other information through existing point-of-sale (POS) infrastructure. This means that swiping the card doesn't provide data that someone could use a second time, reducing the risk of issues such as identity theft. The mutable nature of the data also allows one card to support multiple applications, which eliminates skimming of magnetic stripe card data.

You see MST used with smartphones in applications such as Samsung Pay. The device will first attempt to use NFC to make a payment. If the use of NFC is unsuccessful, the device falls back to using MST. Part of this process is leveraging tokenization so that the vendor never actually has the person's credit card data, but relies on a one-use token instead. You can read more about how this technology works at http://www.nfcworld.com/2015/03/01/334390/mastercard-discusses-how-samsung-pay-works/.

Employing QR solutions

QR codes, those odd-looking pixelated squares, can help you pay for things. All you do is scan the QR code at the register and it performs the transaction for you by associating the physical goods with a digital basket and payment method in the cloud. In some respects, QR codes are temporary because better solutions exist and are making headway in the marketplace. Here are some issues to consider with QR codes:

» QR Codes are simple and cheap

» All you need is QR Code generator software, which is free for the most part

» Marketers and designers do consider them visual clutter (or downright ugly), so they're looking for other alternatives

All this said, QR codes are still popular. The following sections describe a number of popular QR solutions.

Working with CurrentC

CurrentC (https://www.currentc.com/) is the brainchild of significant retailers, such as Walmart, Target, CVS, Exxon, and Sears. These (and other) companies formed the Merchant Customer Exchange (MCX), a consortium of mega-retailers aimed at streamlining customer experiences at participating retailers. The MCX offerings help customers in three ways:

» Making payments

» Obtaining offers (such as coupons)

» Participating in loyalty schemes

MCX has developed and is currently testing the e-payment app, CurrentC. This app is the mega-retailers' answer to other popular payment services. However, you can't use it today.

Working with Walmart-pay

Even though Walmart is part of MCX, it can't wait forever for the solution to launch. Other e-payment app solutions are already out there, and Walmart can't afford to be left behind. As a result, Walmart recently launched Walmart-pay (http://www.pymnts.com/news/2015/walmart-pay-takes-the-field/), which, interestingly enough, also relies on QR codes. The advantage of using QR codes is that a customer can use any payment method and any smartphone running any operating system to pay. Even though Walmart currently views Walmart-pay as an interim solution, it could become Walmart's preferred method, causing Walmart to leave MCX (http://seekingalpha.com/article/3748786-wal-mart-pay-will-have-a-major-impact-on-currentcs-future).

Working with QR Mobile Pay

QR Mobile Pay (http://qrmobilepay.com/) is an option for Business-to-Business (B2B) transactions. Part of QR Mobile Pay's solution is QR Invoice (http://qrinvoice.co/), which provides a way for businesses to create a QR code that, when scanned, generates a secure electronic invoice. A buyer can then pay the invoice using the same mobile device used to access the bill.

REMEMBER

The goal is to provide new levels of security and convenience in B2B transactions. Security is the best part of this particular solution. Payments don't require an exchange of credit card information. In fact, the clients can't even see the credit card number — QR Mobile Pay secures the information in the back end of the platform.

Enjoying NFC Solutions

When working directly with NFC, rather than emulating or interacting with something else, you have a number of native solutions, as shown in Figure 6-6. These solutions let you get the most out of NFC. Each solution provides specific functionality. In addition, the solutions have advantages and disadvantages. The following sections help you understand the NFC solutions in greater detail.

	Apple Pay	Google Wallet	Android Pay	Samsung Pay	Online Wallets (Visa, PayPal, Amazon)	Merchant Apps (Starbucks, Dunkin, CurrentC)
Retail Payments	Yes, NFC only	Yes, NFC only	Yes, NFC only	Yes, NFC and MST (Magstripe Emulation)	No	Only in merchant's own store (via Barcode)
Security	Hardware Secure Element in Phone	Hardware SE in the phone (older models), Software Security via HCE and Tokenization (newer models	Software Security via HCE and Tokenization	Software Security via Proprietary Tokenization	No Credential on the device, Cloud Based	No Credential on the device, Cloud Based
User Authorization	Fingerprint	Password	Fingerprint	Fingerprint	Password and Fingerprint	Password
Internet Payments	Yes, via iOS API	Yes, via Google Wallet API	Yes, via Android API	No	Yes, via merchant API	No
In App Payments	Yes, via iOS API	Yes, via Google API	Yes, via Android API	No	Yes, via merchant API	No
Open NFC API for 3rd Parties	No	No	Yes	No	Not Supported	Not Supported
Compatibility	iPhone 6 and later (2014+)	Android 4 and later (2013+)	Android 5 and later (2015+)	Only Samsung 2015+ devices	All Android and iOS	All Android and iOS
Bank Support	>100	>100	Handful	<5	Mostly All	None
Support of Loyalty	Promised	Yes	Unknown	No	No	Merchant's own card
Peer 2 Peer	No	Yes	No	No	Yes	No
User Adoption	Low but growing	Low but stalled	Just launched	Just launched	High	Very High (Starbucks)

Courtesy of Deepak Jain, co-founder and managing partner of Interact Ventures

FIGURE 6-6: Considering the NFC solutions currently in place.

Courtesy of Deepak Jain

App versus wallet

Figure 6-6 contains two kinds of solutions. The first is a mobile wallet, such as Google Wallet, which lets an app or service allow a user to store multiple virtual cards on their smartphone (with multiple cards serving as a key part of the definition). These solutions tend to provide significant flexibility and always require some sort of bank support.

The second solution is an app that lets a user make a purchase or payment from a smartphone, such as the Starbucks app. These solutions are usually store specific, may not offer any sort of bank support, but do enjoy high user adoption because the solution closely associates with a vendor who can offer perks for using the app. Purely from a usage standpoint, the Starbucks app is currently the king of the hill when it comes to adoption, but you can use it only at Starbucks.

Working with Apple Pay

According to a number of sources, Apple Pay (`http://www.apple.com/apple-pay/`) seems to have the most momentum of any of the mobile wallet solutions so far. In fact, the company claims that $2 out of every $3 spent using contactless payments (using Visa, MasterCard, and American Express) has been with Apple Pay.

TIP

Because this is a field in flux, with plenty of entrepreneurial opportunity, Apple Pay has lots of competition. Things are changing quickly! For example, in February 2015, Google bought Softcard (formerly ISIS) and Samsung acquired LoopPay (now Samsung Pay). PayPal bought Paydiant in March. Consequently, you need to expect adoption rates to change significantly as the technology becomes more embedded with the public.

To use Apple Pay, you begin by entering your credit card information into the Apple Passbook app on your iPhone 6/6s or 6/6s Plus. When you get to the checkout, you simply wave or tap your device on the POS terminal. You must provide a fingerprint on the device (not the POS terminal) to complete the transaction. When using an Apple watch, you provide a fingerprint on the associated device. An Apple Watch lets you make payments with older iPhone 5, 5C, and 5S devices — it acts as an extension to the original device. You can also use Apple Pay on mobile commerce sites and commerce apps accessed through iOS 8.x devices.

Working with Samsung Pay

Samsung Pay (`http://www.samsung.com/us/samsung-pay/`) relies on the Loop-Pay (`https://www.looppay.com/`) mobile payment platform to make a payment possible at just about any POS terminal. It's Samsung's answer to Apple Pay. The payment method is similar to the one used for Apple Pay:

1. Swipe up from the Galaxy S6's bezel to access the Samsung Pay app.

2. Choose the desired debit or credit card.

3. Tap the phone to the NFC point-of-sale terminal.

4. Authenticate the transaction via the Galaxy S6's fingerprint sensor.

This solution also works with standard magnetic stripe readers using LoopPay's Magnetic Secure Transmission (MST) technology. In this case, the transactions rely on credit card numbers stored in an industry-standard encrypted format, unlike the NFC transactions that use secure tokenization. Using the MST option is slightly different from using NFC. In this case, you use the following process:

1. Swipe up from the Galaxy S6's bezel to access the Samsung Pay app.

2. Choose the desired debit or credit card.

3. Hold your phone against the point-of-sale terminal where you would normally slide your card.

   The transaction then continues as if you had slid a card through.

Working with Android Pay

The process for using Android Pay (https://www.android.com/pay) is similar to that for both Apple Pay and Samsung Pay. As previously mentioned, Android Pay is moving toward using biometric authentication (and may have already done so by the time you read this chapter). The big advantage of using Android Pay is that it works with any Android device. Theoretically, this means that Android Pay has a significant jump in market penetration over the other alternatives. Something you'll notice when you visit the Android Pay site is the huge number of stores and banks that are prominently displayed. The strong support for this payment alternative is simply amazing.

Understanding what EMV does

Europay, MasterCard, and Visa (EMV) is the new chip-based strategy used by credit card companies to make your transactions more secure. Figure 6-7 shows the simple process for using these new cards, which is one of the features that make them popular with everyone.

Chip cards are simply standard credit cards with a computer chip inserted into them. You can see the chip when you look at the card. The purpose of using this chipped setup is to

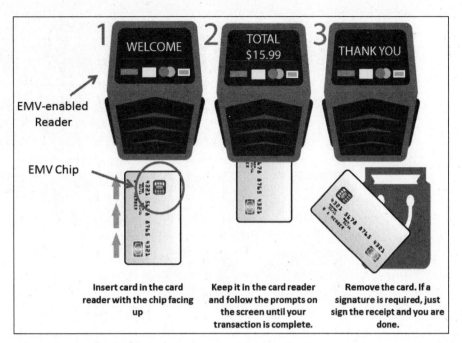

1 WELCOME
2 TOTAL $15.99
3 THANK YOU

EMV-enabled Reader

EMV Chip

Insert card in the card reader with the chip facing up

Keep it in the card reader and follow the prompts on the screen until your transaction is complete.

Remove the card. If a signature is required, just sign the receipt and you are done.

FIGURE 6-7: Understanding the basics of EMV.

>> Increase security

>> Reduce card-present fraud

>> Enable the use of future value-added applications

In some cases, you must provide a PIN to complete the transaction as part of the security requirements. However, the big thing is that the chipped setup provides the means to support dynamic authentication. The older magnetic stripe setup relies on static data, which means that after the data is copied, you can put it on another card and expect it to work. You can read more about the security features of EMV in the very next section.

Grasping why EMV transactions are more secure

Part of the reason you want to use EMV is that it offers better data security. The data flow provided by this chipped technology makes interception of the data less likely. Figure 6-8 shows the data flow used to perform transactions using this approach.

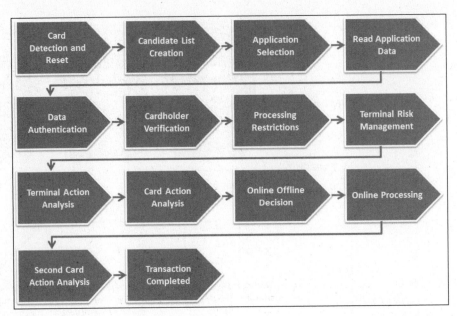

The important issue to consider is that EMV relies on a process in which the terminal questions everything and nothing is static. The most important steps in Figure 6-8 revolve around data authentication and cardholder verification.

Note that the data authentication step includes Static Data Authentication (SDA) for the account number and expiry date. Afterward, however, the process employs Dynamic Data Authentication (DDA) of card and terminal data to verify that the card application and data are genuine. The dynamic nature of the authentication process makes the card more secure. You can't simply copy the card data and expect the card to work.

Verifying the cardholder is also essential. Otherwise, someone could simply steal the card and use it until the actual owner notices. The process leaves the cardholder verification somewhat open. A terminal will have a list of acceptable verification methods. Currently, you can generally use these verification methods:

>> Online PIN (if unattended cash)

>> Offline PIN (if supported)

>> Signature (always)

The process also involves a terminal risk-management phase. Unlike magnetic stripe cards, the terminal now has intelligence to determine when the risk of a transaction is high enough to warrant online authorization. In the past, many fraudulent transactions received local authorization, and this step reduces that risk.

Defining the advantages of using EMV

Consumers will notice that they have a longer wait when using chipped cards in terminals equipped for the purpose. That's because the process for using them is longer (as described in the previous section of the chapter). However, offsetting the time difference are these significant advantages:

>> Safer transactions

>> Easier international purchases because everyone is using the same standard

>> A more thorough authentication process

>> Reduced identity-theft risk

Vendors who accept EMV cards have a definite advantage over those who don't. When at least 75 percent of the vendor transactions are processed through a dual contact and contactless EMV-certified device, the credit card companies will waive the required PCI-DSS audit. Waiving this requirement saves the vendor both time and money.

Of course, there is usually a stick to go with the carrot. Vendors also face a liability shift. In the future, the credit card companies may hold merchants who have not made the investment in chip-enabled technology financially liable for card-present counterfeit and potentially lost and stolen fraud that using a chip-enabled POS system could have prevented.

Card issuers also benefit from EMV. The biggest benefit is the drop in losses from fraud. Studies, such as the one at http://www.gemalto.com/emv/benefits, also say that contactless cards become buyer favorites quite quickly. More spending means that the issuer gets additional payments.

REMEMBER

Although EMV contact (chip card) technology may seem totally different from contactless payment systems, they are very similar, related technologies. Both contact and contactless payments provide the same protections and security, and both qualify under the EMV liability shift. The mobile wallet solutions discussed earlier in this chapter are not significantly different other than the interface (contact versus contactless).

Chapter 7

Employing NFC for Identification

L ife revolves around identifying who you are in a variety of ways in order to perform the tasks needed to keep life moving. For example, you need to identify yourself at work to gain access to your office building. Authentication allows you to enter a room, sign in to your computer, gain access to controlled resources, or work with various devices. Of course, you can use your smartphone to do all sorts of tasks. Chapter 6 discusses using it as a wallet — and this chapter takes its uses even further.

Many of the uses you find for NFC are personal. In fact, personalizing your NFC use should be one of the first things you do after discovering how to use it. NFC also lets you replace your digital keys. After you have access to a device, such as a car, you can sometimes use NFC to perform tasks with it, such as adjusting your seat automatically or presenting your license to those entrusted with enforcing the law. The point is that NFC identifies you to both people and devices in various ways to allow you to complete tasks with far less effort than these same tasks required in the past.

Obstensibly, this chapter focuses on identification. However, the real focus is on getting things done quickly and efficiently. The reason to make yourself known is to gain access. When reading this chapter, your focus is on the identify part of the question, but remembering why you're providing identifying information is essential.

Using NFC for Workplace Monitoring

Workplace monitoring is critical in many cases because, for example, you may need to know where employees are at any given time should an emergency occur. In addition, employees need access to company assets and have methods of reporting issues as they become aware of them. The process is usually simple with NFC; it begins when the employee taps a tag, which brings up the required application at a terminal where the employee can perform additional tasks, similar to the process shown in Figure 7-1.

FIGURE 7-1:
Workplace monitoring is a major use for NFC.

Of course, not every monitoring situation involves a terminal, but the fact that you can use a terminal to obtain additional information is important. Monitoring currently enjoys strong support in a number of fields. You commonly find it used in the following areas:

>> **Security:** Ensuring that assets remain safe is important. Using NFC, guards can log in to show that they actually did make their required rounds by tapping tags that are located along the route they are supposed to be

monitoring. When a guard fails to log in or notes a potential problem, the system can immediately send out alerts to let everyone know. The guard can easily create incidence reports or provide updates on maintenance actions tied to a specific location where the guard has tapped in.

» **Health care:** NFC can be used to help caregivers log into the system, report that they visited with a patient, and easily enter the results of the visit. The caregiver does not have to worry about credentials because NFC provides the credentials for them. Reports can include all sorts of data, including pictures of potential patient issues. If a patient is left too long without being checked or visited, the system can automatically generate messages to those in charge. This type of NFC verification and monitoring works the same for in-home, clinic, and hospital settings, and minimizes employee-training needs. For in-home visits, caregivers can tap to log in, tap to enter in their report, and then tap to log out. These capabilities can greatly streamline reporting, site visit verification, and billing.

» **Cleaning:** You can use NFC to track both inside and outside activities. Tag data can track equipment usage. Workers can tap to check out and check back in equipment used for the day or for a particular job. NFC can also be used for routine maintenance. If a tool or piece of equipment needs to be replaced after a certain amount of time or use, by checking the tool in and out, you can use NFC to help keep track of that usage. The use of programmable locks ensures that cleaning staff members access areas only when and where you want them to. You can even use tags to make ordering supplies easier. You can just tap on an empty container to reorder the product.

» **Real estate management:** Using NFC, you can track when a Realtor shows a property, how long the potential buyers stayed, and where they looked. You can also use NFC on For Sale yard signs so that prospective buyers can quickly and easily get the information on that specific property by just tapping the sign. Keyless locking systems are safer because only someone with the correct credentials can enter the property. By sending secure credentials to a smartphone, NFC can be used to unlock the door for a particular property. You also know precisely who gained access. A Realtor can more easily log buyer comments and assess issues, such as the potential for a sale. It's also possible to log incidences, such as incidental property damage and its cause. NFC makes all this easier because it correlates the user or the person tapping on the tag, with the location via the tag that is being tapped.

» **Other:** Any job can benefit from NFC use. What it takes is thinking outside the box to consider the possible, rather than avoid something because it hasn't been done before. NFC is all about the art of the possible.

Authenticating Users

Authentication has taken on a new meaning in the workplace. It consists of ensuring that only the right people can enter rooms, work with computers, interact with various resources, and use other sorts of devices. The role of authentication is to provide access, but it also makes monitoring access — and determining who has accessed something and when — easier. In addition, because so many forms of authentication now suffer from hacker exploitation, many organizations rely on dual factor authentication, and NFC can provide one of those factors. The following sections discuss various types of authentication in more detail.

Entering rooms

The "Understanding how NFC is deployed in unique ways" section of Chapter 5 describes how an NFC lock might work. The use of NFC allows someone to hold a smartphone against the lock to open it and get a visual indicator that access is successful, as shown in Figure 7-2. The lock can also provide other entry methods, such as a combination.

FIGURE 7-2:
An access panel provides required access to a room.

Using a keyless programmable lock provides some significant advantages. Most of these advantages are security or convenience related, as described in the following list:

- » No keys to lose (or copy)

- » People have their own code, so you know who enters the building and at what time

- » Access is programmable so that people can enter only at specific times

- » Access rights can be changed at any time

- » Remote monitoring becomes possible, so you know precisely when someone is trying to break in

- » You can create a situation in which everyone who needs access has it at any time required, but the door is always locked

WARNING

While NFC provides ease of use, better monitoring, and control accessing your environment, you should use good common sense about your own security. No matter what sort of lock you buy for your door — NFC, keyed, or otherwise — a thief can circumvent your security by using a crowbar or other device to spread the door casement. The best way to overcome this sort of physical attack is to get a long-throw door bolt. Just be sure that the keyless lock you buy provides the capability to move a long-throw bolt out of the way. A long-throw bolt is safer because spreading won't move it out of the door casing — the throw extends all the way through the framing members. Most external doors today are metal fire doors, making it hard to break through them if you have a proper lock in place. You can find some additional tips for making a home (or business) unattractive to thieves at http://www.doityourself.com/stry/preventingburglaries.

Working with computers

The constant barrage of security break-in articles you see in the trade press should tell you something about the state of security today: The current measures aren't working. Users will continue to share passwords, use ineffective passwords, and give their passwords to complete strangers who use them to hack into whatever system the password can access. The proliferation of passwords is also a source of problems for users who have trouble remembering one complex password, much less twenty or thirty of them. The best way to overcome these problems is to provide a solution that doesn't require the user to have to think at all about security, which is where NFC comes into play. Using NFC, a user can simply tap on a computer to unlock it, as shown in Figure 7-3.

When using NFC-based security, the NFC system generates, stores, and presents, on behalf of the user, a long, complex, hard-to-guess password, and the user never has to know or type it. Users can't share passwords because they don't actually know what their password is. Likewise, social engineering attacks become much harder for hackers to implement when the user literally knows nothing of value to tell the hacker. Although NFC won't solve all your security problems, it can go a long way toward making them less likely.

FIGURE 7-3:
Using a combination of NFC and password to provide dual factor logins.

TIP

You can count on users to lose their passwords, even if that password is on their smartphones. NFC can't stop a user from finding a way to cause a security problem, even in the most secure setup imaginable. Combining NFC security with biometric or other security methodologies provides a hedge against the loss of any one security measure. Two-factor security is becoming more common in situations in which data, resources, or environments require high security. Always assume the worst and you won't be disappointed.

Using resources

NFC lets you control resource usage within an organization with far greater precision than previous systems allowed. As shown in Figure 7-4, a user can log into an NFC-enabled device to access it. Using a device in this manner not only means controlling access but also tracking precise resource usage. An organization can potentially determine, for example, how much paper an individual user prints during a particular timeframe.

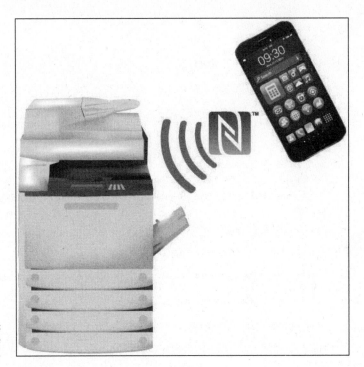

FIGURE 7-4:
Controlling device
access using NFC.

The devices you can access, the methods that you can employ to access them, and the apps that you can use to create the access vary according to vendor. One of the more interesting offerings comes from Hewlett-Packard in the form of Touch-to-Print. You can use Touch-to-Print with these printers:

>> HP Color LaserJet Pro MFP m476dw

>> HP ENVY 7640 e-All-in-One Printer

>> HP ENVY 7645 e-All-in-One Printer

>> HP Officejet 5740 Printer

>> HP Officejet 5742 Printer

>> HP Officejet 5744 Printer

>> HP Officejet 5745 Printer

>> HP Officejet 5746 Printer

>> HP OfficeJet 7510 Wide Format All-in-One Printer

>> HP OfficeJet 7512 Wide Format All-in-One Printer

>> HP Officejet 8040 e-All-in-One Printer

» HP Officejet Pro 8620 Printer

» HP Officejet Pro 8625 Printer

» HP Officejet Pro 8630 Printer

» HP Officejet Pro 8660 Printer

The Touch-to-Print app works the same way on all these devices. To use Touch-to-Print, you follow these steps:

1. **Download and install the HP ePrint mobile app from the Google App Store** (`https://play.google.com/store/apps/details?id=com.hp.android.print`).

2. **Tap the HP ePrint mobile app to open it.**

3. **Tap Photos, File, or Web to open a folder containing items to print.**

4. **Tap the item you want to print.**

5. **Locate the NFC touch zone on the front of your printer.**

6. **Hold your phone against the NFC touch zone.**

   The NFC connection tells the printer what to print, but doesn't send the data to it.

7. **Tap *Print* on the ePrint mobile app.**

   At this point, the printer and NFC-enabled device open another communication channel using Bluetooth or Wi-Fi to transfer the data from the user device to the printer.

Brother and Samsung both offer printers with similar capabilities. You simply place your NFC-enabled device against the printer and tell it to send the files you want to print to the printer.

Working with other devices

You can count on NFC to become a part of working with most devices at some point. For example, Coca-Cola is already using NFC to let you pay for your Coke with a touch of a phone. The short video at `https://www.youtube.com/watch?v=nioHTfqtPfU` shows just how simple this process is and how it lets a vendor add features such as loyalty cards to the scheme of things. Eventually, you'll be able to perform most device interactions using just your smartphone through NFC connectivity.

TIP

This connectivity will offer you the full range of features you expect, such as the ability to use coupons as part of your payment. The important thing is that the way the apps are configured, you might actually find that you save more money than you might otherwise think. For example, you may find that you keep forgetting to use a paper coupon before it expires. Using NFC means that the app will remind you to use the coupon as part of the payment process — no more need to remember to do something.

Using an NFC Phone

For many people, everything now happens on their smartphones. People use the devices for making calls, keeping track of appointments, checking email, surfing the Internet, and playing games when time permits; however, smartphones can provide all sorts of additional functions that affect daily life. NFC makes many of these additional functions possible and provides the flexibility needed to make them work seamlessly with other technologies. The following sections describe just a few of the more popular ways to use NFC with your smartphone.

Authenticating with an access control card

As data breaches become more common, the use of two-factor (dual-factor) authentication is on the rise. Relying on two (or even three) methods of authenticating a user reduces the potential for hackers to gain access to an account without a lot of hard work. Companies such as IBM brought two-factor authentication to mobile devices by combining a password with a special access-control card.

Dual-factor authentication offers more security because it means that a password alone isn't enough to break into another person's account. The password must be supplemented by something a person has, such as a smart card or an NFC-enabled key fob. Using your bank as an example, here is how IBM's dual-factor authentication works.

You open your bank's mobile app on your smartphone. It sends a special challenge number to your phone. Then the app asks you for your password. Here's what is different with dual-factor authentication: After you enter your password, you tap your phone against the NFC-enabled card that your bank gave you. The phone transfers the challenge number to the card using NFC. The card transforms the challenge number through a calculation based on its own key and then sends it back to the phone, which in turn sends it to the bank. Authentication fails if a person types in the wrong password, uses the wrong card, or doesn't have a card at all. You can read more about this at http://www.cnet.com/news/using-nfc-ibm-brings-dual-factor-authentication-to-mobile/.

NFC plays a role by providing access between the smartphone and the smart card — or access-control card — as shown in Figure 7-5. To provide a second authentication factor, you simply hold the card against the back of the phone as shown.

Creating a college campus ID card

Keeping students safe, yet allowing them controlled access to all the resources they require to learn, can be a challenging task. Many of the older methods of performing this task, such as using physical ID cards, are problematic because the student forgets the ID card, it gets lost, or people create fake IDs to gain unauthorized access. Because students are a lot less likely to forget their smartphones at home or lose them, relying on NFC to provide campus credentials makes sense. All students need do is hold their smartphones against a door to gain access to a room, as shown in Figure 7-6. And because the student's identification is housed in the phone, students can also use it to buy items in the cafeteria, check books out at the library, and check in on social media at the football game, all with a simple tap.

FIGURE 7-5:
You can authenticate on your phone using an NFC card and a password.

FIGURE 7-6:
You can store
your college ID on
your smartphone.

Managing hotel room and other access control cards

Instead of having to keep piles of smart cards on hand, a hotel can place the key to a room on an NFC-enabled phone. The user simply taps the door and possibly enters a code, as shown in Figure 7-7. The keys automatically expire when the user's time is up, so the hotel staff doesn't need to worry about collecting anything. In addition, the same key can provide access to hotel resources, such as the swimming pool or gym. As with other smartphone-based uses of NFC, the hotel can track the guests to determine the amenities they're using and when.

TIP

NFC-enabled access also provides the hotel with lots of valuable data. For example, hotels can tell how much time people spend in their rooms as opposed to other parts of the hotel, like the swimming pool. They could tell which amenities are in more use, swimming pool or fitness center. For guests entering their rooms just prior to dinner time, for example, the hotel can send incentives to those guests to visit the hotel restaurant and give them an option to make a reservation. Using NFC in various ways throughout the hotel can enhance the guest experience, increase revenues, and cut costs.

Personalizing NFC Use

NFC doesn't have to be a commercialized proposition. You can also use it for personal needs. The tags aren't so expensive that you can't code some for specific home needs. For example, a tag on the side of the washing machine can place a reminder in your smartphone to buy more laundry detergent (or possibly make the purchase for you). The following sections describe some ways you might use NFC for personal needs.

Using tags to perform common actions

The "Working in reader/writer mode" section of Chapter 4 is one of several places in the book that discuss techniques for creating tags. However, it's a good idea to know why you may want to create a tag. Of course, there are all the business uses for tags discussed so far in the book, but you can also use tags for your personal needs. The following list provides some examples of how you might use tags to address personal concerns:

>> **Reconfigure your smartphone for home:** A tag placed next to your door can reconfigure your smartphone for the home environment. You may want to turn off the Wi-Fi used at the office and turn Bluetooth on instead. Because you won't have your smartphone attached to your hip, you may want to turn off vibrate mode and turn up the volume so that you can hear the smartphone ring anywhere in the house.

>> **Reconfigure your smartphone for the car:** A tag placed on the dashboard can connect your smartphone to the car's systems. You can enable Bluetooth communication and set up the smartphone for hands-free operation. The car can play your favorite tunes right from your smartphone. You can also create a connection to Google Maps so that you can obtain individualized GPS instructions.

>> **Setting up for the gym:** Adding a tag to your sports bag can let you put the smartphone in flight mode so that you're not disturbed during your workout. The same tag can start your favorite playlist so that you have music while working out. Using toggle mode, you can reverse the changes when you're done working out.

>> **Ending your day:** Place a tag on your nightstand to configure your alarm clock and put the smartphone into flight mode. The smartphone can display a clock application while it sits in the charger overnight.

>> **Starting your day:** The tag to turn off your alarm is actually in the bathroom, so you need to get up to scan it. The "Getting a general application" section of Chapter 12 discusses the Puzzle Alarm Clock app, which is an interesting and fun way to wake up in the morning.

>> **Automatically starting your PC:** After a hard day, you come home and want to start the PC that runs your entertainment system automatically. Chapter 12 discusses a number of apps that you can use to help the process along. Even though the process does take a few steps (see the article at https://vv.reddit.com/r/Android/comments/16g1dh/ using_taskerwolnfc_tags_to_auto_start_your/ for guidelines), you have to set it up only once to enjoy the full benefits of automation in your home.

>> **Keeping in touch:** You might not have access to a Wi-Fi hotspot whenever you need it without your smartphone. Add a tag to your PC that turns on your smartphone's Wi-Fi support so that your PC has constant Internet access.

>> **Setting timers:** Creating tags that start a timer app on your phone after you tap a tag is a great way to time things such as cooking eggs or monitoring the wash. You can even add tags to the cases for kid's movies so that you know when the movie ends and you need to check in on how things are going before you resume some activity in your home.

Creating tags to log onto home networks

You may have a lot of different reasons to allow others to share your home network — and with NFC, guests can quickly and easily get onto your home Wi-Fi network. You can even host a movie party (and it is the day and age of the second screen, after all; go to http://www.samsung.com/ie/support/skp/faq/1057791 for details on putting contents you see on your smartphone onto a larger television screen). Of course, you can hand out your login name and password to provide access to the network, but a better option that doesn't require the loss of security is to use NFC to provide the required credentials. Everyone can tap the NFC tag to obtain the required access.

InstaWifi (https://play.google.com/store/apps/details?id=net.jessechen. instawifi) is an app that lets you share your home network login information with ease. It provides both NFC and QR code access, so even people who don't have NFC-enabled devices can participate.

The NFC access is direct when using InstaWifi. When working with a QR code, you create the QR code using InstaWifi and then scan it using a barcode-scanning application such as Barcode Scanner (https://play.google.com/store/apps/ details?id=com.google.zxing.client.android). The result is the same either way: People gain access to your home network without any loss of security on your part.

Replacing Your Car Keys

NFC could eventually replace your car keys and control access to special functionality in your car. Even though some of the technologies in the following sections aren't available for general use today, they do represent some of the things you might do with NFC in the near future.

Gaining vehicle access

If you have more than one vehicle, as many people do, carrying fobs or keys around or remembering entry codes can become quite a problem. The problem becomes larger when you have more people driving the car than you have sets of fobs or keys. The solution is to rely on NFC to provide vehicle access. You just tap your phone against the door (or other marked area), as shown in Figure 7-8.

FIGURE 7-8:
Cars can provide
a number of
levels of access
using NFC.

Adjusting the seat position

After you gain access to your vehicle, you can tap a tag to automate tasks such as adjusting your seat position. Chapter 12 discusses some of the applications you can use to automate all sorts of tasks within your vehicle. The idea is that you not only automate the task (making life easier) but also get consistent setups every time you drive. The consistency of the driving experience can help you feel more comfortable and less distracted, which can improve vehicle safety. The secure experience that NFC provides also allows you to control your car's environment in the following ways:

>> **Defining a custom electronics experience:** The use of NFC can help create an environment in which your personal devices instantly connect to the car's systems. This act enables the car to provide a customized experience based on your personal data.

>> **Improved driving efficiency:** As cars become smarter, NFC will provide secure access to your driving data (possibly stored on a smartphone) through another networking technology such as Wi-Fi or Bluetooth. Companies such as Progressive currently provide lower insurance premiums to drivers who are willing to have their driving behaviors tracked, but the tracking information comes at the expense of privacy. True Mileage (http://truemileage. com/) does the same thing, but without the loss of privacy, because it relies on NFC rather than GPS tracking.

Automating Vehicle Interactions

NFC is also finding use as part of official documentation. For example, French drivers now have multifunction NFC-enabled driver's licenses in place of the paper or plastic cards used in other places. Eventually, you may have a single card or a smartphone app that lets you perform all sorts of tasks related to driving a car, such as presenting your registration and proof of insurance when asked — no more fiddling about in the glove compartment looking for little bits of paper. The following sections present even more ideas about NFC car-related technologies that are close to being used or already in use today.

Presenting a driver's license

Some countries, such as France (`http://www.nfcworld.com/2013/10/23/326507/french-drivers-get-multi-functional-nfc-licenses/`), are now offering NFC-enabled driving licenses. These licenses contain the usual written details, as shown in Figure 7-9, but they also include an NFC chip and two memory areas. The private memory area contains driver-specific information that law enforcement can use to verify a particular driver. Vendors can use the public memory area for any number of purposes, such as storing insurance information.

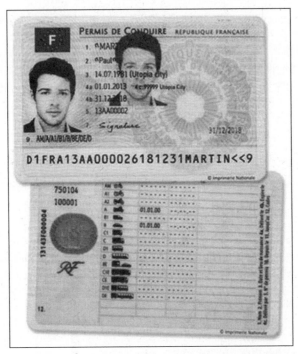

FIGURE 7-9:
Some countries now provide multifunction driver's licenses based on NFC.

Image courtesy of NXP B.V.

TIP

The future may see the NFC-enabled driver's license used for all sorts of purposes. For example, a car rental agency could place the keys for a car right in the public memory area of the license. The driver and the car would be linked, allowing the rental agency to verify precisely who should have possession of the rental vehicle at any given time.

Performing vehicle inspections

One of the more time-consuming vehicle interactions for truck and bus drivers is the vehicle inspection. By adding NFC tags to various locations on a vehicle, a driver can indicate they inspected the area (see http://www.nfcworld.com/2015/06/25/336235/mcgee-group-adds-nfc-inspection-tags-to-trucks/). More important, the tag can open an app that lets the driver note any deficiencies, and even take pictures of them. The information arrives on the workshop manager's system in a matter of seconds, which allows consistent and timely repairs and updates of the vehicle.

Chapter 8

Using NFC in Health Care

NFC has the potential for greatly changing the way in which medical care is offered and how medical professionals interact with patients. A critical part of helping patients get well faster and also reduce medical costs is enabling the patient to do more tasks sooner after an event occurs. In addition, the use of monitoring instead of direct observation gives the patient more freedom and flexibility in determining the course of care.

REMEMBER

One of the issues you must deal with as part of using any new technology in a hospital environment is privacy. Hospitals and other medical establishments have both ethical and legal requirements to keep patient information private. The loss of privacy affects not only the patient but also the doctor, any associated staff, and the organization as a whole because the patient loses the trust required to make medicine work.

This chapter helps you discover the wide variety of medical-related tasks that you can perform using NFC. You may be surprised to find that NFC can directly affect everything from the patient's home care to care in the hospital. In addition, NFC can deal with a patient's daily needs, such as making it easier for special needs people to perform common tasks.

Dealing with Privacy Issues

Privacy is essential to the proper functioning of health care at all levels. Patients are rightfully concerned about the potential losses that can and do occur when anyone involved in the health care industry experiences a data breach. In fact, the consequences of a health care data breach can far exceed those of a financial data breach (see http://www.govhealthit.com/news/5-ways-health-data-breaches-are-far-worse-financial-ones for details) — including everything from loss of status to loss of life. Unfortunately, health care data breaches tend to be huge, such as the Excellus data breach that exposed at least 10 million records (http://www.computerworld.com/article/2983026/cybercrime-hacking/cyberattack-exposes-10m-records-at-excellus.html). Because health care data presents such a rich payback, hackers are focusing a lot more attention on this data today than in the past (see http://www.infoworld.com/article/2983634/security/why-hackers-want-your-health-care-data-breaches-most-of-all.html). The point of all this is that health care data breaches are incredibly messy, long lasting, and far reaching, affecting more than just the patient whose data is lost.

WARNING

NFC does provide safeguards when transferring data. The short signal distance and use of data encryption do help protect the data. However, these safeguards aren't nearly enough security. You must also have applications specifically designed for health care use that provide protections beyond those that NFC provides natively. In fact, you may find new legal requirements in place soon to ensure that the device you own, the application you run, and the security you provide are enough. The National Institute of Standards and Technology (NIST) is currently looking into the problem of using devices, such as smartphones, to work with health care data (see http://www.computerworld.com/article/2951831/healthcare-it/feds-look-to-bolster-security-for-mobile-devices-used-in-health-care.html for details). In fact, you should read and implement the procedures found in the new NIST guidelines at https://nccoe.nist.gov/projects/use_cases/health_it/ehr_on_mobile_devices.

Performing Hospital-related Tasks

If you spend any time at all at a hospital just observing the amount of activity that takes place, you soon realize that hospitals are as much about logistics as about medicine. Coordinating the efforts of all those people, each of whom has a number of patients to deal with, requires a lot of effort. In fact, inefficiencies in managing people and resources create huge costs in hospitals that NFC can help mitigate (eventually reducing the cost of medicine while making patient care timelier and of higher quality). Doing all these things is quite a task, but NFC really can help realize the savings that the medical profession needs. The following sections of the chapter tell you how NFC can make it happen.

Accessing medical records

In a health center, every patient will have a wristband that contains an NFC tag with the patient's ID. To access a medical record or perform other patient-related tasks, a medical professional can read the wristband with an NFC-enabled tablet (https://www.nfcbootcamp.com/favorite-nfc-implementations/ and http://www.rfidjournal.com/articles/view?10511/2), or a peripheral device such as vWand (http://www.vwand.com/) to identify the patient. Figure 8-1 shows how such a device might work.

After reading the ID, the complete medical record appears on the screen of a device, such as a tablet, speeding up the access to the patient's information. The medical professional can perform the task while maintaining patient-information confidentiality because the wristband does not need to contain any personal information. The doctor can see the patient's record and prescribe new treatments and medical tests working with the vWand as a stylus for the tablet.

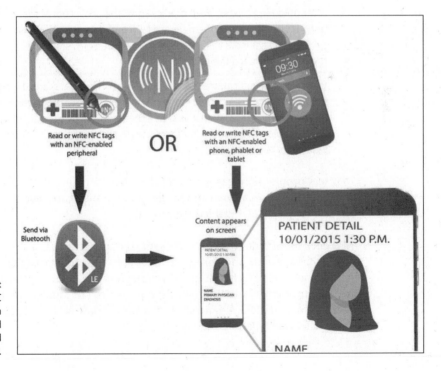

FIGURE 8-1: Combine NFC with Bluetooth to make record access and update faster.

The big thing about using NFC to access medical records is that the medical professional has the information available at all times, in a form that's easy to use, and provides search capabilities as needed. Older medical record technology just doesn't hold up when compared to the innovations that NFC helps create. Using NFC tags helps to ensure that you have the right patient record and that the information is complete. You can read more about this use of technology in the article at http://www.rfidjournal.com/articles/view?10511/2.

Ensuring that patients receive correct medications and dosages

Patients need to receive the right kind of medications in the right dosage at the right time. Otherwise, they might encounter serious medical issues. Using paper records or scanning bar codes doesn't really work as well as it could, and sometimes patients receive the wrong medications. The process for administering medications improves when using NFC. The process is quick and simple, yet less prone to error:

1. The medical professional scans the patient's NFC tag and uses the medical record obtained to get a list of medications a patient needs.

2. After obtaining the required medications, the professional scans each medication in turn, along with the patient's NFC tag. An app displays an error message on the professional's NFC-enabled device when a mismatch occurs between the medication and the patient.

3. When all the medications are correct, the professional scans the patient's ID badge and gives the patient the medication. The patient's medical record now contains what medication was given, the amount given, what time the medication was received, and the name of the person who gave it. The setup allows little room for error.

NFC lets people more easily ensure that they're taking the right medication. As shown in Figure 8-2, you can tap the tag on a medication bottle and learn more about it on your NFC-enabled smartphone.

NFC does more than just check dosages, though. Part of the effort to provide the correct medications and dosages is to supplement the packaging used for pharmaceuticals. An NFC chip in the packaging lets you deter counterfeiting by creating a connection to the Internet, through which the vendor can check and track package information. A vendor can therefore track each package separately and know where each package ends up.

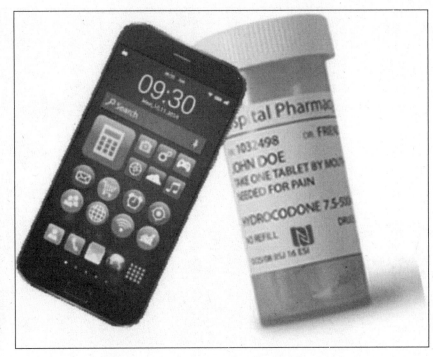

FIGURE 8-2:
Simply tap your
phone on the
medication
bottle to ensure
the correct type
and dosages of
medication.

The patient benefits significantly as well. Instead of having to open a package to see the pamphlet of drug interaction information, the patient can tap a smartphone against the package and see the information immediately, as well as view a video on how and when the medication should be taken. In addition, this packaging technique lets people detect package tampering. If someone has tampered with the package, it will detect it. You can get more details about this particular NFC use at http://www.lfpress.com/2016/01/12/packaging-that-talks-to-your-phone.

Tracking patient progress

Most medical environments require the active participation of a number of professionals including doctors, nurses, dieticians, and therapists of various sorts. Fortunately, most paper record systems are now in electronic format, giving everyone easier access to the same information. No longer are updates floating in limbo. However, accessing these records using a computer that may not be in a convenient place or proves too bulky for some other reason tends to slow things down, and the professionals may not make entries in a timely manner. Using NFC can make keeping records updated significantly easier, as shown in Figure 8-3.

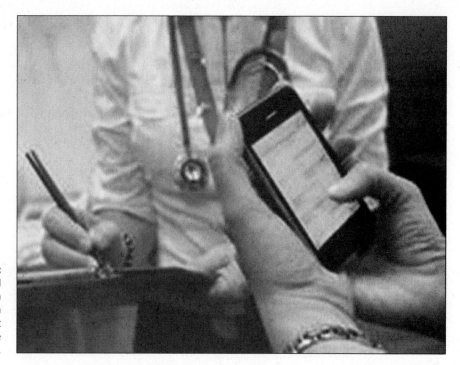

FIGURE 8-3:
Data entered
manually with
a computer is a
thing of the past
with smartphone
access.

Medical professionals say that NFC is the best technology to use because it's available with mobile phones, can be made secure, is cost effective, provides relatively high access speed, and is still simple to use. NFC tags also provide better durability and easier reading than barcodes. In addition, color-coded systems often are not standardized across facilities and require interpretation by the medical professional, so this option isn't the best one to use for identifying patients and ensuring that they receive proper care. By reading the patient ID from a wristband, the information that a medical professional needs about a patient appears on a smartphone screen, making access quite easy.

REMEMBER

The fact that a medical professional must authenticate before receiving the medical information by scanning an ID card means that a smart app can also present the medical information the professional is most likely to need at the outset. The medical professional spends less time looking through medical records for commonly needed information. In addition, the system records each medical record access, so maintaining a secure environment is possible. All this occurs with simple taps of ID wristbands, badges, or cards, so the process is fast and easy.

The tracking process goes still further. Because the entire system is linked, health care professionals know precisely where the patient is at any given time. When the time comes to discharge the patient, all the required information is instantly available, resulting in a complete and highly accurate set of discharge papers.

Medical billing is also connected to the process, so bills for services rendered go out immediately.

Scheduling occupational and physical therapy

Getting patients occupational and physical therapy as needed is essential to recovery. However, coordinating every involved caregiver's time and the resources needed to perform the task are available can become a logistical nightmare. Using NFC tags coupled with other technologies let people track the required time and resources, as shown in Figure 8-4. The figure shows an outpatient scenario, but this appointment scheduling use case can also work for inpatient needs.

The entire process is based on using NFC to make scheduling and tracking tasks quick, easy, and less error prone. For example, a patient can use the following steps to make an appointment:

1. The patient obtains an NFC smart card after registering successfully with the medical care facility. (This step normally happens during the patient's first visit, and the patient continues to use the same card throughout the process.)

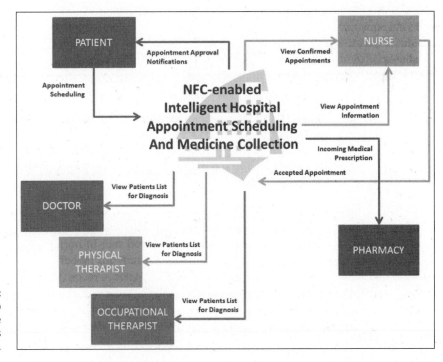

FIGURE 8-4:
NFC can help coordinate the efforts of various professionals.

2. The patient taps the card on a kiosk or smartphone to make an appointment. The NFC-enabled device shows the times and doctors, therapists, or other medical professionals available for the appointment.

3. As part of the appointment process, the patient provides a time window for the appointment. The time window allows the appointment time to slide to meet the medical professional's needs, but also ensures that the patient can actually attend the appointment.

4. After the patient chooses a date, time, and medical professional, the system asks for verification and authentication, which the patient accomplishes by tapping the card again.

5. The NFC-enabled device sends the details of the appointment to the medical facilities server.

TIP

6. On the day of the appointment, if the medical professional becomes overwhelmed, the server automatically prioritizes the appointments by

   - Disabled

   - Elderly

   - Pregnant

   - Infant

   - Normal

7. The system notifies anyone the doctor can't see because the doctor's time slot is used up or falls outside the window provided.

8. Patients can reschedule by tapping their card on the NFC-enabled device and following Steps 1 through 5.

9. Assuming that the appointment works out for everyone involved, tapping the card on the day of the appointment notifies the caregiver that the patient has arrived, allowing accurate record keeping of who actually showed up for their treatment and when. The automation also streamlines billing, as mentioned above.

Not only is the system automated and completely accurate, it also manages to make everyone more efficient and potentially avoid scheduling problems. In addition, neither the patient nor the medical professional becomes stressed over unavoidable delays.

The patient can also use the NFC smart card to cancel or reschedule appointments. Likewise, medical professionals can use their NFC ID cards to gain access to appointment lists, make determinations of time availability, and provide timely cancellations when necessary. The same system makes communication possible between nurses and pharmacists, who have their own NFC ID cards to interact with the system.

Tracking doctors and nurses

Medical facilities have seen all sorts of systems for tracking doctors and nurses. For example, a medical professional presses a button upon entering a room. An indicator lights to show that someone is there; however, this system doesn't indicate who the person is. In addition, forgetting to press the button a second time to turn it off is all too easy, so the light can stay on even when no one is in the room. Most old technology ideas have problems.

When using NFC, a medical professional can tap a wall indicator upon entering a room. Because the tag contains the ID of the medical professional, you know precisely who is in what room — no guesswork involved. In addition, if the medical professional forgets to log out when exiting the room, logging into the next room will automatically log the medical professional out, which means that the location information is wrong for a few minutes at most.

Being able to track the medical professionals makes performing patient billing easier. In addition, the tracking shows who was in the room, when, and for how long, which can be useful when legal issues arise.

Working with Logger Tags

Data logger tags are an essential part of patient monitoring because they can keep constant watch over a patient's vitals. Figure 8-5 shows the typical process of how such a chip works.

The chip itself can contain an internal sensor, such as a temperature sensor. Many chips can also offer access to external sensors that can monitor any element of patient health. The analog data from the sensors goes through an analog to digital (A/D) converter, in which the measurement appears as a numeric value. Each entry is also coupled with a date and time from an internal clock. An ISO 14443A (http://nfc-tools.org/index.php?title=ISO14443) processor provides the control features required to make the tag work. The chip stores the readings in protected memory that is accessible only to someone with the proper credentials. The Analog Front End (AFE) chip provides the NFC antenna interface that makes working with the tag possible. The chip requires some type of power input in most cases — usually 1.5 volts or 3 volts. Now that you have a basic idea of what a logger tag is and how it works, the following sections discuss issues you need to consider when using NFC logger tags.

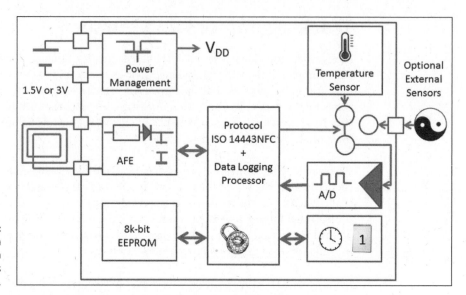

Differentiating between transdermal and subdermal

Logger tags appear in both transdermal and subdermal versions. The transdermal versions work much like an adhesive bandage that you stick to the skin. Figure 8-6 shows such a tag used to monitor a patient's temperature. Passing any NFC-enabled device within close proximity to the tag, coupled with an appropriate application, will display the patient's temperature immediately. When using certain types of tags, you can use NFC to pair the tag with another device, employing another technology such as Bluetooth for remote patient monitoring, all without any wires.

TIP

An advantage of this approach is the capability to monitor patient vitals without waking the patient. The range of available sensors is amazing (see the "Monitoring glucose the modern way" sidebar, later in this chapter, for one such example). VivaLink (http://www.vivalnk.com/) makes the transdermal patch shown in Figure 8-6. The company currently makes two sensors: Fever Scout (http://www.vivalnk.com/feverscout) for constant body temperature monitoring and Vital Scout (http://www.vivalnk.com/vitalscout) for monitoring the following vitals:

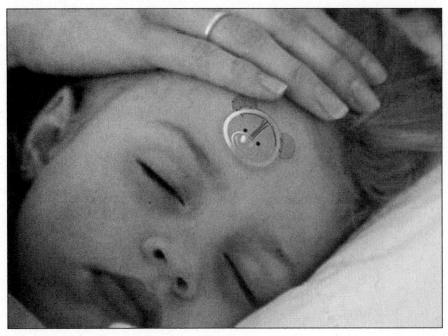

FIGURE 8-6:
Transdermal patches are placed on a patient's skin.

Courtesy of Vivalink

>> Body temperature

>> Respiration rate

>> Sleep status

>> Heart rate and variability

>> Stress levels

>> Activity/training

Both sensors allow remote monitoring through a mobile app. In both cases, you must recharge a battery to keep the tag active, but the charge lasts up to 72 hours, making the charging requirement less of a problem. You can read more about how this application works at `http://www.nfcworld.com/2015/01/06/333385/vivalnk-shows-wearable-nfc-thermometer/`.

A potential problem with transdermal patches is the antenna required to make the NFC connection. Automated Assembly Corporation (AAC) (`http://www.autoassembly.com/`) is working on that problem by creating an antenna that's laid down in the adhesive, rather than in a flexible circuit, which makes the patch considerably easier to wear. The same technology lets NFC chips be embedded into plastic, paper, and cloth. You can read more about this technology at `http://www.nfcworld.com/2015/02/17/334156/aac-to-mass-produce-wearable-nfc-stickers-for-healthcare/`.

An alternative to transdermal patches, which can come off with relative ease (likely at the most inconvenient moment) is the subdermal logger tag. As you can see from Figure 8-7, these tags are extremely small. You inject them below the skin. As with the transdermal patches, you place an NFC-enabled device close to the chip to read it.

Volunteers in the Netherlands are already testing the subdermal version of the tag in the real world. In this case, the volunteers are using the tag for identification purposes. Of course, as with any new technology, the current applications for the tag are limited, but usage will grow with time. The point is that the tag is apparently safe enough for use right now and will make all sorts of medical applications significantly easier.

Making measurements

The capability to measure conditions extends beyond the patient. Many companies are now investigating ways to monitor all sorts of medical needs, such as the conditions under which items such as pharmaceutical goods travel.

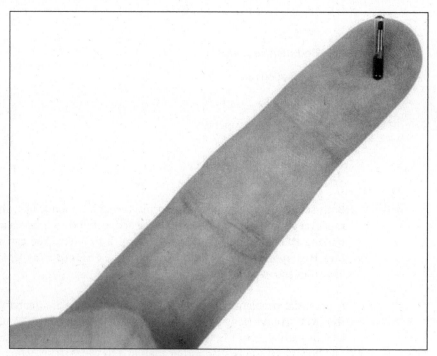

FIGURE 8-7:
Subdermal patches are placed under a patient's skin.

© vetkit/Shutterstock, Inc.

One company in the monitoring business is Blulog (`http://blulog.eu/nfc-data-loggers/`). The interesting aspect of this data logger is that the credit card-sized device incorporates LEDs. Simply looking at the front of the card tells you whether the package has experienced temperatures outside the desired range. Of course, the card also tracks the temperatures. This particular card can hold 48,000 readings. The data on this card is secured using a PIN. You can find additional information about this product at `http://www.rfidjournal.com/articles/view?13621`. A special feature noted by the manufacturer about this product is the access to the temperature data using an NFC connection even if the battery dies, so you never lose access to the detailed log.

MONITORING GLUCOSE THE MODERN WAY

For many diabetics, constantly pricking a body part to obtain a blood sample for glucose monitoring is both painful and inconvenient. Of course, pricking a finger is the most common approach and ends up being the most painful as well, but the other alternatives really aren't any better. That's why companies such as Gentag (`http://gentag.com/`) and Noviosense (`http://noviosense.com/`) are working on methods of obtaining glucose measurements using other approaches, such as measuring the glucose in tears.

Each company has a different method for monitoring glucose. The Gentag approach relies on a skin patch or wireless sensor that a doctor can embed under the skin. These wireless sensors let people with an NFC-enabled smartphone create a connection and read their glucose levels at any time. The advantages are many, including the ability to take forgotten readings from any location before eating or engaging in activities for which glucose level is important.

When using the Noviosense approach, a wireless monitor sits on the lower eyelid and collects tears from the monitor. Patients can read their glucose levels using any NFC-enabled smartphone, making the process extremely convenient. Instead of recording readings manually, the smartphone automatically records them, and because patients will usually have their smartphone with them, the problem of having left the monitor at home goes away and the doctor can easily see the patient's glucose history in a cloud-based application that keeps a record of the readings.

Both companies are coupling the glucose readings taken by a smartphone with insulin delivery. The smartphone does any required calculation, ensuring that the patient receives the proper amount of medication at the right time. You can read more about this innovative approach at `http://www.nfcworld.com/2015/07/22/336759/joint-venture-to-develop-painless-diabetes-monitoring-with-nfc/`.

Chip makers are continuing to develop other solutions that will solve other problems in the future. For example, Delta Microelectronics is producing the Thor chip with a Serial Peripheral Interface (SPI) that allows you to monitor pressure, tilt, voltage, light, and other types of data (http://asic.madebydelta.com/products/thor/). The chip adheres to both the ISO 14443A and ISO 15693 standards.

Monitoring Patients Remotely

Most of the solutions mentioned so far in this chapter include some type of remote monitoring. Remote monitoring is critical unless you want your staff spending a lot of time going to individual rooms. Using wireless pairing technologies, such as Bluetooth, lets staff track patient data from a central location much more easily. However, remote patient monitoring takes other forms as well, as described in the following sections.

Managing patient care

Many monitoring solutions today require the patient to visit the medical facility to provide readings taken at home, or the medical facility must send someone to the patient's home to obtain the readings. Most of the NFC solutions discussed in this chapter, however, involve using an NFC-enabled device, such as a smartphone, and nothing stops the smartphone app from sending its various readings to the doctor in addition to showing them to the patient. This means that a doctor could know about a pending problem before it becomes an emergency. Monitoring software could provide the doctor with an alert the moment the sensors detect a potential problem, prompting corrective action before the patient suffers major trauma.

Verifying health care professional visits

Some situations do require health care professional visits. For example, a patient who is in hospice care or someone dealing with the results of an injury at home may need professional help. Of course, it's important to verify that the health care professional actually makes the visit, that the results of the visit are properly recorded, and that the patient (or caregiver) is aware that the visit has occurred (see Figure 8-8).

FIGURE 8-8:
Simply tap a tag to show that a home health care visit took place.

You can place an NFC tag in the patient's home for use in monitoring visits. In this case, the health care professional would follow these steps:

1. Tap the NFC tag upon entering the home.

2. Tap the patient's tag or wristband before taking any readings.

3. View the patient's medical data when it appears on the NFC-enabled device screen.

4. Make any required entries.

5. Tap the NFC tag again when leaving the home.

Using this approach makes it easy to verify specific visit times because the NFC tag is available only at the home. Various technologies exist to ensure that the tag remains in place and that no one can copy it.

Interacting with Patient Monitors

Making it easy for patients to monitor their conditions is one way to help them regain their health or at least to live higher-quality lives. Of course, the problem is keeping the patient interested and providing good medical input at the same time.

A diabetes study (http://www.imedicalapps.com/2013/01/study-diabetes-mobile-phones-nfc/) that included 403 patients describes a setup through which patients provided diabetes data to a remote location. The patients had the option of using either a web-based reporting application or an NFC-based mobile app. This was a long-term study. After the first 350 days of monitoring, the patients using the mobile app were significantly more active than those who used the web-based application. In short, using a simple NFC-based approach kept patients interested, which likely resulted in better health overall.

Addressing Accessibility Needs

People with accessibility needs require simple solutions that work well and don't require a lot in the way of manual dexterity. The solutions must allow them to perform health-related tasks without undue stress. Fortunately, Android (http://www.apps4android.org/?p=1186) and other vendors are launching initiatives to make working with NFC even easier for those with special needs. These vendors are working on special NFC-enabled devices that help those with special needs more easily use NFC to monitor conditions like diabetes. In addition, these new accessible devices will make it possible to

» Interact with mobile ticketing applications

» Make mobile payments (either credit or debit cards)

» Use electronic ticketing for travel and entertainment

» Use electronic money

» Obtain travel cards

» Interact with identity documents

» Use electronic keys

NFC can also help those with special needs overcome the limitations of devices that vendors haven't necessarily designed for those with special needs (http://uxpamagazine.org/near-field-communications/). For example, people who are blind may not be able to interact with the touch panel of a microwave. However, by putting the settings into their smartphone and then tapping on the microwave, they can still interact with it. The accessible smartphone and associated app lets people perform tasks they couldn't ordinarily perform.

REMEMBER

The same NFC technology allows people with special needs to perform all sorts of other tasks, such as successfully navigate a route on a bus, go grocery shopping, or get a book at the library. Using a specially equipped smartphone, people with a special need can visualize text, understand spoken instructions, or make their needs known. For example, by tapping tagged packages in a store, people who can't actually see the package can hear about the package from their smartphone. Likewise, people who can't hear a sales pitch from an in-store kiosk, can see the text through their smartphone after creating a connection through an NFC tag.

Chapter 9

Considering Other NFC Uses

Previous chapters explore some common and prevalent uses for NFC. However, they don't even show you the tip of the iceberg. NFC is every-where, and you can use it to meet all sorts of needs. In fact, you might be amazed to find that NFC is already at work doing things for you that you really didn't think about before reading this book.

This chapter tells you other NFC uses that the book hasn't covered before now. You explore an interesting array of uses that might help you create the next big thing in your organization or make your personal life better. NFC is there to per-form tasks both public and private — for the good of others and to meet your personal needs.

REMEMBER

This chapter still covers only common uses, though. NFC actually reaches even further than you see in this chapter. Describing all the uses for NFC could require another full book. The point of this chapter is to get you thinking about the ways in which you could use NFC to do amazing things (and some mundane things, too).

Performing Marketing Tasks

Marketers can leverage NFC to get value from the rise in mobile marketing. As mentioned later in this section, the majority of cellular handsets sold by 2020 will have NFC in them. Marketers love NFC because they can interact with people on the go — giving them a direct connection to the consumer. NFC is about creating a customer experience or interaction. NFC allows marketers to gauge intent, garner opt-in permission, create social media buzz, provide exclusive content, give discounts, and more at the point of interaction. A person just needs to tap and get stuff. In addition, NFC can provide the benefit of metrics and actionable data points from the point of tap that marketers rely on to quantify the success of marketing campaigns against strategy and objectives.

Interacting with customers

NFC is directly responsible for increasing sales. Later in this chapter, you discover how NFC works with smart posters; other marketing uses for NFC are described in previous chapters. In fact, you can use NFC in more ways than you might initially imagine. For example, you can use it in your direct mail sales to increase chances of having prospects actually visit your website, download information, or take advantage of a special promotion — all with the simple tap of a smart device. Of course, before you can interact with customers using NFC, those customers have to have a device that's capable of using the technology. Figure 9-1 shows a comparison of the total number of handsets sold per year to the number that are NFC-enabled handsets. As you can see, the prediction is that most handsets will have NFC capability by 2020.

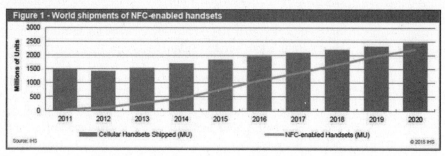

FIGURE 9-1:
The majority of cellular handsets shipped by 2020 will be enabled with NFC.

Courtesy of IHS Technology

You can also find NFC being used in other traditional print channels like magazines. Even though it was the first, the Lexus ad in *Wired* magazine signaled a trend. In this case, you can place your phone on the magazine to test-drive the Lexus Enform App Suite — the app you see in the dashboard of the car when you drive it. The simulation helps you get the feel for driving a Lexus in the real world, which lets marketers woo customers with greater ease. Other vendors, such as *Marie Claire* in the U.K., *Der Spiegel* in Germany, and *Connected Rogers* in Canada, have followed suit. You can read more about Lexus's groundbreaking implementation at `http://hub.tappinn.com/blog/Lexus-Debuts-First-NFC-Tag-in-Wired-Magazine/)`.

REMEMBER

When using tags for marketing, you follow a process that makes implementing any plan a bit easier. The following steps explore one workflow you can use to make interacting with customers through NFC tags much easier:

1. Obtain the correct tag for your particular need.

For example, you may need a tag that works in wet environments or on a metal surface. However, you also need to consider the tag features, visual appeal, and other factors when making a decision.

2. Encode the tag with the information you want the customer to see.

Here are some examples of ways in which you might encode a tag:

- Direct the customer to your website to obtain product information or other sorts of general help.

- Direct the customer to your blog to obtain information through full-length articles. Details obtained through comprehensive articles can finalize a purchasing decision and help solidify the customer's need to know you'll support your product.

- Send the customer to a how-to video. Many people learn better when seeing a process rather than reading instructions on how to perform a task.

- Give the customer an incentive to make a purchase by offering a coupon.

- Provide the customer an opportunity to rate a product or service, or promote you in social media.

3. Place a label over the tag when needed.

The label helps dress up your presentation and lets the customer know precisely where to tap. A label can also describe a reason to tap and make the content appealing.

4. **Track the success or failure of your campaign.**

   In contrast to other strategies, NFC lets you track who is tapping the tags, when, where, and how often they're tapping, and what they do with the information received.

Managing products

Managing any asset is a concern for businesses. Ensuring that the business has accounted for products and other assets helps keep costs low by reducing issues such as theft and loss. The concept of tracking assets isn't new; businesses have done so from ancient times. Recent technologies that have made tracking easier include barcodes and RFID. Both technologies have limitations, such as the lack of storage capability with barcodes or the cost of readers for RFID. NFC solves asset tracking problems by letting you attach more than just an ID to a product. You can also store other kinds of tracking information, which means that tapping a tag provides access to all the information needed, rather than just to an ID that you have to research to learn more.

When using NFC, you can hide the tag within the product. Consequently, someone can't simply come by and remove the tag to hide a potential theft. In addition, NFC tags are extremely durable and come in a wide variety of types, making them attachable to any asset. The low cost of NFC readers (basically free because most smartphones come with an NFC reader) when compared to RFID (which requires expensive fixed or special handheld readers) makes NFC perfect for reading individual items. In addition, NFC allows companies to engage with their customers, so the same tag can be used for both asset tracking *and* for marketing purposes.

Companies such as Selinko (`http://selinko.com/`) and MapYourTag (`http://www.mapyourtag.com/`) provide all the solutions you could ever need, such as the product authentication tag example from Selinko shown in Figure 9-2. The idea is to be able to track any asset in any manner needed. In this case, assets can include equipment, merchandise, or even people. Previous chapters discuss the need to verify a person's location and determine whether the person actually performed a required task (such as a nurse making a home visit).

Having Fun with Applications

Computers are all about the data and the applications that manage the data. Whether you use a computer to play games, work with videos, transfer funds, manage your time, or perform administrative tasks, it all comes down to using applications to manage data of some sort. NFC makes working with data a lot easier because you focus more on the task than the data itself. The change in focus makes doing things like playing games a lot simpler and increases the fun. The following sections describe some of the ways in which NFC improves your ability to interact with applications in fun ways.

Playing games

Game playing of all sorts is big business, but it's also a lot of fun. The toys-to-life genre of games is something new that NFC has helped make possible. You simply put your character onto the gaming device to load it into memory, as shown in Figure 9-3. As you play the game, the characteristics of the game piece change. Instead of storing the game information on disk, the physical toy contains the information, which lets you buy and sell pieces that someone has already aug-mented in some way. The difference is the mixing of the real world with the vir-tual world — you can hold the piece you're playing with in the game.

FIGURE 9-3:
Games use NFC
to register char-
acters to you so
that you can use
them for play.

REMEMBER

You can currently find several of these gaming platforms available for sale. Each of them uses NFC to store character data, but the emphasis of each platform differs. Check out the current offerings to see what is available:

>> **Activision Skylanders:** https://www.skylanders.com/

>> **Disney Infinity:** https://infinity.disney.com/

>> **Nintendo Amiibo:** http://e3.nintendo.com/amiibo/

Producing video greetings and invitations

Digital greetings have become prevalent. Fewer and fewer people use actual cards to send greetings any longer. However, the messages offered by digital greetings remain static for the most part. That's all about to change. Imagine a greeting or invitation that could perform all these tasks:

>> Enjoy the benefits of simplified planning and event execution

>> Include a video of your event and its particulars

>> Obtain timely guest attendance information

>> Share event directions, maps, registry links, or other event-related information

>> Avoid guest discomfort by collecting dietary and meal selection information

>> Customize the manner in which the setup collects and organizes event data

>> Use an app that has a dashboard to view reports for analysis and event monitoring

>> Send the collected data to your favorite app at any time

Even though other vendors might be offering this sort of greeting by the time you read this, the one place you really need to look is TapForMessage (http://www.tapformessage.com/invitation-cards/). This company offers greetings and invitations that someone simply taps with an NFC-enabled phone. The invites have an NFC chip inside, so you can play a video invitation wirelessly and RSVP right from the invitation card. The RSVP form is customizable, so you can relay anything you like for the event, such as the location, registry information, and more. You can see a sample of the physical card in Figure 9-4.

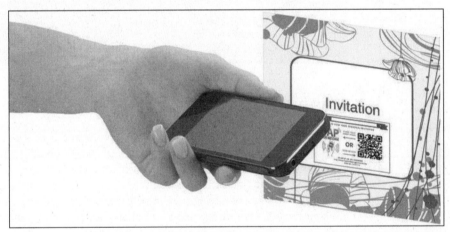

FIGURE 9-4:
The RSVP process is a lot easier when using NFC greetings.

Image courtesy of Tap for Message

Making donations easy

People easily become enthused about a particular community project, national event, or worldwide community effort when they read about it on a poster or in some other location, but then forget to do anything about it later. It happens to everyone. Life intrudes on the best of intentions. Oxfam (http://www.oxfam.org.uk/) and other companies are working hard to overcome that particular problem. Using NFC lets people make a donation when they first learn about the need. All they need to do is tap a poster (as shown in Figure 9-5) or other physical form of public appeal. The amazing part is that the whole process is fast and easy, so life never gets a chance to intrude.

FIGURE 9-5:
Using NFC makes
getting donations
a lot easier.

Keeping track of time

Determining how you spend your day is important because time management begins with knowledge of how you spend it. Of course, you might also have reporting requirements to log how you spend your time for billing or other purposes. No matter the reason for tracking your time, using NFC can make the process incredibly simple. Instead of having to manually log every event, you simply tap a tag and the app records everything necessary about the beginning and ending time of a particular event, as shown in Figure 9-6. This particular app is free for download at `https://play.google.com/store/apps/details?id=com.pascalwelsch.nfctimetracking`.

Managing trees

One of the more interesting uses of NFC is to track trees at Blarney Castle and Gardens. That's right: Each tree has its own NFC tag. The head gardener previously tagged the trees using various labels that ended up damaged or stolen by vandals. Using special tags from ZipNFC (`http://zipnfc.com/`) lets the gardener tag the trees in a manner that is not only easier to work with but also less susceptible to damage or theft. Eventually the gardener plans to tag shrubs using the same technique.

Image provided courtesy of Pascal Welsch

TIP

An advantage of this approach is that the smartphone used to read the tags can also map the precise location of each tree using GPS. In addition, rather than require you to research each tree, the smartphone automatically displays information for that particular tree. You can read more about this use of NFC at `https://igpsblogs.wordpress.com/2014/11/26/tag-my-tree-the-blarney-castle-garden-way-by-adam-whitbourn/`.

Managing Events

An event of any sort can spell chaos. Trying to track ticket purchases, verifying that people actually show up, and dealing with emergencies can create serious problems, especially when you rely on older methods of performing the required tasks. With NFC, you just tap to discover the information you need to perform the required tasks, which speeds information gathering considerably. Every aspect of the event-management process suddenly becomes easier. Sure, you might still have some chaos, but it's easier to control. The following sections discuss how you can use NFC to manage events more efficiently and with far fewer errors.

Purchasing tickets

Using NFC and a mobile app, you can easily purchase a ticket online and not have to worry about using paper tickets. In most cases, vendors such as TicketMaster (http://ayuda.ticketmaster.es/help/faq/printing-nfc-event-tickets/) require that you download a special app to your smartphone to use the NFC option. To use the tickets, you simply tell the app that you want to redeem the ticket and then hold your smartphone up to the device that will receive the ticket, similar to the transfer shown in Figure 9-7. Your device vibrates to tell you that it has made a connection to the other device and then the transfer takes place.

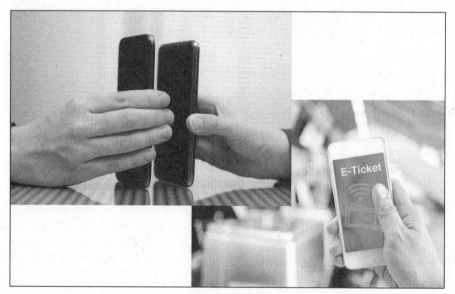

FIGURE 9-7:
Use your phone to transfer your ticket rather than hand over a printed ticket.

© Bacho; © weedezign

Tracking attendance

Companies such as Poken (http://www.poken.website/) specialize in helping you track attendance. However, you can do more than simply tell who attended an event. You can also get a feel for how people interacted with the event, which means that you can collect statistics for different marketing activities you've tried in the course of the event. For example, as described at http://www.poken.website/collecting/, the idea is to turn event visitors into participants. Instead of simply viewing the event, the visitor becomes part of the event — turning a static experience into a dynamic one that the visitor will remember long after the event is over. Pokens actually look fun, so people will want to interact with them, but the biggest reason to use them is that they're both fast and simple.

The techniques you use to track attendance depend on the event. Poken is highly interactive and provides a substantial number of interesting solutions including gamification and social media, easily gathering presentations, brochures and other product information, and more. However, you may also want to view alternatives, such as AllianceTech (http://www.alliancetech.com/solutions/attendee-tracking/intelligent-attendance/overview). This vendor supplies NFC badges that a participant taps for event check-in, booth or kiosk visits, and so on, as shown in Figure 9-8. The more interesting offering, though, is the mat used to track attendance simply by checking who walks over it.

Addressing emergency needs

The use of NFC badges lets officials verify that everyone is out of a building safely in case of a fire. In fact, you can use the badges to help with any sort of emergency by determining who is and who isn't in the right location. You can handle emergency needs quickly and easily, instead of floundering around trying to figure out what to do next.

FIGURE 9-8:
Simply tap to register your presence at an event or event location.

Interacting with Customers

Before the proliferation of mobile technology, you would try a promotion using print, direct mail, email, billboards, and outdoor advertising, or television and radio advertising. All these traditional methods focus on pushing information out to potential customers, but not really interacting with customers. Using NFC with other technologies means that you can create interactions with customers and discover the effectiveness of an approach early in the process. This early information lets you make adjustments to the promotion as needed. You can also tailor your efforts to meet specific customer requirements. The following sections discuss how you can use NFC to improve customer interactions.

Getting and using coupons

Everyone likes saving money. If you want your customers to remember you, find ways to make their purchasing decisions easier and happier. One of the best ways to do that is to send coupons directly to their smartphone, as shown in Figure 9-9. In this case, customers download an app by tapping a smart poster (see the "Developing NFC Smart Posters" section, later in this chapter, for details) upon entering the store. A secondary technology, such as a Bluetooth Beacon actually transmits the coupon based on the customer's location in the store. One of the major vendors creating this kind of solution is Blue Bite (http://bluebite.com/). Its site includes a number of case studies that provide ideas for managing your own customer coupons.

Getting and using gift cards

According to sources such as GiftCards.com (http://www.giftcards.com/gift-card-statistics), consumers spend more than $100 billion annually on gift cards because they provide the one-size-fits-all solution to giving. About 93 percent of consumers receive a gift card in the course of 12 months, including from the 83 percent of corporations that use gift cards as incentives to employees. Stores love gift cards because they represent a guaranteed sale, even if customers don't normally shop at the store. (A successful gift-shopping experience can make them new, satisfied, long-term customers.) The point is, gift cards are everywhere and you need a way to manage them.

FIGURE 9-9:
Mobile coupons
entice potential
buyers without
incurring printing
costs.

Image courtesy of Blue Bite

REMEMBER

Products such as Google Wallet (`https://play.google.com/store/apps/details?id=com.google.android.apps.gmoney`) allow you to store gift cards in digital form so that you don't end up leaving them at home. You can actually see all your gift cards on your smartphone (see Figure 9-10). You can also send some-one a digital gift card instead of a physical one that can get lost. When it comes time to use the gift card, NFC comes to the rescue. All you need to do to use the gift card is tap on the cash register, just as you do when using a credit or debit card. And there is now a solution that allows you to send, receive and switch your e-gift cards from one NFC wallet to another called Swych. You can find out more about how to do it at `http://www.goswych.com`.

Providing a store layout

Malls are notorious for hiding the store you want in plain sight. After looking around for a while, people tend to become frustrated and may even leave before actually finding your store. To keep this from happening, you can give the cus-tomer a way to find your store. Turkish scientists are currently working to com-bine GPS and NFC to create store layout apps like the one shown in Figure 9-11 (`http://www.nfcworld.com/2011/05/19/37492/nfc-indoor-navigation-system-proposed-by-turkish-scientists/`). The app shows customers one or possibly more routes to find a particular store in the mall, reducing the frustration

FIGURE 9-10: Gift cards become even more convenient when used digitally.

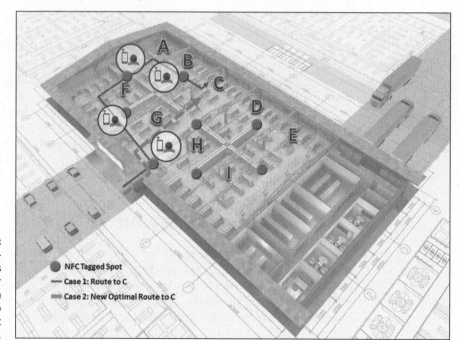

FIGURE 9-11: Tapping strategically located tags updates your position within the store to help you find the best route.

factor. The mall has NFC tags located throughout so that customers can update their position to find the best way to locate particular destinations.

Managing sweepstakes and loyalty campaigns

Some companies, such as Starbucks, are large enough to create their own closed-loop systems to provide payment and loyalty options. However, most organizations that would benefit from this option aren't large enough to support it themselves and require outside help. For example, when Graham O'Sullivan Restaurants (http://www.grahamosullivan.com/) required a closed-loop payment system, they relied on the Escher Group (http://www.eschergroup.com/) to provide it (http://www.nfcworld.com/2013/07/17/325035/irish-restaurant-chain-picks-nfc-p2p-payments-and-rewards/). The solution requires an Android NFC-enabled device to perform tasks and relies on Android Beam to send the customer's information to the point-of-sale (POS) terminal. In this particular case, the solution doesn't require an agreement with the mobile operator. All the customer does receive is a far better experience when visiting the Graham O'Sullivan Restaurants.

Sharing recipes and other supplemental information

If you own a grocery store, the best way to get people to buy more products is to give them an incentive to do so. One method that has seen a lot of use over the years is to provide recipes that contain unusual ingredients that the customer is unlikely to have on hand, but that your store supplies. Of course, these recipes used to hang as tear-off sheets in store aisles. The NFC way is to create recipes that a customer can download simply by tapping a product of interest, as shown in Figure 9-12. The NFC app not only stores the recipe but also creates a list of needed ingredients that shoppers can add to their shopping lists.

Adding tags to items doesn't have to stop with recipes; you can also use tags to provide product information. For example, tapping could display a comparison between a company brand and a name brand to show that the company brand is not only less expensive but also provides precisely the same benefits as the name brand.

TIP

This approach isn't limited to grocery stores. A craft store can use it to provide the customer with craft project ideas. Using the NFC method would keep the store a lot neater and provide the customer with a list of required items to complete the craft project. Home-improvement stores could take the same approach to help customers find items that go well together (possibly getting them to buy a new item rather than continuing to use the old one).

FIGURE 9-12:
Vendors now provide recipes and other information through NFC tag taps.

Managing receipts

With all the buying described in this chapter, customers will require some method of managing receipts. The old method of holding on to paper receipts is error prone. Companies such as Proximiant (http://www.proximiant.com/) provide tag and go receipt solutions that make getting and storing the receipt easier. Depending on the app you use, you may find that you can transfer the receipts on your smartphone directly to your computer. Most products that support this feature, such as Neatdesk (http://shop.neat.com/neatdesk), can directly interface with Excel, Quicken, and TurboTax. Some, such as Shoeboxed (https://www.shoeboxed.com/), also support FreshBooks and Quicken.

Creating NFC Wearable Devices

More and more people are wearing computer technologies. Some technologies, such as Google Glass (https://www.google.com/glass/start/), haven't caught on well, but still have managed to attract some level of users. Of course, the technologies that matter are the ones that eventually reach critical mass and become a must-have item. Interestingly enough, items like Apple Watch (http://www.apple.com/watch/) are becoming popular, and they also incorporate NFC technology (http://www.nfcworld.com/2015/05/01/335048/apple-watch-carries-nfc-components-from-nxp-and-ams/). You can actually use your watch to make payments (http://www.apple.com/apple-pay/). In this case, you just double-click the side button and hold the watch close to the NFC reader. Your watch beeps when the transaction completes.

Google Glass and Apple Watch do have one thing in common — they're relatively expensive technologies that only a few people can really afford. A better example of NFC wearable devices is a simple wristband. You wear it much as you would any other wristband, such as those issued by amusement parks. Figure 9-13 shows an example of such a wristband used by Singapore commuters. You'd expect the technology to have limitations. After all, you're looking at a simple wristband. Yet, the commuters can use this wristband to make purchases at various places, interact with library terminals, and use the transit system. A Singtel mWallet (http:// info.singtel.com/personal/apps-tv/apps/singtel-mwallet) app lets commuters see their current balances for their accounts by viewing the wristband device. You can read more about this particular use at http://www.nfcworld. com/2015/09/01/337402/singapore-commuters-trial-wristband-payments/.

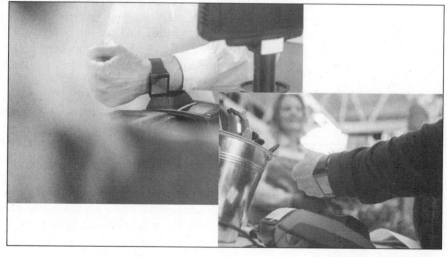

FIGURE 9-13:
Wristbands, jackets, and other apparel can all contain NFC chips.

© Tyler Olson/Shutterstock, Inc.

TIP

Expect to find wristband uses for NFC all over the place at some point. For example, Disney is currently using wristband technology to simplify activities for its customers (http://www.kony.com/resources/blog/nfc-disney-best-wearable-yet) — and you can expect other amusement parks to follow suit. The fact that you can pamper your customer using a custom wristband only makes the experience better. Of course, making payments incredibly easy only encourages the customer to spend more — thereby increasing profits.

You may be surprised to discover that wristbands aren't the smallest device you can use to create an NFC connection. For example, you can use the NFC Ring (http://nfcring.com/). This small ring lets you unlock doors and mobile phones, transfer data, and link to other people. Mind you, this is a tag technology, so your ring never requires charging. You can ditch the keychain and simply wear all your access on your finger should you want to do so.

You can also find headphones now that contain NFC technology. All you need to do is tap a device you want to listen to, and the sound automatically comes through the earpiece. An offering from Asus relies on Bluetooth 4.0 and uses NFC for pairing (http://fareastgizmos.com/computing/asus-launches-worlds-first-bluetooth-4-0-headset-with-near-field-communication-technology-ed50n.php or http://www.crunchwear.com/asus-launches-bluetooth-4-0-headphones-nfc/). The same headphones allow you to listen to any device anywhere in your house or office.

Wearable will take on a new meaning with MC10's stretchable skin (http://www.technologyreview.com/demo/428944/making-stretchable-electronics/). The technology relies on a special stretchable polymer that contains hundreds of gold contacts a few nanometers thick. You can apply it to any part of the body that requires monitoring. The NFC interface allows you to create a connection from the stretchable skin to your smartphone. A doctor can make a connection to provide constant monitoring of your vitals. Using this technology means that a doctor can detect potential health problems before you even know any trouble exists.

In the future, you may not be the only one wearing NFC devices. If you're a pet owner, you can use WoofLinks (http://www.ireachcontent.com/news-releases/wooflinks-dog-information-platform-on-kickstarter-217782051.html or http://www.crunchwear.com/wooflinks-lets-you-store-all-kinds-of-information-on-your-dogs-collar/) to manage your pet's entire life. The collar lets you discover all sorts of information about a pet you find on the street, determine where your pet is at any given time, schedule play dates with other dogs, and even set up a pet babysitter. You should expect to find NFC in all kinds of places that you never anticipated.

Working with Appliances

Appliances are getting smarter all the time. Many now have Internet connections that you can use to perform tasks such as downloading manuals or determining the source of a failure. In addition, many appliances also sport Wi-Fi connections to allow remote interaction. Companies such as LG (http://www.lg.com/us) include NFC connectivity that lets you pair your smartphone with the smart device using Wi-Fi. Consequently, you can tell your robot vacuum to clean the floors before unexpected company arrives home with you. Figure 9-14 shows some of the devices that LG and others are currently NFC-enabling.

FIGURE 9-14:
Tapping an
appliance creates
a Wi-Fi manage-
ment connection.

The interesting part of this technology is that many appliances are now scriptable. You can remotely program them to perform a specific set of actions and then transfer the resulting script to the device. The device will then carry out the actions even if you can't contact the device for some reason.

Developing NFC Smart Posters

Smart posters promise to be one of those NFC solutions that you'll find everywhere at some point. You'll see them in the store, at the park, at the bus stop, in the laundromat — everywhere and anywhere you can imagine. Smart posters are important because you can use them for so many purposes. This chapter alone discusses a number of uses that include getting information and making donations. The following sections help you understand smart posters and their uses better.

Discovering the advantages of NFC smart posters

You have a number of options for distributing information. For example, some people use QR codes to help people obtain additional information. The QR code solution works acceptably in situations in which someone may not be able to access the item directly, such as on the side of a taxi. (The QR code lets you store information such as the taxi's telephone number.) However, NFC smart posters have some significant advantages over other technologies:

>> NFC tags can store more data and more data types.

>> Because the tag resides under the poster, the poster itself can be colorful and attractive.

>> NFC readers are inexpensive and found with many smartphones today.

>> Accessing an NFC tag is easy.

You can easily come up with other reasons, but the point is that NFC makes interacting with poster data fast and simple. You can use the NFC solution to provide everything from coupons to maps of store locations. The smart poster can contain the data locally (within the tag) or point to a website where the person can find quite a bit more information.

Understanding how smart posters work

As previously mentioned, using smart posters is fast and easy. As shown in Figure 9-15, all someone has to do is tap on the poster to receive the desired information. Of course, you need to make sure that it's the right information. The following list provides you with some ideas on how to make smart posters work even better.

>> **Considering user interactions:** The most noticeable part of a smart poster is the interaction that the user makes with it. You need to decide whether to store the information the user needs locally (such as a business card) or to send the user to some other location (such as a website). Also important is to consider the sequence of events that will occur when the user taps the smart poster.

>> **Embedding tags before printing:** An advantage of embedding the tags you use before you print the smart poster is that the embedded tags are completely out of view. The resulting smart poster will have a more professional appearance, and you won't need to get specialized tags.

>> **Attaching tags after printing:** You might have invested in special tags that you want everyone to see. Perhaps the tags have your company's logo on them. In this case, making the tag appear on the smart poster face emphasizes the message you're trying to send and creates a connection to your company or product.

Image courtesy of Blue Bite

FIGURE 9-15: Use smart posters to provide viewers with additional information.

>> **Adding touchpoint indicators:** Users need to know where to touch your poster to receive additional information. For this reason, you need to add *touchpoint indicators* — visual signs that tell users to tap in a certain place.

>> **Using a Smart Poster Record Type Definition (RTD):** The *RTD* verifies the integrity and authenticity of the tag content. This means that your users can be sure that no one has tampered with the smart poster and changed the content to something nasty. The RTD allows you to put content such as URLs, SMSes, or phone numbers on an NFC tag. The NFC Smart Poster RTD Technical Specification (`http://members.nfc-forum.org/specs/spec_list/`) provides more information on how to create an RTD.

>> **Locking your tags down:** Making sure that you lock the tag down so that no one can modify it makes users more comfortable about interacting with the smart poster.

Getting the N-Mark logo

The N-Mark logo (http://nfc-forum.org/our-work/nfc-branding/n-mark/) allows others to recognize your smart poster as an NFC-enabled solution. The logo looks like the one shown in Figure 9-16. To use the N-Mark logo, you must sign the N-Mark trademark license agreement (http://nfc-forum.org/our-work/nfc-branding/n-mark/the-n-mark-license/). After signing, you get a .ZIP file containing the following:

>> Copies of the N-Mark graphic in several file formats

>> An NFC forum N-Mark brand guide

>> The requirements you must meet for compliance

>> A description of the NFC forum device requirements

The main reason to use the N-Mark logo is for identification (http://nfc-forum.org/what-is-nfc/identifying-nfc/). Users can easily identify NFC applications when they see the N-Mark logo. By having a common logo, you let your users know how to interact with your smart posters.

4
Avoiding NFC Issues

IN THIS PART . . .

Getting involved in employing NFC in various environments

Overcoming NFC hardware issues

Overcoming NFC software issues

Ensuring that NFC can communicate properly

Chapter 10

Avoiding the Not-Used-Here Mentality

B y now, you're fully convinced that NFC is an amazing technology that you simply must implement everywhere. However, NFC is a relatively new technology, so not everyone is using it right now. Of course, as the technology proves itself capable, more and more organizations and people will use it. In some cases, you won't have a choice; your credit card provider, vendor, or organization will make the choice for you. In other cases, you'll be the one pushing others to adopt NFC as the right solution for a serious business or other problem. The point is that you need a strategy for working with others who haven't made the move just yet.

One reason that many technologies become successful is that someone develops a killer app that makes life without the technology unthinkable. Often, these apps happen randomly — someone is in the right place at the right time, talking to the right people or thinking the right thoughts. (The three greatest computer killer apps of all time are the word processor, spreadsheet, and database; read more at http://www.pc-history.org/apps.htm). Another way to achieve the same effect is to develop a lot of applications that rely on the technology. The sheer mass of application development often creates a trend that makes the technology successful over the long term. (One of the reasons that the Windows platform remains so successful is the huge number of apps it supports.)

Still, you might face the not-used-here mentality even when you have a strategy for using the technology with others who don't support it and you have all the apps you'd ever need to make the technology successful. Supporters often present this strategy as, "If it ain't broke, don't fix it." Using this strategy would mean that we'd still be using the abacus rather than computers to perform calculations. In many cases, you need to present people with an overwhelming reason to use a new technology that addresses something they want, such as increased profits, reduced costs, or higher efficiencies.

Working with Businesses that Don't Use NFC

Be aware that your enthusiasm for NFC doesn't necessarily spill over onto your business or the businesses of your partners. In fact, you might find that getting these entities to move past paper is a major undertaking, much less getting them to embrace a newer technology like NFC. The problem is one of risk. Many businesses are risk averse to the point of not wanting to adopt any new technology until everyone else has already done so for fear that they'll be left holding the bag when its originator orphans the technology. The following sections discuss some of the issues that occur when working with any entity (your own business or that of a partner) that doesn't embrace NFC or its associated technologies.

Considering the digital payment conundrum

When working in the business-to-business (B2B) or business-to-consumer (B2C) payment space, the paper invoice and net 30-day payment scheme still reign supreme because they allow for larger amounts of floating capital to appear on the books. Before you can get any business to support NFC and other nonpaper payment systems, you need to convince them to use digital payments.

Companies such as BillingTree (https://mybillingtree.com/) are introducing products such as Payrazr (https://mybillingtree.com/payment-solutions/payrazr-portfolio/) to offer Software-as-a-Service (SaaS) as an alternative to incurring a huge risk in moving toward digital payments. By going this route, a company can experiment with digital payments in a safer environment without having to change its current infrastructure completely. If the experiment doesn't work, the company can still fall back to what it had before. The important things to look for when checking out SaaS solutions are

>> How much web support the company provides

>> Whether the company provides the infrastructure needed to support mobile payments

Defining the digital payment benefits

Whether you're trying to convince your own company or that of a partner to go digital, you need to provide a strong incentive to make the change. Nothing speaks more strongly than the bottom line. Making a business case for digital payments means defining a specific payback that is substantial enough to overcome the inherent risk of any change. Here are some reasons to use digital payments:

>> Accelerated availability of funds

>> Reduced costs associated with manual payment processing

>> Improved cash management

>> Integrated processing by managing all payments, returns, and corrections through a single portal

Using NFC in the B2B environment

Much of this book is dedicated to consumer-oriented needs, even when it addresses those needs from the business end of things. For example, businesses create, use, and maintain smart posters, but the target is a consumer of some sort. (Even at a trade show of your peers, the goal is to generate some type of consumer-oriented activity.) Many uses of tags affect consumers as well. The consumer market truly is huge, but the potential exists for an equally large B2B market that you shouldn't ignore when trying to convince an organization to go digital and use NFC technology to make the transition even easier.

Interestingly enough, many companies focus on the B2B market. One such company is FAMOCO (http://www.famoco.com/), which makes a smartphone-like product that relies heavily on NFC to power various apps. The device contains a number of apps, the most common of which do things like the following:

>> Mobile Point-of-Sale (POS)

>> Access control

>> Attendance tracking

>> ID reader

You might wonder why companies such as FAMOCO don't simply use a smartphone to deploy their apps. After all, creating an app to meet just about any need for any smartphone would be relatively easy. Here are the most common reasons to use a dedicated NFC-enabled device in a business environment:

>> **Security:** These devices place an emphasis on security that you could find in a smartphone, but at a considerable cost.

>> **No Street Value:** Stealing the device does the thief no good because it's not usable outside the work environment.

>> **Cost:** The low price of these devices makes them attractive to businesses that don't want to embrace a Bring Your Own Device (BYOD) environment.

>> **Ease of Management:** Most of these devices provide strong over-the-air (OTA) device management support. Given that everyone is using the same device, you also don't encounter the usual surprises that come with a BYOD environment.

Security is the issue that is highest in the minds of B2B users. In fact, you can find specialized B2B security products, such as NFC Secure Channel (`http://www.securenfc.com/b2b/`) that help protect from eavesdropping and data modification. If one of the issues that keeps your organization (or that of a partner) from using NFC is the potential for security mishaps, you need to make your organization aware of the specialized security solutions available for this market.

Many industry pundits see NFC adoption occurring in the small and medium business (SMB) market first because the transactions used by these organizations more directly mirror those used in the B2C market (see `http://ww2.cfo.com/mobile/2015/05/payments-go/` for details). However, as NFC becomes more embedded in the business environment, even large organizations will begin using it for a variety of needs.

To ensure the adoption of mobile payment strategies in the B2B sector, banks such as Wells Fargo are providing new business services designed to meet B2B needs. For Wells Fargo, this service is the Commercial Electronic Office (CEO) Portal (`https://www.wellsfargo.com/com/ceo/ceo-mobile-banking`). The use of CEO Portal can greatly improve employee efficiency, reduce the potential for lost payments, and reduce the amount of accounts receivable (because payments are made at the time of service). The point is that mobile payments are both secure and convenient today, so using them gives a business a significant advantage over competitors who are still stuck using paper.

Developing Apps that Won't Work Without NFC

The best way to encourage the adoption of any technology is to create a killer app for it — one that seems so obvious and simple when you introduce it that everyone must have it. Low-hanging fruit, such as the spreadsheet, are long gone, but the killer app still exists. NFC is a new technology that presents people with a wide range of potential applications. This book presents you with a large assortment of these apps and doesn't even begin to scratch the surface. Of course, the first question is whether any of them is a killer app. Only time will tell whether any of these apps is so universally needed that everyone must have it. A good candidate is mobile payments because everyone has to buy something.

A second question you must ask is whether any of the apps absolutely has to have NFC to work. Chapter 2 of the book compares NFC to various other technologies. Killer apps of the past were unique because they all required a computer to run. Yes, you could write a spreadsheet by hand using a ledger, but it was so inconvenient that businesses rushed to embrace a technology that gave them a significant edge. Spreadsheet apps require a computer. Mobile payments aren't limited to NFC, but perhaps there is some application that will absolutely require NFC to operate.

When you want to overcome the not-used-here mentality, you must come up with a killer app that your business really does need and that addresses an issue not easily dealt with using some other technology. For example, if you ship items that are temperature sensitive, monitoring those items is currently a problematic experience at best. In this case, a killer app might consist of a temperature probe like the one provided by American Thermal Instruments (ATI), Log-IC (`http://www.americanthermal.com/products/log-ic/log-ic_nfc`). In this case, you must have NFC to read the tag data.

The feature that makes Log-IC a killer app is that you can show your client a complete history of the temperature changes that the product experienced. In fact, your customer can monitor the temperatures (if desired) when you export the data to the cloud. This means that temperature-critical items, such as organs for human transplant, are now safer. Your customer knows the precise conditions under which the item is transported so that there is no question about whether the temperatures fell outside the critical range.

GOING PUBLIC

Most people don't plan to go public with their custom app. After all, you created it for your organization. However, the nature of a really good custom app is that it tends to work for more than one organization. Going public with an app means that the money you invested in putting it together is often repaid by the money people pay to get your app.

At one time, it was nearly impossible for small app developers to go public. However, with the proliferation of public, vendor-sponsored venues for uploading apps and making them available to others, nearly anyone can now sell a useful app to anyone else. All you really need is the correct marketing strategy for your app. Of course, the app must also pass any required certifications required of it, which can take time and money to complete. Even so, your killer app could become a money source for your organization under the right circumstances, and NFC provides plenty of opportunities for creating new killer apps.

A disadvantage of the NFC-only app is one of exposure. The way that services, such as Google Play (`https://play.google.com/store`), are configured, only people who have NFC currently available on their device will see your app. Of course, this means that you won't have to deal with anyone asking why your app won't work on their device when it lacks NFC support, but it also means that they won't be encouraged to get NFC support in order to use your app. When you choose to make your app public, you also need to market it in such a manner that people are encouraged to obtain the required hardware.

Creating a Business Plan Showing NFC Advantages

Creating the excitement required to sell NFC to your organization or to partners will eventually come down to writing some sort of documentation showing the advantages of making the move. Previous sections of the chapter give you the sorts of information you need for such a plan — the kind of information that avoids the whole issue of the not-used-here mentality. You have the basis for a strong financial incentive and a setup that makes employees more efficient. In addition, you have already defined the need for NFC as the only viable solution to problems faced by your organization. With this in mind, your business plan needs to cover the essentials of what makes NFC great:

>> Using NFC with the proper app support can improve security because no one will actually touch the credit card or other sensitive information needed to run the business.

>> Monitoring things with NFC is easier than with existing technologies.

>> Employees can use specialized NFC-enabled devices, so you can avoid the whole BYOD nightmare if desired.

>> Relying on NFC saves money by making employees more efficient, reducing friction in almost all organizational processes like inventory management or paper reduction. The point is that contrary to any initial reservations about cost, NFC really does make the bottom line look better.

>> An NFC setup can ease employee training requirements by reducing the complexity of working with required technology. Rather than have to remember complex computer interactions, employees can simply tap their way through the workday.

>> Creating the correct NFC environment can improve management's ability to monitor workflow and fix potential problems before they become issues. Rather than react to problems all the time, management can now intercept problems and deal with them before they become issues that appear on the front page of the trade press.

Making your plan specific to your business is essential. NFC is so flexible that you can probably make a good case for it in any business. However, to convince anyone at your business, the arguments you present must be specific to your needs.

Some vendors make the task of creating specific reasons to use NFC in a business easier by presenting use cases. You can find a typical example of use cases on the vWand site at `http://www.vwand.com/nfc-use-cases.html`. It offers a listing of NFC markets and the way in which this particular product answers needs in that market. Pairing the use cases with specific product suggestions makes your job easier because you can use the information provided to create a presentation for your organization.

Chapter 11

Understanding the Hardware Issues

It would be nice if everything always worked precisely as anticipated, but the real world is filled with glitches, and NFC is no exception. Yes, NFC is an extremely reliable technology, but situations arise in which even NFC experiences problems. Fortunately, most of these issues are easy to correct if you know the right trick, and this chapter contains those tricks. What you find here are answers to the most common issues that people face when using NFC. For example, many people forget to turn NFC support on (or if they do turn it on and NFC requires a related technology, such as Bluetooth, they have forgotten to turn the related technology on to get the full support required).

Some issues are harder to fix. For example, you might encounter a compatibility issue or a problem with a device that doesn't provide the level of NFC functionality you anticipated. Working in environments with lots of metal or water can also pose problems. This chapter also helps you through a few of these issues so that you better understand why NFC is such a great technology.

Ensuring that the Device is Ready

NFC is so good at just working that sometimes people forget that technology underlies the useful functionality. As with any other technology, you can turn it off on most devices. (The iPhone 6 always has NFC enabled, but it also limits NFC accessibility to be used only with Apple Pay for now.). When you turn NFC off, the technology is unresponsive to your needs. Nothing is broken; you just haven't turned it on. When working with NFC, you must consider three levels of device readiness that could make NFC appear unresponsive simply because you haven't turned it on, as described in the following sections.

Turning the device on

Some situations require you to turn your device off, or at least make it pretty much unresponsive. In some cases, you turn the device off to save power or because you lack a signal. In other cases, regulations require that your turn your device off (such as when you're on a plane). Depending on your device and the manner in which you turn it off, NFC can become unresponsive. For example, a smartphone can become unresponsive when you place it in airplane mode. To be sure that you can receive NFC signals, check that your device is physically on and that NFC has been turned on.

Configuring the device to use NFC

No matter what sort of device you have, even if you turn the device on and everything is in place for using NFC, you must still configure the device to work with NFC, in many cases. Some devices do have NFC enabled by default (such as the iPhone 6) and you may not even be able to turn it off. You need to check the instructions that come with your device to be certain. The "Turning On Smartphone NFC Support" section of Chapter 5 tells you how to turn NFC support on for your smartphone.

REMEMBER

All sorts of devices come with NFC support today, including laptop and desktop computers. But why would you want to use your more traditional computer for NFC when you have a smart device? You may want to write to multiple NFC tags rather than just a single tag. However, whether you can actually use NFC with your laptop or desktop depends on its configuration. For example, Microsoft does support NFC with Windows 8 and above. Here is the sequence that most often occurs when installing a new NFC-enabled device:

1. After you connect a device to a Windows system, the operating system automatically detects the device.

2. Windows either installs a device driver or asks you to provide a device driver. Microsoft relies on Independent Hardware Vendors (IHVs) to provide device drivers that implement the Device Driver Interface (DDI) as specified at https://msdn.microsoft.com/library/windows/hardware/dn905575. aspx to create the required support.

3. After you install the device driver, you still must configure Windows to enable NFC support. The methods for performing this task vary by device and vendor, so you need to check the installation instructions for your product.

4. You install an app such as NFC Kits (https://www.microsoft.com/store/apps/nfc-kits/9wzdncrfjqv6) to interact with your new device.

When working with Linux, you need to know about the Linux Near Field Communications (NFC) Project. This open source project lets you add NFC support to various Linux implementations using the library found at https://github.com/nfc-tools/libnfc. When working with a Linux system, make sure that the device you purchase comes with the required drivers, apps, and other support for your particular version of Linux.

The Mac OS X platform relies on some of the same libraries as Linux. You often need to download the support you need separately. For example, the ACR122U USB NFC Reader comes with a Windows installer on a disk. To get Linux and Mac support, you need to go to the Downloads tab of the support page found at http://www.acs.com.hk/en/products/3/acr122u-usb-nfc-reader/#tab_downloads.

TIP

Fortunately, Windows and other platforms support many of the same apps you find for smartphones. For example, all three platforms support TagWriter (discussed in the "Working in reader/writer mode" section of Chapter 4, the "Using a smartphone" section of Chapter 5, and the "Using a tag writer or other utilities" section of Chapter 12). The point is that you must ensure that you have the proper support installed, and that the support is turned on and configured before you try to install an app and use NFC.

Configuring the device to use a related technology

NFC often works with other technologies, such as Bluetooth, to create a complete solution, as discussed often in previous chapters. The whole idea is to make the best use of each technology to perform specific tasks, such as using NFC to create a Bluetooth pairing between devices. NFC starts the job, but then Bluetooth takes over to complete the task. Before a multitechnology strategy can work, however, you must configure the device in question to use all the required technologies and be sure to enable each technology to make it active. Otherwise, even if NFC does its part of the task, the action still won't occur because other technologies are disabled or misconfigured in some manner.

In some cases, you must consider how a device enables NFC functionality. For example, an Android smartphone typically relies on Android Beam (http://www.techradar.com/us/news/phone-and-communications/mobile-phones/android-beam-why-you-should-care-about-this-hidden-gem-1226272) to provide full NFC functionality. Among other tasks, Android Beam speeds file transfers between two phones using Bluetooth after you pair the devices using NFC. If you don't have Android Beam turned on, you may not see full NFC functionality. Fortunately, your smartphone normally enables Android Beam automatically when you turn on NFC support.

REMEMBER

Things can become a little tricky with these related apps. For example, Android Beam works completely only with other Android smartphones. High-end Samsung smartphones (such as the Galaxy S3, http://www.samsung.com/global/galaxys3/) come with S-Beam (http://androidfact.com/what-is-s-beam/). Android Beam and S-Beam are similar but not precisely the same, so you might encounter issues such as slower data transfers. Newer Android smartphones actually support both Android Beam and S-Beam. The big difference is that S-Beam uses Wi-Fi rather than Bluetooth to perform data transfers. (The video at https://www.youtube.com/watch?v=MItjKitDUlI shows just how easy using this technology is.)

The problem becomes more apparent when working with some other smartphones. Modestly priced Samsung and the Microsoft version of the Windows Phone don't come with any support alternative to Android Beam or S-Beam, so you can't perform file transfers using this shortcut without doing some extra work. The Tap+Send app that comes natively with Windows Phones works only with other Windows Phones. Fortunately, you can download ATIV Beam from the Windows Phone Store and install it on your Windows Phone to gain the needed functionality (http://www.windowscentral.com/samsung-releases-ativ-beam-so-you-can-send-files-android-hardware).

Using the Device Correctly

No matter what mode you use for your device to interact with other NFC-enabled devices, you must use the device correctly to obtain the desired results. Depending on your device, you may have device-specific needs to consider. However, for most devices, you need to think about the following issues when using the device to ensure that it works properly:

» Turn both devices on.

» Configure both devices to provide the proper support.

» Install the required apps.

» Select data items you want to work with, such as the file you want to transfer from one smartphone to another.

» Tap or place the devices close enough to initiate an NFC connection.

» Wait until the NFC action completes (such as a pairing of two devices to transfer files) before separating the devices. (You don't need to wait until the actions that rely on other technologies, such as a file transfer, complete before separating the devices.)

When trying to read NFC tags, you must remain aware of the position of the antenna in the phone. Some things can go wrong when establishing contact. For example, you might not find the sweet spot for the two devices (see the "Finding the Device Sweet Spot" section, later in this chapter, for details). When this happens, you need to move the two devices apart and try again. The devices normally give you both visual and aural cues when the connection process is successful.

Depending on your app, you may also find that selecting data for transfer can be error prone. For example, when beaming, you hear a two-part tone that tells you the files are transferring. A four-part tone indicates that you selected the data item incorrectly and need to start beaming the files again. Selecting outside the files simply results in no transfer occurring. In many cases, a timer will lapse and you need to start the beaming process again.

REMEMBER

Wireless technologies are subject to the same rules as any other radio frequency transmission. You may see commercials that quote data rates as high as 300Mbps when using S-Beam. However, interference, distance between devices, and other factors can reduce transmission speed. When you get a lower transmission rate, you need to consider the environment in which you're working. Remember, you use NFC only to make the connection. Higher-speed technologies like Wi-Fi or Bluetooth are used to actually transmit the data.

Understanding Odd Device Behaviors

You might encounter a situation in which you've turned everything on and are using the device correctly, yet the device still fails to work as anticipated. Of course, these situations are frustrating because you know you're doing everything correctly, so it should work. It really should work, but sometimes the device still fails to work because of some odd circumstance that's beyond your control. The important thing is not to get frustrated. Device issues normally have a reasonable and logical explanation, even if you can't always fix them. Getting upset simply means that you'll have a harder time fixing the problem — assuming that a fix exists. The following sections describe a few odd behaviors you need to know about.

Considering the MIFARE Classic tag compatibility issue

At one time, MIFARE Classic was the only tag in town and was compatible with every NFC device. That's no longer the case. Newer devices tend not to work well with MIFARE Classic. Many smartphones no longer work with MIFARE Classic, including (but not limited to)

» Google Nexus 4, 5, 7, and 10

» LG G2 and G3

» LG Optimus L7 II

» Moto X

» Samsung Galaxy Ace 3, Express 2, Mega, Note 3, S4, and S5

» HTC One M8

If you continue to use the MIFARE Classic tag, you need to be aware of this issue. The simplest fix is to use a universally compatible NFC tag in its place, such as the NTAG213, NTAG215, or NTAG216 (among many others). This chapter doesn't have the space to list all the compatible tag combinations, but you can check tag compatibility with specific smartphones on sites such as http://rapidnfc.com/nfc_enabled_phones.

Determining device functionality

Not every device works with every tag. The issue may not be with the tag's compatibility or with the device's operation. Some devices, such as the iPhone 6, don't support the functionality required to access certain types of NFC connectivity such as discovery mode or peer to peer. This means that you can tap all day long and the device will never react. When working through an odd behavior issue, first verify that the device will actually support the action you want to perform.

Finding the Device's Sweet Spot

Every device has a sweet spot for reading NFC tags. The sweet spot is created by placing the reader, in this case a mobile phone, in the exact, optimal location of the object being read, in this case an NFC tag. The key to finding the sweet spot is to know where the antenna resides in your smartphone. Smartphones can present a challenge because the antenna might be anywhere on the device. Figure 11-1 shows the potential location of an antenna on several makes and models of smartphones. Not knowing the location of the antenna on your device can make the difference between a great NFC experience and a frustrating one at best.

Most smartphones and many other devices place the antenna on the back of the device so that you can see the screen when you tap. If you find that you have problems getting NFC connectivity to work, look through your documentation to ensure that you know where to tap.

FIGURE 11-1:
The antenna's location can vary by make and model of smartphone.

Photos courtesy of NFC Ring Forum

Unfortunately, you may not find the location of the antenna listed in the documentation (or you might have misplaced your documentation). In this case, if you have an NFC tag handy, you can move it along the back of your smartphone until you hear the beep indicating that the smartphone has made a connection. This will be the sweet spot on your smartphone. Another alternative is to use an NFC-enabled wristband or other device and follow the same process. The point is to ensure that you know where the antenna is on your device. The alternative is to spend a lot of time trying to get a good read by lots of trial and error.

Considering Other Tag Issues

The interaction between the device and the tag usually works precisely as planned after you've addressed all the basics, such as finding the sweet spot and knowing that the device is working properly. However, sometimes a tag fails to work as anticipated. Nothing is wrong with your device — the tag itself has some sort of problem that keeps it from responding as expected. The following sections discuss the most common tag issues you encounter. By knowing about these issues, you can quickly determine whether there is little or nothing you can do to read the tag.

Determining when a tag is simply broken

NFC is a simple technology when you think about it. When it comes to tags, you're really just looking at an antenna, IC, and inlay — that's it. Just three parts. The whole thing is relatively reliable because it's simple. However, you still have to have those three components in good working order to make the tag work. Depending on the kind of tag and how someone uses the tag, you might find that it doesn't take much to damage one. Simply damaging the inlay or breaking one of the extremely fine lines in the antenna can cause the tag to break.

In some cases, you can see the tag damage. Perhaps the tag has scratches or some other obvious imperfection.

The problems occur when you can't see the tag. Perhaps the tag is mounted on a poster and the poster was damaged in the tag area in the back (causing damage to the tag). You might not be able to see the damage from the front of the post, but it still exists and the NFC connection still won't work. When you're with someone else who has a different kind of smartphone, you can ask that person to try the tag. If that person also can't read the tag, the tag may be at fault, not your device.

Tags do wear out. According to the documentation found at http://www.nxp. com/documents/short_data_sheet/NTAG203_SDS.pdf, an NFC tag will retain data for about five years. After that time, you could have problems reading it, even if the tag is physically intact. Tags also have a limited number of write cycles. Most wear out after 10,000 writes. Of course, not many tags are likely to see that many writes, so the five-year data retention limit seems to be the one that you must think about when working with NFC.

TIP

Some forms of damage that you normally associate with electronics are less likely to happen with NFC. For example, Electro-Static Discharge (ESD) can fry most electronics quite easily, but most NFC tags would require an extremely high voltage to get fried. When working with implementations such as rings, the fact that the ring is encased in plastic makes it even less likely that ESD will be a problem. In short, what you really need to worry about in most cases is physical damage of the kind that you can see.

Reading tags on metal

NFC tags work by electromagnetic induction. This means that placing a tag on metal can be problematic. You can never read an NFC tag through a piece of metal. The metal will reflect the electromagnetic signal, making the tag difficult, if not impossible, to read.

You must use special tags designed for use on metal. A ferrite foil barrier shields the tag from the reflecting qualities of the metal underneath.

REMEMBER

Even when you use tags designed for use on metal, you can still encounter problems getting NFC to work. According to http://rapidnfc.com/on_metal_nfc_tags, tags located on a metal surface often have only half the performance potential of tags located elsewhere, and creating the connection in the first place might be harder.

Reading tags near water

Water can be challenge when using NFC because water tends to absorb RF signals. However, you can find special tags and NFC tokens that can work in or near water. For example, GoToTags (http://buynfctags.com/tags/blank-tags/blank-nfc-tokens/) provides a number of waterproof tag options, including use on laundered wearables. You just want to be sure to use a waterproof tag or one designed for outside use in a wet or humid environment.

You may be surprised to find out that NFC tags can survive and even work in a wet environment. The video at `https://www.youtube.com/watch?v=ANSzMAw1sdU` shows someone who has placed a tag in a block of ice. You can see him program and read the tag. In this case, the demonstration shows the tester making a phone call, but tags should work for other purposes, too. After the ice melts, the tag still works just fine. The tester shows you that the tag is still accessible even in a bowl of water. The interesting part about this video is that the tester then proceeds to burn the tag (right on his stove, no less). The tag still works.

IN THIS CHAPTER

Getting the software you need

Discovering the functionality your device supports

Using biometric authentication

Ensuring your app sources are reliable

Chapter 12

Understanding the Software Issues

Without software, the hardware you own is useless. Yes, the hardware provides the ability to perform a given task. However, without the instructions needed to perform the task, the hardware will just sit there waiting for input. An issue many people face when working with a new technology is a lack of the right software to make the hardware perform the required tasks, so that's the first area this chapter tackles.

Software is a series of instructions. It tells the hardware precisely what to do and determines when to do it based on user input. Put another way, the software is the brains and the hardware is the brawn of a computer. Software and hardware must understand each other in order to work together, which means the developer must know the capabilities of the device. Of course, the user must also understand these capabilities or risk being surprised when the software reports that a particular feature is unavailable.

Whenever an application discovers a need for security, such as when you want to use a credit card to pay for something, the application needs to verify that you really are the right person to perform the task. It has become more popular over the years to eschew passwords and other forms of authentication in favor of *biometrics* — a kind of authentication that relies on verifying a body part, such as a fingerprint. No authentication solution is perfect, however, so this chapter views a few of the issues you might encounter when using biometric authentication.

Poorly written software that lacks the right instructions will cause the hardware to fail, behave erratically, or simply become frustrating. Software issues can include everything from causing system lockups to allowing hackers to break into the device and steal your data. This chapter helps you understand the details of software issues and provides you with input on how best to deal with the issues associated with errant software.

Installing Needed Software

Applications are a sort of canned knowledge. The developer who writes an application provides instructions that the computer turns into actions. What many people don't consider is that the manner in which a developer puts an application together partially reflects the developer's knowledge about a given topic. The better a developer understands the topic at hand, the better the application tends to be. So users don't just need software, they need the right software with the knowledge appropriate to the user's needs. The following sections provide some strategies for obtaining and installing the software needed to perform NFC tasks.

Getting a general application

The app you need for your device depends on what you do with it, the relationships you have with vendors, and the requirements of the device. Android and Apple products appear to be the most popular when it comes to applications, but you can find applications for any NFC-enabled device out there. Sometimes it just takes a bit of searching. Of course, your device may already come with all the apps you need, so downloading and installing anything else becomes unnecessary. The book covers some general apps, such as the various payment applications like Apple Pay, Android Pay, and Google Wallet in Chapter 6 (read the comparison of Android Pay and Google Wallet at https://www.google.com/wallet/faq/). This section deals with other sorts of general applications that you may want to download and use, such as the following:

>> **Trigger** (http://gettrigger.com/)**:** This app helps you automate daily tasks. You can tap your way through life. Tap one tag and Trigger silences your phone before you got to bed; tap another and you connect to your car's Bluetooth. Trigger lets you use NFC for a wide assortment of tasks, automating each one as needed. This app is a free download.

>> **Tasker** (http://tasker.dinglisch.net/)**:** You use Tasker to automate tasks based on contexts (application, time, date, locations, event, or gesture). This app goes well beyond simply relying on NFC. It provides a range of options for controlling automation and makes working with your Android

device a pleasure. You can obtain a free trial version of this product at `http://tasker.dinglisch.net/download.html`, but you must purchase the product after the trial period expires (currently seven days).

» **Tasker Plug-ins:** In contrast to many other apps, you can expand Tasker to perform additional tasks using plug-ins such as the NFC Locale Plug-in (`https://play.google.com/store/apps/details?id=se.badaccess.locale.nfc`). The majority of these plug-ins require that you buy them before you try them. However, they do extend an already useful app and help it perform other tasks. Here are some of the Tasker plug-ins you might consider obtaining:

- **AutoVoice** (`https://play.google.com/store/apps/details?id=com.joaomgcd.autovoice`)**:** Helps you control Tasker using Google Now commands.

- **Secure Settings** (`http://securesettings.intangibleobject.com/`)**:** Lets you take complete control over the settings on your device.

- **Tasker App Factory** (`https://play.google.com/store/apps/details?id=net.dinglisch.android.appfactory`)**:** Lets you create an app from a task or project, which means you can send your best tasks or projects to a friend — even one that doesn't have Tasker.

- **Bluetooth Auto Connect** (`http://www.uniqtec.eu/applications/bluetooth-auto-connect.html`)**:** Automates your Bluetooth connectivity using Tasker events.

» **Puzzle Alarm Clock** (`https://play.google.com/store/apps/details?id=com.wroclawstudio.puzzlealarmclock`)**:** If you're one of those individuals who has a hard time getting up in the morning, this may be the app that changes your life. It makes you solve a puzzle (ensuring that you're actually awake) or tap an NFC tag to turn this one off. This app is a free download for the standard version.

» **InstaWifi** (`http://www.instawifi.jessechen.net/`)**:** Sharing a Wi-Fi connection with family and friends can prove difficult because you often need to spell out the password before anyone can connect. This app allows you to write your Service Set Identifier (SSID), security technology (such as Wi-Fi Protected Access, or WPA), and password to an NFC tag. When friend or family members want to connect to your Wi-Fi network, they simply tap the NFC tag to do it. This approach is not only faster but also more secure. The app is a free download.

Using a tag writer or other utilities

Some apps that you install on your phone are more utilitarian than fun. You still need them, but they serve specific purposes such as reading or writing tags.

To use NFC effectively for business tasks, you need one or more of these apps installed on a device that you have available during work hours. The following list provides you with some ideas of what is available in the way of tag writer or other utility-like apps:

» **NFC TagWriter** (`https://play.google.com/store/apps/details?id=com.nxp.nfc.tagwriter`): You can use this app to record contacts, bookmarks, geographical locations, Bluetooth Handover, Short Message Service (SMS) texts, Mail, text messages, and many other data types to any NFC-enabled tags. It also works well with posters, business cards, watches, and other NFC-enabled electronics. This app is a free download. Make sure to check out the tutorial at `http://rapidnfc.com/how_to_encode_nfc_tags` to see how easy this app is to use.

» **NFC Tag Info** (`https://play.google.com/store/apps/details?id=com.nxp.taginfolite`): This app lets you read the content of any NFC-enabled tag, poster, business card, watch, or other NFC storage device. This app is a free download.

» **NFC Tools** (`https://play.google.com/store/apps/details?id=com.wakdev.wdnfc`): This is another app that lets you read, write, and program NFC tags. With the programming feature, you can easily perform tasks such as to turn on Bluetooth or turn on an alarm. This app is a free download.

» **NFC Tasks** (`https://play.google.com/store/apps/details?id=com.wakdev.nfctasks`): This app is an extension to NFC tools that focuses on programming functionality. Using this tool lets you create scripts to automate any complex task that NFC can perform. You can even use it in combination with Tasker to gain even more functionality. This app is a free download.

» **NFC ReTag Pro** (`https://play.google.com/store/apps/details?id=com.widgapp.NFC_ReTAG_PRO`): You may have a host of already-used, write-protected tags at your disposal. Don't throw them out! Using NFC ReTag Pro lets you reuse those tags and mark them with one or more standard activities. You can also use this app in combination with Tasker to create complex scripts. The best part is that you don't need to write anything on the tag. Instead, this app uses the tag ID for any required information. This makes NFC ReTag Pro a great way to work with smaller tags. The vendor does provide a free trial version of this product (`http://www.apk20.com/apk/197601/`), but you need to deal with advertisements when you use it.

» **NFC Kits** (`https://www.microsoft.com/store/apps/nfc-kits/9wzdncrfjqv6`): This app allows you to read and write tags from proximity devices. The app works only on Windows 10 systems. You use it to write tags that perform all the usual tasks. In addition, it lets you launch an application. However, it doesn't allow actual scripting. This app is a free download.

Encoding tags using a USB tag reader/writer

You may not want to have a special app installed on a device, such as a smartphone, for reading and writing tags. In fact, if you're a developer, you may want some method for interacting with a USB reader at your desktop or laptop computer instead. In this case, you need a USB tag reader/writer from a company such asGoToTags(http://buynfctags.com/hardware/desktop-hardware/desktop-nfc-readers-and-writers/).

The device you receive plugs into a USB port. When you plug the device into a USB port, your system normally recognizes it automatically. Most reader/writers come with an application that you install on your system to read and write the tags. Some setups, such as the one from ACS, come as a kit, so you get a sampling of NFC chips as part of the package. Depending on your system setup and the installation you use, here is a typical set of instructions for encoding tags using a USB reader/writer:

1. Choose the kind of chip you want to use.

As noted in previous chapters, NFC supports a wide range of chip types, so choosing the correct type for your application is important.

2. Start the encoding application.

The application should recognize that you have the reader/writer attached to the system.

3. Place the chip on the device.

Some devices have a specific sweet spot you must use. The sweet spot normally has some sort of printed indicator. When you place the chip properly, the device reads it and displays the chip type on the encoding application.

REMEMBER

If the tag already has information written to it, you see that information as part of the initial display. Most tag reader/writer applications won't modify content on a read-only tag. One exception to this rule is NFC ReTag Pro (see the "Using a tag writer or other utilities" section, earlier in chapter, for details).

4. Fill out the information you want to write to the tag.

How you do this depends on the application. Most applications rely on multiple tabs, each of which contains a type of information required to create a complete tag. For example, if you want to create a tag that contains a Uniform Resource Identifier (URI), you use the tab for URIs to provide the locations you want to use.

TIP

Some applications let you write multiple kinds of information to the same tag. Whether you can actually write multiple information types depends on the kind of tag you select, the amount of data you want to write, and the memory space the tag has to offer.

5. **Determine whether you want to make the tag read only.**

   Most tag applications provide a simple check box to make this determination.

6. **Click Write Tag (or a similar button) to write the tag information.**

   In most cases, the application closes the writing dialog box and reads the tag. You see the content you just wrote to the tag.

7. **Test the tag by reading it with an NFC-enabled device, such as a smartphone.**

   The device should read the tag and offer to perform a task based on the tag content.

UNDERSTANDING THE NEED FOR MASS PRODUCTION

Reading and writing individual tags may seem fun at a first, but these tasks quickly become chores when you need to create multiple copies of the same tag. Fortunately, sites such as GoToTags have your back with products such as the Reel-to-Reel NFC Encoder (https://gototags.com/products/reel-reel-nfc-encoder/ or http://buynfctags.com/gototags-reel-reel-nfc-encoder/). This device can encode two tags per second, which makes writing the same information to a roll of tags quite fast. The device plugs into your PC and works about the same as using an individual USB tag reader/writer device and associated software. Of course, when using this kind of solution, you must obtain tags that come on a roll — but not all tags do.

Another mass-production option is to have someone else produce the tags for you. For example, Automated Assembly Corporation (AAC) can create wearable NFC tags for a number of uses — most notably for health care (http://www.nfcworld.com/2015/02/17/334156/aac-to-mass-produce-wearable-nfc-stickers-for-healthcare/). Moo.com (https://www.moo.com/us/products/nfc/business-cards-plus.html) also mass produces NFC-coded custom business cards. The interesting thing about this offering is that the business cards come with multiple designs in the same box. Make sure to check out GoToTags (https://gototags.com/), RapidNFC (http://rapidnfc.com/), and Tagstand (http://www.tagstand.com/) for additional mass production ideas.

Knowing the Modes Your Device Supports

Not every device supports every kind of tag available today. In fact, your device can exhibit some odd behaviors that depend on the vendor's implementation of the NFC standards. The "Understanding Odd Device Behaviors" section of Chapter 11 describes these particular issues from a hardware perspective. NFC is moving toward standardized support in every possible area, but you still have compatibility issues to consider. As a result, you need to know the level of support your device provides from a software perspective, too.

Software has limitations as well. When obtaining software for your device, you need to obtain the right kind of app. For example, some apps support only Android devices, others only Windows devices. In addition to platform, you need to consider the app specifications to be sure that your device can support it. This is especially true when working with Windows; many NFC apps require that you have Windows 10 installed.

The level of support that software provides varies considerably as well. Developers are always designing new apps that perform some tasks better than others, which means that the app may not use all the functionality that your device hardware can support. Compare the functionality provided by NFC TagWriter (https://www.microsoft.com/store/apps/nfc-tagwriter/9wzdncrdcr11) when compared to NFC Kits (mentioned in the "Using a tag writer or other utilities" section, earlier in this chapter). The NFC TagWriter app works quite well for the tasks that it's designed to perform but lacks much of the functionality provided by NFC Kits. The trade-off is that the NFC Kits app requires more system resources and is harder to use. Neither app is a bad choice — it comes down to what works best for your particular need. Whenever possible, try to obtain a trial version of the software for testing before you make a purchase.

REMEMBER

Many of the sites that offer apps for download also provide the means for creating reviews. Some people put a lot more faith in the reviews than they warrant. A review is an opinion — and often a misinformed one. An app that didn't work well for someone else may work fine for you. The best way to ensure that the app you get for managing tags and performing development tasks will do what you need it to do is to test it on your setup. You may find gems of applications that others have rejected.

TECHNICAL
STUFF

If you're involved in a large-scale project using a host of devices, you may need to perform actual device testing to make sure that you understand how each device will work with your application. Normally, this sort of testing isn't required unless you plan to create application software or build a device of your own, but it helps to know that testing resources of this type are available. One such company is

Rohde and Schwarz (http://www.rohde-schwarz.us/en/solutions/wireless-communications/nfc-rfid/in-focus-nfc/testingnfcenableddevicesinlisteningmode_101091.html). The instructions provided on this site show you how to create a test setup to determine how a number of NFC-enabled devices perform when passive. A similar set of instructions (http://www.rohde-schwarz.us/en/solutions/wireless-communications/nfc-rfid/in-focus-nfc/nfc-polling-tests_101090.html) shows how to test devices in active mode.

Providing Biometric Authentication

Knowing for sure that the person performing a task is the person who is authorized to perform the task can be a difficult issue to resolve. In fact, even when vendors, users, and developers find a workable solution, not everyone will agree that it's the best solution.

Biometric authentication uses a body characteristic for identification purposes. The characteristic need not represent a visible body part. For example, you can use the way a person walks as a means of identifying that person, even though a manner of walking isn't associated with one specific body part.

In many cases, biometric authentication augments an existing authentication method such as a Personal Identification Number (PIN), password, or passphrase (a sentence or other complex human-readable text that is hard to guess). Some vendors are using two-factor authentication to reduce the chance that the inadvertent disclosure of one authentication technique will automatically open data sources to hackers. In fact, a few vendors even rely on three-factor authentication (http://www.pearsonitcertification.com/articles/article.aspx?p=1718488), in which one factor is an input, a second factor is a body characteristic, and a third factor is a physical element (such as a smartcard). The following sections give you an overview of biometric authentication.

Considering the types of biometric authentication

You may think that biometric authentication begins and ends with the fingerprint, but that's not the case. Over the years, science has developed all sorts of biometric authentication techniques. Of course, some are far more popular than others. The following list offers some ideas of the kinds of authentication that your body can support (generally in order of usage):

>> **Fingerprint recognition:** The most common form of biometric authentication in use today, this visual biometric relies on an analysis of the ridges and values found on the surface tips of the finger. Because this particular physical characteristic is easy to mimic, hackers can readily fool the authentication.

>> **Signature recognition:** A visual and behavioral biometric technology that combines statistical handwriting analysis with the actual act of creating the signature. The statistical analysis portion (also called static checking) compares a scanned signature with a base signature kept on file. The behavioral component (dynamic checking) verifies the signature based on how the person creates the signature. Combining the two elements makes forging someone's signature quite difficult. Unfortunately, many applications use only one of the two biometric verification strategies (normally the static check).

>> **Facial recognition:** A visual biometric that relies on a statistical form of pattern recognition of specific features. Most of these systems rely on *eigenfaces*, which is a math-based technique used for facial recognition (`http://www.pages.drexel.edu/~sis26/Eigenface%20Tutorial.htm`), or a local feature analysis. The fact that this is a statistical check means that someone can potentially fool it unless the analysis is complete enough.

>> **Eyes (iris matching):** A visual biometric involving a specially designed camera that takes a picture of the iris pattern. The issue with this biometric is that the iris can change over time or be affected by disease (`http://webvision.med.utah.edu/2012/05/iris-changes-complicate-biometric-scans/`).

>> **Eyes (retina recognition):** With this visual biometric, a specially designed camera takes a picture of the veins in the back of the eye. This approach uses a pattern-recognition technique that may not work properly when diseases such as diabetic retinopathy and glaucoma cause changes to or occlude the retina vein pattern.

>> **Finger geometry recognition:** An upcoming form of authentication that relies on both visual and spatial biometric techniques. Because of how this authentication method works, a hacker has a much harder time fooling it.

>> **Hand geometry recognition:** A visual and spatial biometric authentication technique that uses features of the entire hand for identification. The technique can combine finger geometry recognition with hand features such as the length of the fingers or the breadth of the hand. Depending on the implementation, fooling this recognition technique can be quite difficult.

>> **Voice or speaker recognition:** A technique for authenticating people based on how they speak and what they say. The technique measures characteristics

such as cadence, voice inflection, and accent. It also relies on a unique pattern of words in many cases. You can divide this biometric into two distinct types:

- **Voice (speaker verification and authentication):** An auditory biometric that relies on matching the vocal characteristics to create a voice print or voice model. The speaker must use a specific phrase when talking and attempt to say the phrase in the same manner each time. The technique relies on performing statistical analysis to ensure that the speaker's voice and voice print match within a reasonable auditory range. This technique assumes that the speaker is aware of the authentication process. You see it used for secure access of buildings or when obtaining access to specific resources.

- **Voice (speaker identification):** An auditory biometric involving an unknown speaker. The technique begins by creating a template that is then matched against like templates, looking for a match within a statistical range. The authentication technique works without the speaker's knowledge and gets used in security applications, such as when a police officer makes a stop.

>> **Vein recognition:** A visual biometric that uses the vein patterns in a finger or the palm of the hand for authentication. Interestingly enough, a number of vendors, such as Fujitsu (`http://findbiometrics.com/solutions/vein-recognition/`), have made this particular kind of authentication available. The authentication technique finds common use in hospitals (see the PatientSecure system at `https://www.imprivata.com/imprivata-patientsecure`).

>> **Ear:** With this visual biometric, a camera takes a picture of the shape of your ear. The technique works similarly to fingerprint analysis. The presence of external factors, such as earrings, makes using this technique difficult.

>> **Typing recognition:** A behavioral biometric that relies on statistical sampling of how a person types. It measures such factors as the amount of finger pressure used and the angle at which the fingers strike the keys.

Discovering the problems that could occur with biometric authentication

A problem with biometric authentication is that it's an evolving technology. If a person loses a finger and that finger happens to be the one that was used for the fingerprint reader, the person also loses access to anything that the fingerprint could access. An accident can cause other body characteristics to change. For that matter, something as simple as getting arthritis can cause problems with biometric authentication, depending on the sort of authentication you use.

Odd as it might seem, it's perfectly normal for body characteristics to change over time or sometimes disappear altogether. For example, a man from Singapore lost his fingerprints as a result of cancer treatments and ended up being detained when entering the United States (http://www.scientificamerican.com/article/lose-your-fingerprints/ and http://time.com/3823350/cancer-patients-fingerprints/). However, losing your fingerprints as a result of working with pineapple long term is a myth (https://www.quora.com/Does-long-term-pineapple-cutting-get-rid-of-your-fingerprints and https://www.youtube.com/watch?v=U7eLBwCAwmo). The point is that even if you manage to keep all your digits, you can still lose your fingerprints.

Understanding how hackers overcome biometric authentication

Hackers see biometrics as an interesting challenge, but that's about it. People who think that any form of security exists that is completely safe are only fooling themselves; hackers will always find a way to circumvent any security measure you put into place. About the only way you can potentially keep data safe is to make the data of low enough value and the obstacles large enough that hackers will go after lower-hanging fruit. Increasing the time required to break into your system also helps because it gives the alert and astute administrator time to discover the hacking.

Of all the biometrics, the fingerprint has received the most hacker attention. You can even find instructional videos on how to do it (http://www.instructables.com/id/How-To-Fool-a-Fingerprint-Security-System-As-Easy-/). In fact, hackers have found more than a few ways to make fingerprints useless as a biometric authentication aid (http://www.networkworld.com/article/2293129/data-center/120606-10-ways-to-beat-fingerprint-biometrics.html). The problem with fingerprint identification is increasingly becoming an issue: Hackers recently obtained 5.6 million of them, some from people with high security clearances (http://www.wired.com/2015/09/opm-now-admits-5-6m-feds-fingerprints-stolen-hackers/).

WARNING

Some biometrics may seem impossible to overcome. For example, creating a duplicate of someone's eyes would be hard in real life (movies notwithstanding). The actual hack for eye scans is interesting — you use a picture (http://www.forbes.com/sites/thomasbrewster/2015/03/05/clone-putins-eyes-using-google-images/). In fact, the high-resolution images available through Google today let people circumvent nearly any form of biometric authentication that relies on a physical attribute such as a fingerprint. The ongoing effort to circumvent biometric authentication techniques is the reason that vendors are constantly looking for other ways to provide application security.

Getting Apps from Reliable Sources

As you build your infrastructure for working with NFC in various ways, you need to consider the software you use to interact with the hardware you own. More than one vendor produces great application software to use for a variety of purposes, but not all vendors are reliable. The reliability of your vendor affects the software in a number of ways:

- » **Security:** Apps can contain a wealth of security woes. In some cases, the app contains malware designed to infiltrate your system. Even if you know that the app doesn't normally contain malware, downloading the app from a locations you don't recognize can cause problems because you don't know that the third-party site hasn't tampered with the app's code. Security woes can also include advertising software that the app developer includes in order to pay the bills.

- » **Standards:** As you might have guessed, obtaining software that follows the various NFC standards is essential because the standards have evolved over time, and some software hasn't kept up. Unless the software and hardware both adhere to the current standards, you'll likely encounter problems trying to implement your NFC solution.

- » **Functionality:** Software varies considerably in the way of functionality. Some people feel that more features are better, but this isn't always the case. A less functional app may use fewer resources, prove easier to use, or work more reliably. Depending on the software, you may find that the vendor provides plug-ins and other means of customizing the software. Extending your software through plug-ins helps you get precisely the right match. The point is to get software that meets your needs, rather than looking for software that provides the most features.

>> **Timeliness:** Because NFC is a moving target, you need a vendor that will provide timely updates. You need to know that the vendor will help you get through the various changes and provide software that continues to meet standards, yet takes advantage of the latest hardware advances.

>> **Longevity:** A problem with emerging technologies is that vendors simply disappear — sometimes overnight. Choosing a vendor with a larger installed base and a good reputation is often more important than locating one with the glitziest apps. You want to be sure that the vendor will be around to support your decision after you do decide on a product and have it implemented in your solution.

>> **Expandability:** The capability to expand the application using techniques such as plug-ins or additional modules to support new features in the future is always good to look for. As your organization grows, so do the needs of your users. Unless you want to change apps on a regular basis, looking for an app that expands to meet your needs is the next best bet.

>> **Scalability:** Your application will have to scale to support more users and a great workflow at some point. Think positively! Your business is definitely going to grow, so you need a way to support all that additional activity.

TIP

In most cases, the best place to start searching for that perfect app is at the vendor store. Most vendors today provide a store where you can shop for apps that have gone through a certification process. The apps are free of major flaws, embedded security issues, and reliability problems. Of course, a vendor can't ensure that the app will meet your needs; only you can do that. Certification also doesn't guarantee that the vendor will release updates in a timely manner or that you'll find the vendor around the next time you need to make a purchase. You still need to consider all these issues, but starting at the vendor store at least removes a few of the most egregious problems from the pile.

Chapter 13

Considering Networking Problems

A number of chapters in this book discuss how you use NFC to pair one device with another using another networking technology such as Wi-Fi or Bluetooth. You could perform the pairing using the native network technology, but doing so is time consuming and error prone. When using NFC, you simply tap and NFC makes the connection for you. You may not even realize that you're connected to another networking technology until you move the NFC-enabled device away and see that the connection is live and working with something like Wi-Fi or Bluetooth.

In most cases, you find that these technologies work together amazingly well. It may surprise you when they don't (assuming you ever see it happen). As with any other technology, sometimes things break, and you need to have some idea of what is going wrong to fix it. Fortunately, given the reliability of the hardware produced today, most of the problems are relatively easy to fix as well.

This chapter views potential networking problems in three different ways: hardware, environment, and security. You see how to solve the most common problems for two types of hardware: Wi-Fi and Bluetooth. By the end of the chapter, you should be able to fix a considerable number of user-fixable networking problems. Of course, other sorts of issues can (and do) happen, but often they require help from a vendor or professional to fix.

REMEMBER

This book focuses on NFC specifically, so you may see other solutions for technologies such as pairing. In addition, networks have various layers. Pairing for communication using another wireless technology is an application-layer use case that may or may not use NFC. In addition, the physical layer might use NFC to exchange configuration data to enable such communication. Precisely how NFC affects pairing depends on which network layer uses it.

FOCUSING ON THE RIGHT ELEMENT

Remember that NFC works with other technologies on a regular basis. Even though the user may see a single package, multiple technologies must work together in the background to create that package. Because users understand that NFC is starting a particular conversation, providing the required pairing with another technology, users tend to blame NFC for every networking ill. People may not even understand that the true culprit is another technology, such as Wi-Fi. Consequently, when a user reports a problem, the support person hears all sorts of input about NFC. Unfortunately, NFC isn't even involved.

When working through networking problems, teasing out the correct element to focus on is essential. Otherwise, you'll never fix the problem. As long as the pairing occurs, you know that NFC is doing its job. The pairing might not succeed, but that may not be a problem with NFC. Consider these kinds of questions when a network connection almost but doesn't quite work:

- Does the user know all the technologies used to create a pairing (or is the user aware of only NFC)?

- Does the user understand the other technology's role in the conversation?

- Has the user turned the other technology on?

- Has the user configured the other technology?

- Is the technology working with other sorts of connections?

- Does the pairing require special settings that NFC must provide?

- Has anyone verified that the NFC card provides the special settings to the other technology?

By going through a list of questions that breaks the problem down into smaller pieces, you can usually reduce the number of elements you must troubleshoot to find the source of a problem. In addition, you can also reduce the number of dependent technology events that you must research to ensure that the related technology can perform its job.

Understanding the Cost of Using Wi-Fi

Wi-Fi enables the transfer data between devices at a relatively high rate of speed using equipment that is becoming ever more popular and available at a low cost. However, working with Wi-Fi can become complicated, especially as you add security features to keep the network safe. NFC makes the complications of working with Wi-Fi less apparent by automating many of the tasks you have to perform. All you need to do is tap, and the Wi-Fi bends to your will — at least, most of the time. The following sections discuss the issues you might encounter when using NFC to pair with Wi-Fi and Bluetooth.

Comparing Wi-Fi and Bluetooth

This book discusses both Wi-Fi and Bluetooth pairing with NFC for good reason. The two technologies can help you perform certain tasks, but Wi-Fi is actually better suited to the needs of a full-scale network, while Bluetooth is better suited to ad-hoc short term networks. Wi-Fi requires greater knowledge to use and presents a more complicated setup; Bluetooth is simpler and less likely to cause problems from purely a configuration standpoint. Knowing something about how these two technologies compare will help you make a better choice when selecting one for pairing with NFC. Table 13-1 contains a quick overview comparison of the technologies. You can use the material in the remainder of the chapter to refine your view of the two technologies for your particular need.

The statistics in Table 13-1 are subject to change as the specifications for each technology change. However, you can see that each approach has distinct advantages. For example, Bluetooth uses less power, which can be a significant benefit when working with battery-powered devices. On the other hand, Wi-Fi offers far greater range and bandwidth.

TABLE 13-1: **Wi-Fi versus Bluetooth**

Feature	Bluetooth	Wi-Fi
Frequency	2.4 GHz	2.4, 3.6, and 5 GHz.
Cost	Low	Moderate to High.
Bandwidth	Low to Moderate (800 Kbps to 24 Mbps)	Moderate to High (11 Mbps to 100 Gbps).
Specifications authority	Bluetooth Special Interest Group (SIG)	Institute of Electrical and Electronics Engineers (IEEE) and Wireless Ethernet Compatibility Alliance (WECA).
Security	Low	Moderate with proper configuration.
Development Year	1994	1991
Primary uses	Mobile phone, mouse, keyboard, and office and industrial automation devices	Notebook computer, desktop computer, server, TV, mobile phone.
Hardware requirements	Bluetooth adapter on all devices	Wireless adapters on all devices, wireless router and/or Wireless Access Points (WAPs) (unless you create a Wireless Ad Hoc Network, WANET, using NFC for configuration purposes).
Range	5 to 30 meters	Varies by network specification, location, hardware, and frequency used. For example, an 802.11n network at 2.5 GHz has a typical range of 70 meters indoors and 250 meters outdoors. Using a 5 GHz frequency increases this range. The types of antennas used can also increase the range.
Power consumption	Low	High

Pairing with consumer electronics

Consumer electronics that support NFC pairing normally use a specialized chip, such as the NXP NTAG21xF series (https://nxp-rfid.com/new-nxp-tags-enable-simple-wi-fi-and-bluetooth-pairing-via-nfc/). These tags automatically turn on the device when they sense an NFC-enabled device. What makes these tags different from other NFC tags is that they have an extra output signal to the device that indicates when the tag detects RF. The additional output allows the device to turn on automatically when the user presents the NFC-enabled device. The same tags work with both Wi-Fi and Bluetooth in many cases. Using these kinds of tags can greatly decrease the work required to make the pairing after the device and the NFC-enabled devices are both configured correctly.

A problem is that the hardware functionality might be there, but the application support is often lacking or you need special knowledge to make it work. For example, when creating a pairing between a smartphone and a camera, you often need a special application to make the pairing work (such as the PlayMemories Mobile App, `https://www.playmemoriescameraapps.com/portal/`). You need to have Wi-Fi connectivity enabled and to turn off airplane mode. So far, nothing is too odd about the setup. The bit of secret knowledge is that you usually have to disable any smart-switch functionality that the smartphone might provide because a camera doesn't qualify as a smart switch. (A *switch* provides network connectivity between devices, and a *smart switch* provides this functionality in a semi-unmanaged mode so that you see connections automatically.)

Device stands (a cradle, charging station, or other physical entity used to hold the device) can also cause problems. You might find that the sweet spot for a device (that is, the area that makes the connection with the other device — see "Finding the Device's Sweet Spot" section of Chapter 11 for details) actually appears at the back of the device in a location that the device stand makes inaccessible. Depending on how the devices are set up, you might actually need to remove the device from its stand every time you want to perform a pairing (which naturally is inconvenient). The device-stand problem happens more often than not when you use a third-party stand to hold a particular device. The third-party vendor may not know which device you're using with the stand and hasn't designed the stand appropriately.

Pairing with a network

Pairing Wi-Fi with NFC is a great way to share your network with a guest and perform a wide variety of network-related tasks. Of course, you need some way to log in your guests to your network. Logging your guests in is much easier if you write a tag for the purpose or provide the guest with a QR code. The NFC Forum Connection Handover Technical Specification (`http://members.nfc-forum.org/specs/spec_list/`) does provide you with the information you need to perform this task with most smartphones.

The problem is that the technique doesn't always work. For example, some people have complained that the techniques for writing the tag don't work with Android smartphones. You also need a specific app to make the connection work, and the connection is only for short-term peer-to-peer connectivity. By the time you get through all the caveats, you wonder just how well the whole thing will work. The point is that the technique does work, but you often need to spend time working through the details to ensure that it works as expected. In the case of Android, a number of developers have mentioned using a three-step process to write data to a tag to ensure success, as follows:

1. **Create a tag that contains the appropriate connection Uniform Resource Identifier (URI) (such as** `wifi://[network ssid]/[wep|wpa|open]/[network key]`**).**

2. **Add a record to the tag containing the required credentials.**

3. **Build a Java app record for the tag that defines an Android Application Record (see** `http://developer.android.com/reference/android/nfc/NdefRecord.html#createApplicationRecord(java.lang.String)`**).**

TIP

Newer versions of the Android smartphone do come with a useful alternative. You can use the technique described at `http://www.androidpolice.com/2014/06/27/android-1-feature-spotlight-write-wi-fi-passwords-to-nfc-tags-directly-from-android/` to create an NFC tag directly from the smartphone. Of course, you need to have an Android smartphone to make this technique work. In addition, you likely need a special app to perform the task, such as InstaWifi (`https://play.google.com/store/apps/details?id=net.jessechen.instawifi`). The article at `http://fieldguide.gizmodo.com/share-your-home-wi-fi-easily-using-an-nfc-tag-or-qr-cod-1624327128` describes how to use this utility to make accessing your home network considerably easier. The article specifically mentions that the techniques involved require your friends to also have an Android smartphone or have a smartphone that can read a QR code that you create.

Make sure that your platform also provides the required pairing support. For example, when working with Windows, you have to have a special driver or Windows 10 installed. The newer version of the operating system provides pairing support through the Wi-Fi alliance's Wi-Fi P2P Carrier Configuration Record (`https://msdn.microsoft.com/library/windows/hardware/dn481543.aspx`). If the pairing isn't working, you need to look beyond NFC in most cases to find the cause.

Understanding the Cost of Using Bluetooth

Bluetooth is used in an amazing array of devices. In most cases, you use Bluetooth to create ad-hoc networks (see Table 13-1, earlier in this chapter, for a comparison with Wi-Fi). Pairing Bluetooth devices using NFC can take some unexpected twists and turns. The following sections provide you with some insights into working with NFC and Bluetooth.

Pairing with consumer electronics

NFC-enabled pairing can sometimes take unexpected turns when dealing with Bluetooth because sometimes the product advertising is a bit misleading. Consider the case of a tablet connection to some Bluetooth speakers. A vendor advertises that a speaker can connect to a tablet using either Bluetooth or NFC. However, it turns out that the speaker always creates the connection using Bluetooth; NFC provides an intermediary step that's probably not necessary in many cases. (You can read more about this issue at http://forums.androidcentral. com/google-nexus-7-tablet-2012/352863-how-do-i-pair-my-nexus-7-tablet-nfc-enabled-speakers.html.) This particular issue may take some people by surprise, but it happens often enough that you really need to know about it.

When you do have all the appropriate hardware features for using NFC to create a pairing between two devices, remember that you likely need to download an app to make the functionality work. After the app is downloaded, installed, and configured, you may still need to wait several minutes before the pairing completes (so, patience is a virtue). Many devices can be paired with only one device at a time. If you have already paired a device (such as a smartphone) with another device (such as a watch), you may need to reset the primary device (in this case, the smartphone) before you can pair it with another device (say, a different smart watch).

The instructions for the SmartWatch 3 are typical when pairing devices using Bluetooth. To set up a smart watch, you need to do a couple of things:

1. **Connect your phone or tablet to a Wi-Fi network (you must remain connected throughout the entire set-up process).**

2. **Turn on the NFC function.**

3. **Ensure that the device screen is active and unlocked.**

4. **Place your phone or tablet over the smartwatch so that the two devices can detect each other through NFC.**

   After the device is detected, the applicable download page for your smartwatch application appears on your phone or tablet.

5. **Follow the download instructions provided by the download page.**

   The app eventually appears on your device.

6. **Turn on Bluetooth when prompted.**

7. **Choose your smartwatch from a list of available devices.**

   It's like pairing your smartphone with your car.

You can obtain additional information at `http://support.sonymobile.com/global-en/swr50/userguide/Setting-up/`). Interestingly enough, this is one of the few times that you must have both Wi-Fi and Bluetooth support to make the connectivity work.

REMEMBER

Sometimes no precise cause exists for a pairing problem. You may not even be able to get the problem to repeat after you fix it. For those situations in which pairing fails for no apparent reason at all, you can try these fixes to see whether the pairing will eventually succeed:

>> Turn off the two devices, wait a few seconds, and then turn them back on. A soft reset often gets the devices talking.

>> Remove the device from the pairing list. For example, when working with iOS, you can remove a device by tapping its name and then Forget this Device. When working with Android, tap a device's name, and then Unpair. After removing the device from the list, add it again to see whether the pairing succeeds the next time.

>> Verify that the two devices really can connect. If you don't see the device pairing in your user manual, check with the vendor. A support person often knows the secret words that you need to whisper to the device to get it to work.

>> Download a device driver when needed to get a pairing to work with your PC.

>> Update the hardware's firmware. Sometimes you need to take the device to a professional to make this happen. The *firmware* is a permanent sort of software that determines the Bluetooth characteristics for a device. Unless the firmware provides the correct instructions, your device will never pair with certain other devices even if you have the correct hardware and platform.

Detecting the Bluetooth version problem

A common problem today is that both Microsoft and Apple are shipping products that work only with Bluetooth 4.0 devices. This means that you can do everything right, but your older Bluetooth 3.0 device will never connect to the Bluetooth 4.0 device. To detect this problem, try to create the connection manually first and then determine the source of the problem when you see it. The following list describes the common issues you may face when working through this problem:

>> **Device lacks the correct hardware:** The vendor specifications tell you what level of Bluetooth support your hardware device supports. When your hardware doesn't work with Bluetooth 4.0, your only option is to get new hardware.

>> **Platform lacks the required drivers:** Even if your device provides Bluetooth 4.0 support, it can't connect as a Bluetooth 4.0 device without the proper platform support. Older versions of Android lack the support, so you need to wait for an update. Android 4.3 and above provide Bluetooth 4.0 support.

>> **App lacks the required functionality:** Just because your hardware and platform provide the required support doesn't mean that the app you're using does. When you do need an app, make sure to obtain one that provides the required Bluetooth 4.0 support.

TIP

Some smartphones actually do have all the Bluetooth support that you need, they just don't know it. In some cases, you need an app such as NFC Easy Connect (`https://play.google.com/store/apps/details?id=com.sony.easyconnect`) to make the NFC pairing work. When obtaining an app for your smartphone or other NFC-enabled device, make sure that the app actually works with that specific device and that you actually need an app (rather than just a setting change).

Making devices discoverable

Your Bluetooth device may have everything needed to create a pairing and still not create one because it isn't discoverable. Depending on the device, you may actually have to change a setting to make the device discoverable. Most smartphones and other Bluetooth devices automatically detect any discoverable devices within their range. When your device is within range and doesn't detect the device you want to pair with, check to ensure that the device is discoverable using the method prescribed in the user manual. Some devices are set not to be discoverable on purpose for convenience or security reasons.

Dealing with Environmental Factors

Environmental factors can contribute to issues with any sort of RF signal — not just NFC, Wi-Fi, Bluetooth, and the like. In addition, environmental factors can affect all application use cases and not just pairing. Unless you deal with the environmental factors, you will notice a serious drop in performance or potentially no signal at all.

REMEMBER

Of course, before you can diagnose any problem with your NFC connection, you need to verify that your underlying network (the one you want to use for pairing) is actually working. Otherwise, no amount of effort on your part will make the NFC part of the picture work. Users generally conclude that any failure of making the connection using NFC is specific to NFC, so you won't necessarily know at the outset that the problem is actually with Bluetooth or Wi-Fi.

After determining that your underlying network is working, you can begin tackling any NFC-specific issues. The following sections give an overview of some of the environmental factors to consider when working through networking problems of various sorts.

Considering the effects of water

Water and water vapor can cause all sorts of networking problems. From an NFC perspective, you need to ensure that any tags you use in a moist environment are rated to perform in that environment. Oddly enough, weather plays an important role. Consider any environment in which the outside air strongly interacts with materials you use to create an NFC environment as potentially moist. Even high humidity has been known to cause paper to become damp — not to the point of being wet, but wet enough to cause problems with the tags that you're using.

However, it's not just your NFC devices you need to consider, but the effects on the supporting technologies as well. For example, a damp environment can cause problems for antennas, access points, devices, and even cabling that isn't specifically designed for such environments.

REMEMBER

Water also tends to complicate RF transmission. You can't transmit any signal through a water environment — the water simply absorbs the energy (which is why microwaves work as they do in cooking food). Sometimes the presence of water is obvious, such as a swimming pool. However, you might not consider the fish tank that you set up to entertain customers as much of a threat, even though it can cause problems. Water tanks and other sources of water (or water-like substances) can also cause problems, and sometimes they're hidden in plain sight (such as the commode tank that interferes with line-of-sight connectivity).

Considering the effects of metal

Metal can be a huge problem for networks. Unfortunately, business environments are surrounded by metal, and you find metal in all sorts of other places, too. In fact, metal often hides in places you might not expect. For example, some plastics for electronics are painted with a metal to reduce electromagnetic interference.

REMEMBER

NFC isn't affected by metal as much as other wireless technologies because you aren't working with large distances. However, as noted earlier in the chapter, users commonly associate problems that occur with other kinds of networks in pairing scenarios with NFC, so you need to know a little more than just the NFC-specific metal issues. Here are some common mistakes to avoid if you want your NFC pairing with other RF technologies to work as expected:

- >> Placing access points, antennas, tags, or any other stationary item required to make communication next to a thick wall often causes loss of data rate because the wall absorbs part of the signal.

- >> Misdirecting a directional antenna causes the signal to go in the wrong direction, sometimes making communication impossible.

- >> Painting any access point, antenna, tag, or other stationary item required to make communication often results in the failure of the device (or at least an inability to communicate with it).

- >> Using a metal enclosure to hold any communication device (including user terminals) results in the Faraday cage effect (http://science. howstuffworks.com/faraday-cage.htm), in which the enclosure absorbs all the signal.

- >> Ignoring the effects of human usage often causes communication devices to fail in unexpected ways. For example, a hand next to a headset can interfere with the antenna, as can trying to move the signal through someone's head (where the signal has no direct path to travel, except through a person's head).

TIP

You need to think outside the box when it comes to signal issues. Some ceramic tile contains metal, as do decorations such as mirrors. Changing the locations of devices, antennas, and decorations can sometimes fix a seemingly unsolvable problem. The important thing is to change one item at a time and perform your tests again. Otherwise, you'll never know what is causing your problem and may eventually cause it again by moving the item back into the wrong place.

Eliminating sources of interference

Remember that RF energy doesn't understand that it shouldn't mix with the signals from that microwave. Likewise, the garage door and other gizmos you rely on daily don't mean to cause interference. Any device that produces RF energy can interfere with your ability to pair NFC with other technologies to produce a useful result. In many cases, ensuring that the line-of-sight transmission path is clear keeps this interference from happening, but you need to perform tests to be sure.

You may also have to consider using multiple channel devices. When a device detects that it has problems using one channel, it can automatically switch to another to keep the connection working. These devices normally allow you to manually select a channel as well, so you can help things along by making the channel used for communication the one with the least interference.

Considering Potential Security Issues

This chapter doesn't discuss security from the perspective of data loss or corruption, but the issues discussed in the chapter can also affect your data. For example, a hacker who has installed applications on various devices under control steals resources that will cause the network to run slowly or perhaps not at all. Even if an application isn't causing any other damage, the loss of resources is a problem that many people don't think about.

You can also have direct hacker threats to your network. For example, a hacker can launch a Distributed Denial of Service (DDOS) attack that uses all the bandwidth your network has to offer. Unfortunately, sometimes the issue isn't caused by a hacker and isn't truly a DDOS attack, either. An incorrectly configured device can continue pinging the network and cause it to fail. The effect is the same — you can't get the network to work, but the causes are different.

Wireless technologies invite all sorts of problems. One of the most common problems is that other people tend to use your resource uninvited. At one point, businesses had to deal with the whole issue of warchalking (http://www.computer weekly.com/feature/The-demise-of-the-warchalkers), the act of marking a building to show whether it offered open Wi-Fi service. Of course, now you can get free Wi-Fi in so many places that activities such as warchalking are no longer needed, but people still borrow network bandwidth nonetheless (sometimes inadvertently when the network is configured incorrectly).

The best way to overcome these kinds of problems is to ensure that you properly secure your network by requiring a password to access any resources. Of course, you also need to secure all the networking elements, such as the network router. Make sure that any devices you use rely on WPA2-PSK (AES) security. Any older technologies are insecure at this point and will cause you problems.

REMEMBER

Security and speed usually conflict with each other. The same is true for any networking connection you create. Adding security reduces network speed. However, you need to contrast this slight loss of speed with the major loss of speed that occurs when someone attaches to your network and uses the resource it provides. Generally, losing a little speed to ensure that your network remains secure is better than losing a lot of speed when someone decides that your network looks like a dandy place to use for nefarious purposes.

5

The Part of Tens

IN THIS PART . . .

Discovering where you can find ten really interesting sources of NFC information

Understanding how the right NFC resource can give you a competitive edge in the marketplace

Locating ten amazing NFC implementations

Considering ten NFC trends that truly speak about the viability of this technology

Finding out about ten influential NFC companies

Chapter 14

Ten Places to Find NFC-Specific Information

This book helps you gain an understanding of everything NFC. It points out all the practical benefits of using NFC for all sorts of tasks in your organization and including it in your personal life. The technical topics show you how NFC works, and you discover how to troubleshoot issues when the technology stops working as you think it should. In fact, reading this book makes you ready to use NFC to do all sorts of amazing things. Of course, NFC is a growing technology. It changes almost daily to meet new needs and answer new questions. With this in mind, you also need to know where to find the latest insights into how NFC is changing, which is what this chapter provides. Using these ten resources to keep your NFC information updated will make you stand out from everyone else.

REMEMBER

Of course, the NFC Bootcamp (http://www.nfcbootcamp.com) is also constantly updating its information. Not only can you get additional NFC training, but you can find lots of great articles on the blog (https://www.nfcbootcamp.com/blogs/). Make sure that you also keep up with the latest NFC Bootcamp resources (https://www.nfcbootcamp.com/nfc-resources/), videos (https://www.nfcbootcamp.com/videos/), press releases (https://www.nfcbootcamp.com/press-releases/), and events (https://www.nfcbootcamp.com/event-registration/). Make NFC Bootcamp the first place you visit when you need to know more.

NFC Forum

http://www.nfc-forum.org/

The NFC Forum is the first place you should go for insights into everything regarding NFC standards and applications. This site provides you with these kinds of information:

>> NFC basics

>> N-mark basics and usage

>> Products that use NFC

>> Developer resources for NFC

>> NFC specifications

>> NFC certification

The site also provides a blog that discusses the latest advances in NFC technology. You can learn about NFC events and discover NFC news.

Smart Card Alliance

http://www.smartcardalliance.org/

Smart cards are an important part of NFC because they appear in so many forms and vendors use them in so many ways. The Smart Card Alliance makes keeping up with the latest developments in smart card technology easy. In fact, the section devoted to white papers and case studies can also provide ideas for smart card uses for your organization.

TIP

Interestingly enough, you can find NFC-specific topics such as Mobile/NFC and Transit/NFC. Make sure to check out the NFC Resource page at `http://www.smartcardalliance.org/smart-cards-applications-nfc/` for NFC specifics. The amount of NFC information on this site might surprise you because it's not something that most people would expect to find.

The Smart Card Alliance is active in hosting events, including the annual NFC Solutions Summit conference, which is the largest NFC-focused event in the United States. Separate sections on government uses for smart card technology will interest anyone who works with the government or has government contracts. In short, this is the place to go when you need to do anything with smart cards, NFC, or payments.

Groupe Speciale Mobile Association (GSMA)

`http://www.gsma.com/`

This is the place to go if you need to learn more about mobile standards. The organization was formed in 1995 to promote the use of GSM technology, which has become the most widely accepted technology used for mobile phones throughout the world. You can probably find a listing for nearly any topic on this site. However, the top-level topics include issues such as

>> Network 2020 (the future of mobile computing)

>> Personal data

>> Digital commerce

>> The mobile economy

>> Mobile for development

REMEMBER

When visiting this site, you find a number of NFC-specific areas mixed in. For example, you can find a discussion of NFC and digital commerce at `http://www.gsma.com/digitalcommerce/nfc-in-digital-commerce`. Make sure to check out the NFC-related topics in the newsroom at `http://www.gsma.com/newsroom/tag/near-field-communications/`. In addition, seminars (such as the one at http://www.gsma.com/digitalcommerce/near-field-communication-can-mobile-nfc-enrich-transportation-services) provide you with the latest information about applying NFC in various situations.

NFC World

http://www.nfcworld.com

This site provides you with a major source of news for NFC-related product topics (with other sorts of news mixed in). In fact, you see links to this site in a number of places in this book. In addition to news, you also have access to the following:

>> Webinars

>> Whitepapers

>> Various resources (such as determining whether your smartphone has NFC support)

>> Events

>> Partner resources

>> Support (through an expert question blog)

NFC Times

http://www.nfctimes.com

Whereas NFC World provides quite a lot of product news, this site is more oriented toward technology news. You also find feature length articles, blogs, and event listings. A profile listing tells you about companies and organizations that are involved with NFC development. A project listing describes ongoing NFC products that help you see the direction that NFC is taking. You can also get the content sent to your inbox simply by registering for it.

NearFieldCommunication.org

`http://nearfieldcommunication.org/`

Every technology requires an educational site, and this site is it for NFC. The goal of this site is to educate everyone about the benefits of using NFC in various ways to meet specific goals. Even though it might initially look like a site for organizations and companies, you can find helpful resources for just about anyone. The educational content of this site is split into three areas:

>> **How it works:** Provides discussions of how NFC works and how it compares to other technologies.

>> **Using NFC:** Describes how to use NFC to perform practical tasks. It also tells you where you might find NFC used today.

>> **Technology and alternatives:** Specifies how NFC compares to other technologies. You gain an understanding of where NFC works best, times when you combine NFC with other technologies, and cases in which alternatives might provide a better answer.

Pymnts.com

`http://www.pymnts.com/`

The emphasis of this site is on telling you how people are paying for things today and how they'll pay for them in the future. It may not seem as though paying for things would take up much space, but this site tells you that the whole process involves more than meets the eye. For example, you can learn about the latest in virtual reality payments. You can also discover the ins and outs of using Bitcoins. The site is divided into the following areas:

>> News

>> Opinion

>> Exclusive series (longer articles)

>> Data and research

>> Media center (where you can watch webinars)

>> Company spotlight (where you can learn more about the players)

>> Events

Many of the articles go beyond just paying for things. For example, you find articles about the ethical way of handling problems. Some articles discuss topics on how to handle promotions or dealing with consumer passions. You even find advice on how to fix things when a marketing effort goes wrong.

EverydayNFC

http://everydaynfc.com/

This site is essentially a blog that provides you with helpful insights into everything NFC. The articles touch on various NFC topics that express an informed opinion on the direction that NFC is taking. You also find links for

» Events

» Resources

» Use cases

Gartner

http://www.gartner.com/it-glossary/near-field-communication-nfc

Gartner is known for the trend-based research it provides. You find the results of Gartner researches everywhere — even outside the IT community. It's not surprising, then, that you can find NFC-specific research on the Gartner site. At the top of the page, you find a basic NFC definition. However, the list of research papers and webinars is what you really want to look at.

REMEMBER

As with many of the offerings Gartner provides, you must pay for the pleasure of reading the NFC research. The webinars are also paid experiences, and you must sign up to attend. However, if you look at the right side of the page, you see a Free Research link that you can click to find useful information that costs you nothing to view.

IHS Technology

`https://technology.ihs.com/Search?q=Near+Field+communication`

IHS Technology is a global information company that provides most of its resources as a paid subscription. The company gives you global market, industry, and technical expertise to help make important business decisions. The NFC-related materials help you decide between various products and technologies that emphasize the way you do business. As with many sites listed in this chapter, IHS Technology provides you with solutions for specific needs and hosts events that emphasize specific technologies.

REMEMBER

The number of articles that any search turns up will likely be more than you want to check. Fortunately, you can use the filters on the left side of the page to reduce the number of articles you need to check. For example, you might choose to limit the results to a particular kind of research (such as reports) or a particular industry (such as consumer electronics).

Chapter 15

Ten Really Cool NFC Implementations

E ven though the book shows you an abundant number of uses for NFC, space doesn't allow me to provide you with more than a glimmer of all the uses currently available. NFC truly is appearing in all sorts of places that you'd never think about because it provides such a flexible method for sharing data of various sorts. Previous chapters focus on specific examples of NFC technology that help you understand how NFC works and how you can use it to perform useful work.

REMEMBER

This chapter views NFC product uses from a different perspective. In this chapter, you discover some of the cool uses for NFC that makes it a technology to not only meet but also truly exceed your expectations. The point of the examples in this chapter is to demonstrate that you can make NFC perform tasks that no one has thought about yet, and expect it to fulfill the needs of those tasks completely. The only thing that limits your use of NFC technology is your imagination. This chapter is all about demonstrating that if you can imagine a use, you can probably make it happen.

Harvard Medical School and Brigham and Women's Hospital

Anyone who has visited a hospital knows that every patient has a wristband that provides identification information. In recent years, that wristband has sported a bar code that the health care professional scans to record a patient's identity. The only problem is that bringing in the scanning equipment and performing the actual barcode scanning is a cumbersome and time-consuming process. NFC is being piloted to reduce the time involved in identifying and verifying that the right patient is getting the right medication.

Harvard Medical School's teaching affiliate Brigham and Women's Hospital (BWH) now uses an NFC setup in place of the bar codes (http://www.brighamandwomens.org/about_bwh/publicaffairs/news/publications/DisplayCRN.aspx?articleid=2106). A health care provider taps a Google Nexus 7 tablet (https://www.asus.com/us/Tablets/Nexus_7/) on the patient's wristband, on the medication, and on the health care provider's badge. The new system verifies that the patient is receiving the correct medication, at the correct dose, at the right time, and verifies who is giving the medication. In short, the system reduces the time it takes to administer medications to patients and eliminates the need for specific barcode reading equipment.

Blue Bite

The Rock the Vote campaign (https://www.youtube.com/watch?v=UhU4tV2KPew&feature=player_embedded) provides an example of NFC used to make people aware of a campaign (political, in this case) and to help them engage in it. People simply tapped their phones against the smart poster to load an app that allowed them to register to vote. It didn't matter where users lived; the app worked fine for any state. In short, the app made registering easy because the user didn't have to go anywhere special or do anything hard to register to vote.

TIP

Businesses are always looking for new ways to target consumers, and this NFC use does just that. An ad on a smart poster can engage consumers or educate people about specific needs. The technology works the same in any case — only the targeting of the smart poster differs. Because the cost of this sort of campaign is relatively small, even out-of-home businesses can use it to offer all sorts of things:

>> Special offers

>> Coupons

>> Social media check-ins

>> Event networking and information

>> Anything else you can imagine

Galatea: Jewelry by Artist

Imagine being able to create a beautiful piece of jewelry that does more than just look good. This use of NFC is probably one of the most personal you will find online right now. The jewelry, an artistic pearl called Momento (http://galateausa. com/videos/momento-introduction-135.html), contains an NFC chip that you can encode with a message. Tap the jewel against your NFC-enabled device and you

>> Hear the message that the sender wants to provide

>> View images of special importance

>> Watch videos of a special event

You can read more about this offering at http://www.nfcbootcamp.com/nfc-can-capture-moment/ and http://www.jckonline.com/2015/06/09/wearable-tech-on-your-ring-finger-one-ring-to-hold-your-memories-other-to-track-your-partner. The point is that NFC provides the means to record media that someone can enjoy for a lifetime. Because NFC doesn't require a battery, you never need to worry about losing that special message, even when the loved one is gone.

NFC Ring

Most people associate rings with decoration or possibly with a special event (such as marriage or graduating from college). However, rings now have taken on a new meaning. Instead of being a passive item to wear, a ring can also unlock doors and mobile devices, transfer information, and link people when it sports NFC technology. Amazingly, just about anything you can do with an NFC tag is potentially possible with an NFC ring. The advantage of wearing an NFC ring is that it's always available. In addition, you're less likely to lose it. You can wear it all the time, just like any other ring. Check out the additional information available for this product at `https://www.kickstarter.com/projects/mclear/nfc-ring-2016-range-one-smart-ring-unlimited-possi`. And I wouldn't be surprised to see these NFC rings being used for making payments in the future.

Khushi Baby

Ensuring that a child receives proper vaccinations can be hard, especially in the developing world. The child may not see the same medical provider all the time, and obtaining records may prove difficult at best. The Khushi Baby device (`http://khushi-baby.blogspot.com/`) makes tracking which vaccinations a child has had easier. The child wears an NFC pendant or bracelet containing all the required vaccination information so that it doesn't matter which provider is offering service. You can read more about this use of NFC technology at `http://www.dnaindia.com/lifestyle/report-that-thing-around-their-necks-2119889`.

Rémy Martin

The product of interest is cognac, but it applies to the alcohol industry as a whole, and quite possibly far more than that. Producers of spirits are becoming more aware that customers want some sort of digital connection with the vendor, so they have started spending more on digital media (`http://www.warc.com/LatestNews/News/Booze_brands_back_digital.news?ID=34944`). However, the direction that this form of marketing is taking could apply to just about any other product. Expect to find NFC used to provide shoppers with all sorts of incentives at some point. You simply tap the box on the shelf to determine whether the vendor is offering loyalty points, coupons, or some other incentive to buy. Tapping a ready-made pie crust could put a recipe for using it on your smartphone — the possibilities are endless.

REMEMBER

What makes the Rémy Martin offering interesting is that the NFC chip also lets you determine whether the cognac is authentic and the bottle unopened (`http://www.geek.com/mobile/remy-martin-puts-nfc-chip-in-its-cognac-to-prove-they-are-genuine-1626926/`). Given the cost of the cognac, providing this authentication feature is important. As this use of NFC develops, expect to find it with medical supplies and then with other products. At some point, tapping a product will tell you whether anyone has tampered with it so that you can make your purchase safely.

Tracking the Things You Love

Whether your children are your actual offspring or of the four-legged variety, NFC provides solutions that make tracking them down quite easy. In addition, the information that someone can obtain about the child or pet is significantly greater than other sorts of tracking devices provide. The following sections describe two such devices (one for children and another for pets).

Tappy

All parents' nightmare is going to an event with lots of crowds and losing their children. Over the years, parents have tried all sorts of methods for keeping track of their children (even putting them in a harness and attaching a leash). With the Tappy NFC hat, you don't have to tether your children to keep track of them. If they wander, someone just needs to tap the child's hat to discover how to contact you. You can read more about this product at `http://www.gizmag.com/tappy-nfc-hats-find-lost-chidren/38150/`.

PetHub

Pets often go for a walk without their master's knowledge. After all, there is that interesting tree across the street that master has never deigned to visit or the squirrel that keeps taunting a poor dog. Of course, cats need to visit with the wonderful woman across the road because she gives such wonderful treats. The reasons for pets wandering off are many, but the results are always the same. The family spends a great deal of time worrying and wandering the streets looking for the lost pet. Sometimes, the pet never comes home because no one knows quite where it belongs.

WARNING

Embedded chips have been around for a long time. However, they come with some issues — the most important of which is that you need a reader to interact with one. An embedded chip can also cause problems for the pet, such as irritation and infection (`https://www.vetinfo.com/the-side-effects-of-microchipping-dogs.html`). Even though embedded chips look like a good alternative (and they do have the advantage that they remain with the pet no matter what), you need to consider the health risks before getting one.

The NFC solution provided by PetHub (https://www.pethub.com/) solves these issues. Anyone can read the chip using an NFC-enabled device, and the tag doesn't cause any problems for the pet. You can even obtain a free, basic ID tag to start. The free tag provides you with the opportunity to determine whether the tag solution will work with your pet. You can read more about this product at http://www.prweb.com/releases/2013/4/prweb10613712.htm.

London History Museum

For some people, spending an entire day or two or even three at a museum is sheer joy. Reading everything possible about each of the exhibits helps a person picture the history of the offering in question. It's not enough to simply know that the offering existed, but also who used it, who created it, why it was created, how it worked, shortcomings, and on and on. A curator could possibly write a *War and Peace*–length novel about each item and still not satisfy the hungry mind. Making more information available to these rabid consumers of knowledge is just one way in which NFC can make a visit to a museum more delightful.

The London History Museum has installed NFC RFID tags in both of its locations, according to the article at http://www.rfidjournal.com/articles/view?8705/2. The tags allow users to do all sorts of interesting things. Here are a few of the ways in which you might see the tags used:

>> Getting vouchers for discounts at the museum shop

>> Linking to a museum server site where users can purchase special exhibit tickets

>> Obtaining exhibit-related information that isn't printed on signs in the museum

>> Linking users to social media sites

>> Viewing photos of art objects or artifacts in the museums' archives

Anyone could use these same sorts of ideas to extend the effectiveness of any informational presentation. Imagine how much more effective a kiosk becomes when linked to outside sources in various ways. Trade shows take on a new meaning when the results of viewing items in a booth continue long after the show is over.

Oxfam

All sorts of organizations vie for the few dollars you can afford to donate to a worthy cause. The problem is trying to figure out which of these organizations provides the best use of your dollars to support a cause that interests you. In most cases, you learn of new organizations through posters or through other supporters who really can't tell you the whole story. Even when they can provide you with a decent amount of information, you still don't know where to send a donation.

The NFC-based app provided by Oxfam (`http://www.civilsociety.co.uk/directory/company/305/oxfam`) solves these issues. You can tap a smart poster or the bracelet worn by a supporter to gain additional information about the organization. The associated app also lets you make a donation after you see what the organization is doing with the funds. You can read more about this application at `http://www.civilsociety.co.uk/fundraising/news/content/19470/oxfam_trials_tap-to-donate_technology`.

TIP

An interesting aspect of this particular NFC use is that it could apply to all sorts of fundraising. The emphasis is on the low cost of the advertising and the potential for a good payback. As the technology comes down in price, you can expect to find it in other places. For example, imagine a school or other organization using wristbands to help parents and other supporters obtain the information needed for a fundraising effort. An app could allow parents and other interested individuals to sign up to help with various activities. No longer would anyone have to rely on word of mouth to get the job done (often with a lot of miscommunication involved). The app could even do things like update the parent's calendar. (No more forgotten school events.)

Skylanders Superchargers

Skylanders is an incredibly popular gaming technology that embeds NFC technology in the gaming pieces. I also mention this game in the "Having fun with games" section of Chapter 1. Of course, there is a lot more than meets the eye with this game. The "Playing games" section of Chapter 9 provides you with additional information of just how this technology works. If the characters don't provide enough fodder for your imagination, you need to check out the video at `https://www.skylanders.com/?utm_campaign=skylanders-superchargers-launch-us`. Skylanders Superchargers offers you the capability to use your characters in ways you hadn't really imagined before, and it has vehicles that take you just about anywhere by land, sea, and air.

Imitation is the sincerest form of flattery (cliché, but it expresses the idea well). Given that Skylanders has become so incredibly popular, you can now find similar offerings from other vendors. For example, you may have wanted to become Captain Jack Sparrow for a day (go ahead, admit it) after seeing him evade the blundering British Navy so many times (well, not always). Disney has the solution you need at http://www.theverge.com/2013/8/21/4643924/disney-infinity-review, along with a host of other characters. You can let your imagine provide you with hours of fun, all courtesy of NFC-based characters.

Those of you who grew up playing Nintendo games, such as Super Mario Brothers (and all the other Mario offshoots), will love the idea of having your own NFC-based Super Mario Brother. Nintendo has also gotten into the game with all its offerings, as described at http://www.gamesradar.com/what-is-amiibo/.

Of course, you may like all three offerings but aren't sure which one to invest in first. Fortunately, you can find reviews of these various products online and a great comparison of them at http://www.gamesradar.com/amiibos-vs-skylanders-vs-disney-infinity/. The bottom line is that Skylanders is setting the bar for NFC-based toys, but that all the offerings have one thing in common: They're a ton of fun to play.

Chapter 16

Ten NFC Trends

Trends help you predict the future of a technology. A trend is a sort of crystal ball that helps you determine where to place time and resources in making the best use of a new technology to meet specific needs. Of course, you have to know what those needs are before you can make such an assessment. The rest of this book helps you see the benefits of NFC for businesses of various types and provides you with examples of how NFC technology is being used today. This chapter is all about creating a crystal ball so that you can see how NFC will be used in the future.

REMEMBER

Be aware that the NFC market is growing. According to a report recently released by Report Linker, forecasters expect the market to reach $21.84 billion by 2020, at a Compound Annual Growth Rate (CAGR) of 17.1 percent between 2015 and 2020, with the retail and consumer electronics industries currently dominating the NFC market.

The retail industry is one of the most prominent applications of the market because mobile commerce and cashless transactions are growing worldwide. In 2014, the retail industry accounted for a 60 percent share of the total market. Retail owners and many other stakeholders also support deploying NFC to help streamline purchasing and reduce the use of cash and plastic credit cards, the latter because it is plagued by fraud. Consumer electronics applications also held a prominent share of the NFC market with the demand for NFC technology in devices such as wearable electronics, cameras, mobile phones, and others supporting the growth of the market. You can read more about the NFC market at http://www.prnewswire.com/news-releases/near-field-communication-market-by-operating-mode-product intelligent NFC PoS terminals--software-industry-and-geography---global-forecast-to-2020-300182256.html.

You should also realize that many nonpayment use cases exist for NFC that require some form of user credential such as a ticket, identity badge, or loyalty card. The whitepaper at http://www.smartcardalliance.org/wp-content/uploads/NFC-Non-Payments-Use-Cases-v23-121715-clean.pdf provides you with a great discussion of these uses. Now that you have your appetite whetted for some interesting NFC trends, read the sections that follow to get a better picture of where they might fit within your business or personal needs.

Moving from Tap-to-Pay to Tap-to-Buy

It's no secret that people are increasingly using mobile payment options. According to the article at http://dazeinfo.com/2015/11/23/apple-pay-android-pay-samsung-pay-lg-pay-nfc-mobile-wallet-industry, NFC and mobile wallets are ready to take over retail.

At the forefront of the mobile payments revolution is the United States, with a staggering 61 percent of its population owning a smartphone. In 2015 alone, mobile payments have accounted for a total of $8.71 billion worth of transactions in the United States, with users spending an average of nearly $376 annually, using their mobile phone as a payment method. This number is expected to rise to $27.05 billion by 2016, with users spending an average of $721.47 annually.

Another trend emerging at the same time is online one-click buying. Amazon is spearheading this movement. When you see something online that you want to buy, you can just click and buy it. We see the convergence of these two trends with NFC again bridging the real world and the digital world. A precursor of this change is technologies like those offered at http://www.powa.com/powatag/ where you can scan a QR code on a product in a window display and buy it. In fact, this site offers solutions for

>> **Scanning:** Transforms existing marketing media such as billboards, printed materials, and ads into dynamic and immediate points of sale.

>> **Touching:** Allows the consumer to check out instantly online with one touch using a mobile or tablet device.

>> **Listening:** Embeds inaudible audio watermarks into any live or recorded broadcast, letting consumers purchase spontaneously and immediately.

>> **Interacting with social media:** Embeds URLs into social media feeds for easy impulse purchases.

>> **Interacting with email and SMS:** Embeds contact information in emails and SMS, providing an elegant scan or touch buying experience.

>> **Employing beacons:** Delivers personalized greetings and promotions to customers in physical locations using beacons (discreet low-power Bluetooth devices).

NFC can take this trend another step further. Imagine that every item sold is embedded with an NFC tag. So, if you see a friend wearing something you like, you can just tap it and buy it instantly. You won't need to go to the store or look online for the product. It's fast, easy, and extremely accurate. In this example, every piece of clothing becomes a digital sign and sales opportunity for the brand. In addition, consumers get convenience and accuracy in their shopping experience.

TIP

You can extend the embedded NFC tag approach to almost anything. For example, when visiting a friend's house, you might like a print hanging on the wall or a piece of furniture in the living room. All you have to do is tap it, buy it, and the store sends it to your house. It's guaranteed to be the exact product you want because the product info is in the product. Even if the manufacturer has discontinued that product, you can get suggestions as to a newer or similar version of that product.

Enhancing the Gaming Experience

NFC can create a new gaming experience for you — one that no one would have imagined even a few years ago. Companies such as Amiibo, Disney Infinity, Skylanders, and Lego Dimensions are creating these new toys that turn inanimate objects into the subjects of interactive video games (see the story at `http://www.polygon.com/features/2015/12/14/9868062/amiibo-disney-infinity-skylanders-lego-dimensions-a-guide-to-gaming`). The idea is that you load your character into the game using the physical toy. In fact, toys are big news. Online magazines, such as NFC World (`http://www.nfcworld.com/technology/toys/`) and Giant Bomb (`http://www.giantbomb.com/near-field-communication/3015-7431/games/`) provide heavy coverage of the topic.

Products such as Skylanders are examples from the gaming world that you've seen covered in other chapters of the book. However, the technology can do a lot more than simply offer a new kind of gaming experience. The video at `https://www.youtube.com/watch?v=c6ATOgEcR1U` provides a good example of how NFC can turn an everyday experience like eating at McDonalds into a fun experience for your kids, turning a static piece of furniture (a table) into an interactive digital experience. The Happy Table actually looks like a whole lot of fun — expect to see a few adults checking it out, too.

REMEMBER

NFC allows you to take any ordinary, everyday physical object and give it a digital expression. Another item around gaming is gamification (essentially turning a site or other entity into a gaming-like experience in which people can interact with objects in a richer way). Check out `http://www.poken.website/gamification/` as an example of how some companies are developing an inclusive gamification model. According to the article at `http://knowledge.wharton.upenn.edu/article/gamification-still-a-gamble-but-one-with-real-payoffs/`, gamification offers measurable results, and many companies see it as a means for improving employee productivity.

Improving Health care

Health care consumes a considerable amount of cash and resources. It makes sense, then, that the use of mobile technology to reduce costs and to add efficiency is gaining support from insurance companies and enterprises. For example, insurance companies will use mHealth Apps (such as the one supported by iMedicalApps, `http://www.imedicalapps.com/`) to gather health data about customers and reward or penalize them. You can read more about the use of mHealth Apps and other trends shaping the mobile application industry at `http://www.huffingtonpost.com/young-entrepreneur-council/3-trends-shaping-the-mobi_b_8774786.html`.

Direct savings from things like health initiatives are just the tip of the iceberg, however. It's also important to ensure that patients get the right kind of medication, at the right time, and that the medication isn't tampered with in any way. Smart e-labels, such as those produced by Shreiner MediPharm, help ensure the quality of care that patients receive when it comes to medication. You can read more about this use of NFC at `http://www.packagingeurope.com/Packaging-Europe-News/65854/Mobile-Authentication-for-Product-and-Brand-Protection-in-the-Pharmaceutical-Industry.html`.

Just reducing the amount of health care paperwork is something that NFC can help accomplish. For example, every time you go to see a doctor, you have to fill out at least five pieces of paper on allergies, previous medical conditions, and so on. If all you had to do was tap your phone to have it automatically transfer your health care history to the doctor's office, everyone would realize a huge time and cost savings, not to mention a much-improved customer experience. More important, you can ensure the accuracy of the information recorded. You can read more about e-health care records at `https://www.cms.gov/Medicare/E-Health/EHealthRecords/index.html?redirect=/ehealthrecords/`.

Finally, you can find all sorts of products today that allow elderly and special-needs people live in their homes in relative comfort. Products like Life Alert allow a loved one to call for help when needed. Some devices are so feature rich now that the person doesn't even need to press a button; the device automatically senses a fall or some other tragedy. In the future, you can expect to find devices that sense problems, such as a stroke or heart attack, before they even happen. Of course, these devices get the emergency responders to the door, but that's not the end of the story.

REMEMBER

After the emergency responders gain access to the person, they need to know as much as possible about the person's needs. An emergency responder could have all sorts of questions, such as the kind of medications the person is taking. Unfortunately, the patient may not be able to respond, which is where EMS SignPost (`http://emssignpost.com/`) comes into play. This vendor produces a refrigerator magnet that provides emergency responders with all those crucial bits of information needed to save a life (read more at `http://www.rfidjournal.com/articles/view?13162`). The emergency responder just taps the refrigerator magnet, and the required information appears on a smartphone or other NFC-enabled device.

Creating New Marketing Strategies

Marketers are constantly developing new ways to make you aware of products you must have (even when you really don't need them at all). Personalizing the experience is one way that marketing has made the buying experience better. Your smartphone represents a personalized experience for you. It's where you keep your most personal information in many cases. That's why marketers are working hard to come up with mobile sales strategies that focus on deepening human relationships and leveraging the best that mobile has to offer to do so. Having a real human connection with someone who has taken time to get to know you is important.

The personalized touch will translate into more *Out-of-Home (OOH) marketing* (forms of marketing that people see or hear when they are outside their homes, such as, on buildings or public transport) as the use of ad blockers makes web advertising less effective. Imagine being able to tap with your smartphone to learn more about any product you see and then being able to buy that product without ever visiting a store. Now, imagine that beacons tell the user about store locations, discounts, and promotions to further enhance this experience.

Another NFC use to consider with marketing is the use of Digital-Out-of-Home (DOOH) technology, such as the use of smart posters to download exclusive content. Comicon used NFC a couple of years ago for content for the TV show *Under the Dome*, and Disney has advertised in Europe using NFC enabled tables at cafes. The options for keeping a potential customer's focus on your product are nearly limitless using a combination of OOH and DOOH.

After you begin acquiring sales potential, you need automation to perform tasks such as email automation, automated social post, and automated data entry. Tying up staff to address these needs is a poor use of resources. You need your staff to focus on extracting the most from customer feedback, interactions, budgets, criticisms, challenges, and failures. Of course, gathering all this information translates into the potential for using data analytics to make decisions on what actually happens to marketing efforts, rather than reacting to what you expect to happen.

Another powerful use of NFC as part of a marketing strategy is to gain highly personalized data at the point of interest that can move people to action. Basically, NFC provides *small,* highly personal data from individual interactions, which in turn power *big* data and analytics. Every tap of a smart poster logs data on location, opt-in information, contact info where provided, and more, providing a clearer picture of customer behavior through analytics, providing your marketing staff with actionable information to make decisions on what actually happens with your marketing efforts instead of having to react to what you expect to happen.

Managing Events

You're sponsoring an event and you want the whole thing to go off flawlessly. Yet, many events start by making the whole sign-in experience as error ridden and hopelessly slow as possible. Now imagine that your attendees have a wearable

NFC device. You can now offer a streamlined response to the attendee's registration, payment, and engagement needs. In addition to making the attendee's experience better, you can also make your organization's experience better with nonintrusive automatic tracking. Employees can literally watch the event statistics arrive in real time so that they can handle glitches before anyone even notices. You can read more about how NFC can improve the attendee experience by automating transportation, improving attendee tracking, and providing smarter breakout scheduling at http://ungerboeck.com/fr/blog/the-effect-of-near-field-communication-on-the-events-industry.

Theoretical uses of NFC to make event hosting better is one thing, but finding real-world examples is another. Fortunately, you can find a number of such examples, including the use of NFC RFID for the Salt Lake Comic Con FanX event (http://www.rfidjournal.com/articles/view?12664). In this case, the technology reduced the length of lines in front of the venue's entrance, prevented fraud, and collected information regarding attendees during the event. In fact, the technology has proven so successful that is has been used for three such events, and the host plans to increase the use of NFC RFID for other purposes.

By now, you might be wondering where you can get some of these technologies for your own use. Check out Poken (http://www.poken.com) for all sorts of event management, gamification, and related technologies. They're the experts at helping you make your event a success.

TIP

NFC technologies are helpful in allowing you to go green by reducing all the excess paper normally found at events today (such as all those brochures you pick up at a trade show and then throw away). In addition, the exhibitor can capture your interest in something by you tapping to collect brochures electronically versus picking something up and sticking it in a bag. The point is that you can make your event even more attractive by making attendees aware of the fact that you're working to keep the planet clean, while also attending to their needs in a more efficient way.

Enhancing the Effects of Mobile Commerce

Mobile commerce (payments, loyalty, and couponing) makes it possible for you to offer potential customers incentives for buying your product or service in real time. A recent Business Intelligence (BI) report states that by 2020, mobile commerce will make up 45 percent of total e-commerce, equaling $284 billion in sales. That exceeds expectations for 2016 by more than three times: BI Intelligence predicts mobile commerce will hit 20.6 percent of overall e-commerce, or $79 billion (see `http://www.startupsmart.com.au/technology/mobile-ad-spending-lags-behind-usage-six-key-digital-trends-from-kpcb/2015052814831.html` and `http://digiday.com/brands/mobile-commerce-going-2016/` for additional details). In fact, it's important to realize that people use their smartphones a great deal — with Americans spending an average 5.3 hours per day on the Internet, and 51 percent of that time (or 2.7 hours) spent via a mobile device, according to StartupSmart.com/au. They may as well be learning about your product or service, too. Given the impressive growth of mobile commerce, it could potentially surpass e-commerce someday. Even if it doesn't, you definitely want as many venues as possible for making a sale.

Of course, NFC is a big part of this picture, as described in other sections of the chapter. For more information on current mobile commerce trends, visit `http://www.moovweb.com/blog/mobile-commerce-trends-2016/`. The point is that you need to embrace NFC as part of your mobile commerce strategy because it's easy to get people to tap on smart posters and other forms of communication to get the information they need.

Making the Most of Wearables

Even though you may not know too many people using wearables today, the use of wearables will increase. For example, a wearable allows people to easily make payments. A watch is on your wrist at all times. The watch company Swatch is making it easy to keep track of the time and make payments using a single device that you don't have to constantly worry about losing (`http://www.pcmag.com/article2/0,2817,2495803,00.asp`). The same NFC technologies that work for your smartphone also work for a wearable, so it doesn't matter how you create the connection, just as long as the connection is made when making a payment. Manufacturers have created all sorts of other options for wearables that you can use to make payments, as shown in the following list (along with an article that gives you more information):

» **Rings:** `http://www.creditcardguide.com/credit-cards/pay-by-ring-jacket-cuff-lines-between-fashion-finance-blur.html`, and `http://www.wareable.com/fashion/house-of-hollands-lfw-ss16-nfc-rings-shoppable-catwalk-1713`

» **Smart Watches, Fitness Trackers, and Payment Wristbands:** `http://www.prnewswire.com/news-releases/wearable-payments-contactless-nfc-rfid-and-qrbarcode-payment-technologies-for-smart-watches-fitness-trackers-and-payment-wristbands-300186376.html`

>> **Glasses, Band-Aids, and Other Future Wearables:** http://www.information-age.com/technology/applications-and-development/123460636/current-and-future-applications-wearable-technology

Interacting with Smart Appliances

Smart appliances may not seem very exciting at first because some of the ways in which manufactures designed them in the past provided features that weren't necessary or easy to use. However, new ways to interact with smart appliances really are smart and useful, too. For example, in the future, you might tap your new appliance and the application will prompt you to register for the product warranty. Of course, that's usually just a single use. But it could help with things like automating annual maintenance issues like changing air filters, lubricating parts, and so on. Another smart appliance use comes when you get an error message on the appliance. Instead of going to YouTube to figure out how to fix it, you just tap the machine. The machine responds by asking whether you want to see videos on how to fix it, call customer support where the problem is pre-identified to the customer service rep, automatically order the replacement part and have it shipped to your house, or set up an appointment for the repair person to come out.

The smart home appliance market is expected to reach $38.35 billion worldwide by 2020 (http://www.wdrb.com/story/30693200/smart-home-appliances-market-is-expected-to-reach-3835-billon-worldwide-by-2020). In other words, many people already realize the potential of smart appliances to make life easier. Some pundits attribute the growing interest in smart appliances to energy costs. After all, if your air conditioner can find a way to save money while keeping your home cool, it's a win for everyone (except maybe the utility company). Of course, NFC will come into play by helping you monitor the various smart appliances in your home. A tap with your smartphone will make it possible for you to verify that your air conditioner actually is saving you money. Tapping your other appliances to create a connection could allow you to automate some tasks and perform others manually from a remote location. The idea is that the application would be able to communicate with you as needed but also take over many of the tasks that you must perform manually today.

REMEMBER

To actually make these technologies useful, every appliance will need to communicate in the same way and in a manner that your smartphone understands. Consequently, new standards for creating these communications (such as the one discussed at https://ec.europa.eu/digital-agenda/en/blog/new-standard-smart-appliances-smart-home) are important. Eventually, you can expect NFC to let you connect your smartphone to every appliance in your home so that you don't ever have to worry about the system that failed and left ice-cream dripping all over the floor.

Authenticating Products

Counterfeit products have always been a problem. Previous chapters have discussed the problem with products such as wine. However, you need to be able to authenticate all sorts of products to ensure that you know what you're getting. A global economy brings global counterfeiting. Fortunately, companies such as NXP are working to let you easily authenticate products (read the details at http://media.nxp.com/phoenix.zhtml?c=254228&p=irol-newsArticle&ID=2118076). You simply tap the side of an item with your smartphone to determine whether it's authentic.

Most of the products that use authentication today are wines and spirits. The reason alcohol is attracting this sort of attention is simple: Financial losses due to counterfeiting and related activities globally have been accelerating at an alarming rate since around 2013 and are forecast to continue to grow at an annual rate of around 15.6 percent through 2019. That's an estimated annual loss of more than $1 billion, which means that any measure taken to easily distinguish fake from real products is enormously valuable.

Considering B2B Trends

Businesses have special needs that NFC can answer as well. Some of these needs fall into the areas of Occupational Safety and Health Administration (OSHA) compliance, attendance, paper reduction, and asset management. For example, Flexstr8 offers NFC-enabled labels for chemicals, pharmaceuticals, and consumer products. These on-demand labels make it easy to meet new (and upcoming) government and business regulations. You can read more about the specifics of this product at http://www.rfidjournal.com/articles/view?13368.

REMEMBER

Labeling requirements will continue to evolve. For example, in June 2015, OSHA updated the U.S. requirements for the labeling of hazardous chemicals, in accordance with the Globally Harmonized System of Classification and Labeling of Chemicals (GHS). The new labeling requires a product identifier, supplier information, a hazard and precautionary statement, and other details for each chemical product. Companies that sell such hazardous chemicals must not only print a large amount of information on a label attached to each product's container but also provide an application sheet to users of that chemical. The application sheet includes directions indicating how to handle and store the product, personal protection requirements, accidental release measures, and other precautions. And all this information must be kept with the product and accessible at all times, especially in case of an emergency. NFC can help solve these challenges by making that information readily and easily available in the cloud and accessible with the simple tap of a smart device.

Chapter 17

Ten NFC Companies You Need to Know About

Every technology has its list of businesses that influence the direction that the technology takes. For example, when you think about online application development, many developers immediately consider the effect Google has had on the industry. Likewise, many people would agree that Microsoft still owns the desktop. Of course, no single business influences technology in a vacuum, which is why you need to consider businesses other than Google and Microsoft when thinking about their respective fields of expertise. The same holds true for NFC. Some businesses provide enough influence to affect the direction that NFC takes as the technology matures. By knowing the names of these businesses, you gain an advantage over a competitor who isn't quite so aware. This chapter provides you with the names of ten companies that you really need to know about when it comes to NFC.

Blue Bite

http://www.bluebite.com

It probably hasn't escaped your notice that the world is becoming increasingly mobile. People use their mobile devices for everything. That's why you need to support mobile technology in every way possible. Any business that wants to remain relevant in today's world will have a mobile strategy. Blue Bite can help you create a viable mobile strategy with a lot less effort than you might otherwise need to expend. This site specializes in these areas:

>> mTAG

>> Analytics

>> Design

>> Deployment

TIP

Make sure that you don't get stuck looking at just the top of Blue Bite's page. The middle of the page contains some interesting case studies, and you can see the impressive list of brands that Blue Bite has worked with below that. At the bottom of the page are pictures of the people you'll work with — none of whom look like they'll bite. Hover your mouse over each picture, though, to have a bit of fun.

NXP

http://www.nxp.com

Despite every effort to shrink hardware into nonexistence, the world still relies on it to make technology work — and NFC is no different. Fortunately, you have access to NXP, a company that delves head-first into hardware of all sorts. In fact, here is a list of the sorts of products you can obtain from NXP (including those required to meet your NFC needs):

>> Amplifiers

>> Audio/radio

>> Bipolar transistors

>> Data converters

>> Diodes

>> ESD protection, TVS, filtering, and signal conditioning

>> Identification and security

>> Interface and connectivity

>> Logic

>> MOSFETs

>> Media processors

>> Microcontrollers

>> Power management

>> RF

>> Sensors

>> TV and STB front ends

>> Thyristors

One of the more important links on the site for anyone using NFC is NFC Everywhere (http://www.nxp.com/techzones/nfc-zone/overview.html). Make sure to check out this link for ideas on how NXP can meet your specific NFC hardware needs. NXP offers NFC help in these areas:

>> Controller solutions

>> Frontend solutions

>> Connected tags

>> Demo boards

Flomio

http://flomio.com/

This site is oriented toward the needs of developers and proximity ID technologies. You can find NFC, Bluetooth Low Energy (BLE), and Ultra-high Frequency (UHF) Radio Frequency Identification (RFID) solutions all in one place. As noted in other chapters in the book, these technologies often work together to create a complete solution, so it's nice to find them all in one place. The site design helps reduce the complexity normally associated with developing a solution by dividing solutions into four areas:

>> Tags

>> Readers

>> Middleware

>> Web services

TIP

One of the more interesting aspects of this site is the tags. Yes, you can find the usual assortment of chips, wristbands, and tags, but you also have access to dimensional solutions, such as Dorus the dragon (http://flomio.com/shop/nfc-tags/dimensional-nfc-tags/). The dimensional tags add the fun into creating an NFC solution. Interestingly enough, you can send Flomio your design for any 3D object (.STL format only) and Flomio will print some NFC solutions for you. The company even provides you with a few pointers to ensure that you get a great result.

Smartrac

https://www.smartrac-group.com/

Smartrac has the distinction of creating the fanciest and smartest phone case ever built (https://www.smartrac-group.com/the-fanciest-and-smartest-phone-case-ever-built.html). Many of the solutions you read about promote connectivity using more than one technology. In this case, the smartphone case incorporates a combination of NFC and RFID technologies.

REMEMBER

Even though the Smartrac site may initially seem to revolve around RFID, you can find plenty of NFC offerings as well. Check out the NFC inlays and tags at https://www.smartrac-group.com/nfc-inlays-tags.html. Most of these solutions are for serious business uses. For example, Smartrac stocks NFC tags on a roll that you can use to create multiple duplicate tags when necessary. Smartrac addresses a number of market segments, including

- >> Animal identification
- >> Automatic vehicle ID systems
- >> Car access
- >> Electronics and gaming
- >> Enterprise access control
- >> Government eID
- >> Health care
- >> Industrial applications
- >> Leisure and entertainment
- >> Media and document management
- >> Payment
- >> Public transportation
- >> Retail
- >> Supply chain and asset management

HID Global

http://www.hidglobal.com

If it has anything to do with identity, HID Global has a solution. NFC appears in the forefront on this site, so you can wade right in looking for the solution you need. The vendor provides support for all sorts of ID solutions, including

- >> Asset tracking
- >> Access control
- >> Border protection
- >> Caregiver visits
- >> Identity management
- >> Embedded solutions

- » Resource access
- » Secure transactions
- » Visitor registration

HID Global has the solution you need for any sort of identity requirement. It also works with a broad range of industries, including

- » Banking and financial
- » Education
- » Enterprise and corporate
- » Government
- » Health care

One of the best parts about working with HID Global is the large number of partners it works with. You can find a partner company for any additional needs at `http://www.hidglobal.com/partners`. The fact that you can go to this single site for a complete solution (even if doing so requires working with a partner company) means that you can save considerable time and effort creating a solution.

Poken

`http://www.poken.com`

Making any event a success means creating connections that last and generating buzz that keeps people talking about your event for a long time afterward. NFC can help make that happen by reducing the effort required to obtain information from other people. A simple tap of two NFC enabled event "Pokens" makes it possible to exchange information, and tapping a smart poster provides long-term access to helpful information. Poken provides the resources to make events fun, successful, and much easier than in the past. Not only do the attendees benefit, but your organization benefits as well through additional tracking capability and reduced paperwork. When working with Poken, you obtain a complete event experience that includes

- » Networking
- » Digital collecting
- » Event management

- » Online visitor portal

- » Digital check in

- » Attendee tracking

- » Match making

- » Meetings manager

- » Registration

- » Gamification

- » Mobile apps

- » Sponsorship

Cellotape

http://www.cellotape.com

If you need to print it, Cellotape has a solution to do it. You can find any printing solution you can imagine and more than a few solutions you never thought about on this site. They are the leaders in custom NFC–embedded printing solutions. They can embed NFC into practically anything that you want or can imagine. All you really need to be able to do is describe what you need printed in order to begin creating your NFC solution. After you have some idea of precisely what Cellotape can do for you, you can obtain a quote for the work at http://www.cellotape.com/html/request_a_quote.html.

Advanced Card Systems (ACS) Holdings Limited

http://www.acs.com.hk/

Has ACS got a smart card solution for you! In fact, if you can't find it here, you're not likely to find it anywhere else. You can find cards in all sorts of form factors, including

- » Contact interface

- » Combi interface

>> Contactless interface

>> USB token

After you have a smart card solution in mind, make sure to get a reader in the form factor you need. ACS also has a broad range of readers that can meet just about any need. The reader form factors include

>> PC-linked smart card readers

>> PC-linked readers with mass storage

>> Contactless readers

>> Mobile card readers

>> Smart card readers with PIN pad

>> Dynamic password generators

>> Smart card reader modules

REMEMBER

In addition to selling you the hardware, ACS provides services, solutions, and support. For example, ACS performs card printing. They also offer product customization and new product development to meet specific solution requirements.

Thinfilm

http://www.thinfilm.no/

Browsing this site takes a while because you're too busy gawking at all the interesting uses of NFC technology it contains. Some of the technologies, such as smart medical injection devices, are potentially expected and perhaps even a little mundane. However, other technologies, such as the smart bottles, are both interesting and unique. Many of the solutions you find on this site revolve around anticounterfeiting, but they also include providing information to the product users.

Smartwhere

https://smartwhere.com/

Proximity solutions let you extend your reach directly to the consumer from a product shelf. Consider the advantages of being able to send a customer an ad or a coupon that directly relates to the product the customer is viewing at any given time. The use of this technology will increase sales because you're giving the customer a strong incentive to make the purchase. After all, few people can resist a combination of a good argument to buy a product and then a certain amount off to make the purchase as well. The suggested venues for this kind of technology include

>> Retail campaigns

>> In-store experiences

>> Museums

>> On-site mapping and Blue Dot

>> Events and venues

>> Integrated print campaigns

>> Social media campaigns

Index

G

G&D (Giesecke & Devrient), 44

Galatea, 235

games. *See also specific games by name*
  gamification, 244
  general discussion, 239–240, 243–245
  market trends, 242–243
  overview, 13, 159
  platforms, 160

gardening, NFC for, 162–163

Gartner, 230

Gemalto, 44, 74

Gentag, 149

gestures, showing intent with, 23–24

GHS (Globally Harmonized System of Classification and Labeling of Chemicals), 250

Giesecke & Devrient (G&D), 44

gift cards, 90, 166–167, 168

GiftCards.com, 166

glasses, 249

Globally Harmonized System of Classification and Labeling of Chemicals (GHS), 250

glucose monitoring, 149

Google devices, HCE support on, 87

Google Glass, 170, 171

Google Play, 184

Google Wallet, 42, 112, 113, 167

GoToTags, 195, 201, 202

Graham O'Sullivan Restaurants, 169

greetings, digital, 160–161

Groupe Speciale Mobile Association (GSMA), 227–228

gym, personal smartphone settings for, 131

H

hackers, 24, 127, 207–208, 222

half-duplex mode, 71–72

HALT command, 50

hand geometry recognition, 205

Happy Table, 243

hardware. *See also* antennas; NFC tags; operating modes
  adding NFC to existing devices, 73–75
  audio jack NFC readers, 92–93
  communication between devices, 71–73
  communication modes, 64
  controller chip, 58–62
  correct use of, 190–191
  development of, 80
  device readiness, 188–190
  emitters, 63
  glitches, 187
  interrogators versus tags, 68–69
  odd NFC behavior, 192–193
  overview, 57–58, 59
  sweet spot, 24, 191, 193–194, 215
  transfer of power, 70–71
  updating firmware, 218
  USB NFC readers, 92

Harvard Medical School, 234

hazardous chemicals, 250

HCE. *See* Host Card Emulation

headphones, 172

health care. *See also* data logger tags
  accessibility needs, 152–153
  Brigham and Women's Hospital, 234
  market trends, 242–243
  medical record access, 139–140
  medications, administrating, 140–141, 234, 244–245
  monitoring with NFC, 121
  overview, 137, 138–139
  patient progress, tracking, 141–143
  privacy issues, 138
  remote patient monitoring, 150–152
  scheduling therapy, 143–145
  stretchable skin, 172
  tracking doctors and nurses, 145

Hewlett-Packard Touch-to- Print app, 125–126

HID Global, 35, 42, 255–256

High Frequency Radio Frequency Identification (HF RFID), 35

PCD (proximity coupling device), 50

PCs. *See* computers

peer-to-peer communication mode, 9, 18, 36, 38, 67–68

Personal Identification Number (PIN), 43, 89

personal needs, using NFC for, 130–132

personal networking, 12

PetHub, 237–238

pets, NFC technology for, 172, 237–238

physical therapy, scheduling, 143–145

PICC (proximity inductive coupling card), 50

PIN (Personal Identification Number), 43, 89

PlayMemories Mobile App, 215

point-of-sale (POS) terminal, 11, 81, 82, 104, 107

Point-to-Point Encryption (PTPE), 90

Poken

 general discussion, 247, 256–257

 smart posters, 9

 tracking event attendance, 164–165

POS (point-of-sale) terminal, 11, 81, 82, 104, 107

powa.com, 242–243

power, transfer of, 70–71

presentations, exchanging, 12

Primary Account Number (PAN), 89, 104

printers with NFC capability, 125–126

producers, 19

products

 authentication, 236–237, 250

 management, 158

 tap-to-buy technology, 243

Professional NFC Audio Jack p2 reader/writer, Advanced Card Systems, 93

Progressive, 133

proprietary technologies, 35, 42, 48

Proximiant, 170

proximity cards, standard for, 38–39

proximity coupling device (PCD), 50

proximity ID technologies, 78, 97

proximity inductive coupling card (PICC), 50

PTPE (Point-to-Point Encryption), 90

Puzzle Alarm Clock plug-in, 199

Pymnts.com, 229–230

Q

Qfuse, 94

QR (Quick Response) codes, 26, 111–112, 132

QR Invoice, 112

QR Mobile Pay, 112

R

Radio Frequency Identification (RFID), 8, 16, 25–26, 40

Radio Frequency (RF) communication, 23, 220

RapidNFC, 93, 202

RBC (Royal Bank of Canada), 86

read and write mode, 18, 36, 65–67

reader chips, NFC, 61

readers, 16, 23, 24, 49

readiness, levels of, 188–190

real-estate management, 121

real-time tag tracking, 94–95

receipts, managing, 170

recipes, sharing, 169

Record Type Definition (RTD), 52, 175

records, NDEF, 52–54

Reel-to-Reel NFC Encoder, 202

Remember icon, 3

Rémy Martin, 236–237

Report Linker, 241

Request (REQA) command, 50

resellers, 80

resource usage, controlling with NFC, 124–126

retail industry, NFC in, 242

retina recognition, 205

RF (Radio Frequency) communication, 23, 220

RFID (Radio Frequency Identification), 8, 16, 25–26, 40

rings, 171–172, 235–236, 248

Rock the Vote campaign, 234–235

Rohde and Schwarz, 204

room entry systems, 122–123, 129

rooting, 86

Royal Bank of Canada (RBC), 86

RSVP process, 161

RTD (Record Type Definition), 52, 175

S

V

vaccinations, tracking, 236
vehicle-related technologies, 132–135
vein recognition, 206
vendors
  APIs, 96
  EMV cards, 117
  marketing strategies, 245–246
  patent protection, 39
  proprietary technology, 35, 42
  reliable sources of apps, 209
  use cases, 185
Ventra, 44
verification, cardholder, 116
video greetings, 160–161
Virtual Target Emulation, 85
Vital Scout, 146
vital signs, monitoring, 146, 172
VivaLink, 146
voice recognition, 205–206
voting campaign, 234–235
vWand, 139, 185

W

Wakeup (WUPA) command, 50
wallets, mobile. *See* mobile wallets
Walmart-pay, 111–112
warchalking, 222
Warning! icon, 3
watches, smart, 217–218, 248
water, problems due to, 195–196, 220
waving phone to connect, 24
wearables
  event management with, 246–247
  general discussion, 170–172
  market trends, 243, 248–249
  mass production of tags, 202

web versus mobile apps, 97–98
Wells Fargo, 182
Wi-Fi (Wireless Fidelity)
  versus Bluetooth, 213–214
  home networks, logging into, 132
  versus NFC, 28
  pairing devices, 172, 213–216
  unauthorized use of, 222
Wi-Fi P2P Carrier Configuration Record, 216
Windows, Microsoft, 188–189, 216
Windows Phone, 85, 190
wireless connections, ad-hoc, 12–13
Wireless Fidelity. *See* Wi-Fi
WoofLinks, 172
workplace monitoring, 120–121. *See also* authentication; hospitals
wristbands, 171, 248
writing data to tags
  on Android devices, 215–216
  apps for, 198–200
  general discussion, 91–93
  mass production, 202
  overview, 16
  steps in, 66–67
  TagWriter app, 66, 91–92, 189, 200, 203
  with USB reader/writers, 201–202
WUPA (Wakeup) command, 50

Y

Yeager, Doug, 85–86

Z

ZipNFC, 162
zone, interrogation, 24

About the Authors

Robert P. Sabella is a serial entrepreneur, investor, inventor, and author. He has started several companies, invested in a few more, and invented some products along the way with two current patent-pending applications. This is Mr. Sabella's second published book, his first being the *RFID+ Exam Cram*. He is passionate about start-ups, both as an entrepreneur and an investor. Mr. Sabella's focus is on all things related to mobile, specifically proximity ID technologies (NFC, RFID, BLE), and mobile commerce apps.

Mr. Sabella founded the NFC Bootcamp (www.nfcbootcamp.com) in 2011 and has since trained hundreds of individuals and organizations around the world on NFC and related proximity technologies and the solutions they enable.

Mr. Sabella created and cofounded AccelerateNFC (www.acceleratenfc.com), a seed accelerator program focused exclusively on proximity ID technologies, and he is the co-organizer of the global hackathon series TrackHack: The Proximity ID Hackathon (www.proximityhack.com).

Mr. Sabella is also the cofounder and Managing Partner of Interact Ventures (www.interactventures.com), a seed round venture capital investment firm focused on proximity ID technologies (NFC, RFID, BLE), IoT, and mobile commerce.

Mr. Sabella holds bachelor's and master's degrees in Philosophy and a Juris Doctor from Boston College.

John Mueller is a freelance author and technical editor. He has writing in his blood, having produced 99 books and more than 600 articles to date. The topics range from networking to artificial intelligence and from database management to heads-down programming. Some of his current books include books on Python for beginners, Python for data scientists, and MATLAB. He has also written a number of hardware-related texts, including one on building custom PCs and another on home security. His technical editing skills have helped more than 60 authors refine the content of their manuscripts. John has provided technical editing services to both *DataBased Advisor* and *Coast Compute* magazines. Be sure to read John's blog at http://blog.johnmuellerbooks.com/. When John isn't working at the computer, you can find him outside in the garden, cutting wood, or generally enjoying nature. John also likes making wine, baking cookies, and knitting. When not occupied with anything else, he makes glycerin soap and candles, which come in handy for gift baskets. You can reach John on the Internet at John@JohnMuellerBooks.com. John is also setting up a website at http://www.johnmuellerbooks.com/. Feel free to take a look and make suggestions on how he can improve it.

Dedication

This book is dedicated to my loving wife, Beth, and awesome children, Sofia, Gianluca, and Giovanni. Every meal a feast, every day a celebration. I love you guys the most!

Acknowledgments

Over the years, I have had the great fortune of working with some of the best minds in NFC, many of whom have helped make this book possible. I am very grateful for their friendship and their contributions. I want to especially thank my technical editors and contributors Robert Palmer, Miller Abel, Michael Gargiulo, and the technical folks at NXP for the detailed feedback and extraordinary patience in the process of writing this book. There is no way this book could have been written without their help.

I also want to thank some of the many friends I have come to know over the years who have helped with the NFC Bootcamps, AccelerateNFC, and TrackHacks, and who have helped in one way or another with this book: Deepak Jain, Tony Sabetti, Mikhail Damiani from Blue Bite, Richard Grundy from Flomio, Mark Robinson from HID Global, Randy Vanderhoof from The Smart Card Alliance, Stéphane Doutriaux from Poken, Nick Testanero from Cellotape, Sophie Mausolf from NXP, Bob Whalen from Smartwhere, Chi Ho Wong and Bob Merkert from ACS, Jim Ellis from ABNote, Theresa Gordon from Near Field Connects, Jason Wimp and Alex Howard from TX Systems, and The NFC Forum, especially Lisa Gundlach.

And I especially want to thank Tracee Lee Beebe and John Mueller for all their hard work in helping me get this book done. If it weren't for them, I am not sure I would ever have made it through the process.

Publisher's Acknowledgments

Acquisitions Editor: Katie Mohr

Project and Copy Editor: Susan Christophersen

Technical Editor: Robert Palmer

Editorial Assistant: Matthew Lowe

Sr. Editorial Assistant: Cherie Case

Production Editor: Antony Sami

Cover Image: ©bgblue/Getty Images, Inc.

NEW PRACTICE READERS
THIRD EDITION
BOOK E

Project Management and Production: Kane Publishing Services, Inc.
Cover Design: Pencil Point Studios
Text Design: Craven and Evans, Inc.

ISBN 0-7915-2121-4

3 4 5 6 7 8 9 0 02 01 00

NEW PRACTICE READERS

THIRD EDITION

BOOK E

S0-BBC-523

DONALD G. ANDERSON

Associate Superintendent, Retired
Oakland Public Schools
Oakland, California

CLARENCE R. STONE
with ELLEN DOLAN

Phoenix Learning Resources
New York • St. Louis